Innovation and Dynamics in Japanese Retailing

 **University of Hertfordshire**

College Lane, Hatfield, Herts. AL10 9AB

Learning and Information Services
de Havilland Campus Learning Resources Centre, Hatfield

For renewal of Standard and One Week Loans,
please visit the web site **http://www.voyager.herts.ac.uk**

This item must be returned or the loan renewed by the due date.
The University reserves the right to recall items from loan at any time.
A fine will be charged for the late return of items.

Innovation and Dynamics in Japanese Retailing

From Techniques to Formats to Systems

Hendrik Meyer-Ohle

First published 2003 by
PALGRAVE MACMILLAN
Houndmills, Basingstoke, Hampshire RG21 6XS and
175 Fifth Avenue, New York, N.Y. 10010
Companies and representatives throughout the world

PALGRAVE MACMILLAN is the global academic imprint of the Palgrave Macmillan division of St. Martin's Press, LLC and of Palgrave Macmillan Ltd. Macmillan® is a registered trademark in the United States, United Kingdom and other countries. Palgrave is a registered trademark in the European Union and other countries.

ISBN 1–4039–1128–2

This book is printed on paper suitable for recycling and made from fully managed and sustained forest sources.

A catalogue record for this book is available from the British Library.

Library of Congress Cataloging-in-Publication Data
Meyer-Ohle, Hendrik, 1965–
    Innovation and dynamics in Japanese retailing : from techniques to formats to systems / Hendrik Meyer-Ohle.
        p.   cm.
    Includes bibliographical references and index.
    ISBN 1–4039–1128–2 (cloth)
    1. Retail trade—Japan.   2. Retail trade—Technological innovations—Japan.   3. Marketing channels—Japan.   I. Title.
    HF5429.6.J3M49 2003
    381'.1'0952—dc21   2003044165

10   9   8   7   6   5   4   3   2   1
12   11   10   09   08   07   06   05   04   03

Printed and bound in Great Britain by
Antony Rowe Ltd, Chippenham and Eastbourne

Contents

v

List of Tables

List of Figures

Preface and Acknowledgements

This book concludes a decade of research on Japanese retailing, incorporating research for my PhD thesis that focused on the emergence of modern Japanese retail institutions and later research that discussed the development of Japanese retailing in the 1990s. In the course of my research results were presented at various conferences such as the Association of Japanese Business Studies, Euro Asia Management Association and the European Association of Education and Research in Commercial Distribution. I would like to thank all reviewers and participants for their helpful comments. I would also like to thank all the people I interviewed in the course of my research and who provided me with valuable background information.

Special thanks go to the institutions where I worked and studied in the course of my research, beginning with the Centre for Japanese Studies of Philipps-Universität Marburg, where I did my PhD studies, and here especially to Erich Pauer, my supervisor, continuing with the German Institute for Japanese Studies in Tokyo, where I worked for five years as a research associate, and finally the Department of Japanese Studies of the National University of Singapore which I joined three years ago. I thank all former and current colleagues for their continuous encouragement and friendship.

I thank Tawnya Hartberger for proofreading the final manuscript and Palgrave Macmillan for a speedy and efficient publishing process. The mistakes are all mine. Finally, I thank my wife and my children for sharing my curiosity for all things Asian and having followed me to Tokyo and Singapore.

HENDRIK MEYER-OHLE

Part I

Introduction

1
Innovation and Dynamics in Retailing

Japanese retailing and distribution systems have been described variously as a non-tariff barrier to market entry for foreign products, an appendix to Japan's social security system and labor market by providing work for a high number of employees, a highly service-oriented environment neglecting aspects of costs and efficiency, or a residue of the Japan of the past. Anyone who has been to Japan will certainly find most of these assumptions to contain some truth.

While some elements of Japanese retailing might appear as traditional and somewhat outdated at first sight, it has to be recognized that tremendous change has been taking place over the past fifty years. New retail techniques and retail formats have been introduced continuously. Many innovations were borrowed from or inspired by developments in foreign countries but quite a few also occurred within Japan. Some of these innovations failed outright, some needed to be adapted to the Japanese environment, and some of them eventually even proved to be adequate for transfer to other countries. Successful innovations, while often seen mainly as a result of a favourable environment, were usually to the same degree due to the ingenuity and perseverance of entrepreneurial individuals and companies.

Half a century of innovation and dynamics in Japanese retailing

This book looks at the innovative forces underlying the development of Japanese retailing over a period of fifty years. It starts by describing the removal of restrictions on retailing after the period of war and occupation, then discusses Japan's period of high growth in the 1960s, the oil shocks of the 1970s, and the bubble economy of the late 1980s, before finally engaging in a detailed discussion of retail change and strategy within the prolonged period of economic stagnation of the 1990s and the turn of the millennium.

In retailing, the introduction of certain techniques such as self-service, self-choice and chain store management during the 1950s marked the beginning of the first phase of development. Initially, these techniques were introduced separately or in combination in stores handling a variety of product categories. Out of the combination of techniques and product categories two main formats emerged during this period: the general superstore and the food supermarket, with the first format in particular becoming the symbol of Japanese retail modernization. These developments were driven by powerful entrepreneurs and happened in an environment that was characterized by fast economic growth, the formation of modern consumer markets, the availability of new technologies, and conflicts between retailers and manufacturers.

The beginning of the second phase can be seen in the early 1970s. During this period the spectrum of retail formats widened further. From today's perspective the most important retail format introduced at that time was the convenience store, though at the time the emergence of discount stores and home centres received more attention. Food supermarkets developed into a distinctive Japanese format and, from the 1980s on, larger category-oriented stores began to challenge the dominance of general superstores and small traditional retailers alike. Retail regulation became a major factor after a law was introduced that regulated the opening and activities of all large-scale retail stores. Change at that time was again driven by ambitious entrepreneurs either starting out afresh or aiming to further develop their businesses by pursuing ambitious growth and diversification policies. The later measures culminated in the 1980s in the emergence of retail and leisure-related empires, increasing the complexity of competitive patterns in Japanese retailing. The initial successes of these strategies, ambitious future plans, and also the bold attitude of the companies involved and their representatives led observers during the late 1980s to conclude that the Japanese retail sector had matured, would finally manage to shed its largely passive and adaptive role, and might even play a leading role within the future development of the Japanese economy.

On entering the 1990s, however, with the burst of the bubble economy, many of these diversification plans proved to be costly failures, being built on common expectations of continuously rising land prices, the availability of inexpensive financing and finally the continued willingness of Japanese consumers to easily part with their money. In the difficult economic environment of the 1990s, new qualities defined success in the retail sector. So far, companies had tried to capture as large a share of the retail market as possible by offering a wide selection of merchandise in ever-larger stores in favourable locations, being to a certain extent protected from competition by the provisions of the Large Store Law. Companies concentrated on the merchandising side, largely collaborated with wholesalers and manufacturers and overall tended to ignore profit and cost considerations to pursue increased sales and store networks. In the 1990s, this paradigm of focusing on the purely consumer-oriented retail format was challenged by foreign and local companies that had accumulated capabilities in category management and were able to coordinate activities tightly along the whole value chain. Being able to pass the advantages of this systematic attempt on to increasingly mobile and selective consumers, these companies quickly gained general and sometimes even enthusiastic acceptance. While it seems too early to judge the long-term success of individual companies, they nonetheless initiated a widespread trend among Japanese retailers towards reexamining and restructuring their operations with the aim of gaining strength in every area of their businesses including the newly emerging one of e-commerce.

Describing and analyzing the above developments in detail, the approach taken in this book is in a long tradition of looking at patterns and underlying factors of dynamic developments in retailing. Outlining some of the findings of this discourse before discussing developments in Japan will show the complexity involved in the analysis of processes of entrepreneurship and innovation in retailing, and will also help the reader to judge the developments in the Japanese retail scene.

Approaches to innovation and dynamics in retailing

Schumpeter (1926:100) defined five cases of innovation, and of these, two are of special relevance for retailing: (1) the production of a new type of product, meaning one unknown to consumers, or a new quality of a product, and (2) introduction of a new method of production, based on new scientific advancement or new methods of dealing commercially with a product. The introduction of a new product is equivalent to the introduction of a new retail format. However, while product innovations consist of the provision of material goods, format innovations deal with the provision of immaterial services (Kuhlmeier 1980:32). Process innovations can be closely related to format innovations in retailing, often providing the basis for these (Etgar 1984:47–9).

The next question is, what is really new and innovative? Schumpeter (1926:100) was concerned mainly about the relationship between the new and the existing, and regarded phenomena that were not the result of continuous adaptations as new and innovative. El-Ansary (1984:470) regarded innovation as an activity that has disruptive effects in the market. He pointed out three levels of innovation: continuous innovation that does not affect markets to a large extent, dynamic continuous innovation that leads to some degree of disturbance but does not disrupt existing patterns of consumption and competition, and finally discontinuous innovation that leads to disruptive results.

The theoretical occupation with innovation in the retail sector has focused mostly on the innovation of new retail formats and the development of hypotheses about the processes surrounding the introduction and development of these retail formats. This field of research is even characterized as one of the most prominent within marketing research (Savitt 1989:336). While it is not the aim of this book to develop a new theoretical framework, a short introduction to these theories seems to be helpful in understanding the many issues involved in the dynamics of retailing.

As already been pointed out, the study of the processes of retail format development is a popular one. Brown, in 1988, came up with 150 articles on this topic, starting in the 1930s. After a peak in the 1960s, it received renewed interest in the late 1980s and early 1990s, and the discussion is bound to come up again soon. Brown (1988:19) described contributions in this area as having four possible approaches: cyclical, environmental, conflict-oriented and integrated.

The most popular concept of retail evolution and change was introduced with the location of a pattern of cyclical development called the 'Wheel of Retailing'. In 1931, based on observations from the American department store and chain store industry, McNair proposed three stages of development (McNair 1931:39). In the first stage, new retail formats are introduced based on low prices and overheads. In the next stage, companies improve the quality of products handled, which leads to a certain loss of price competitiveness. In the third stage, retail formats change their focus to an expansion of services offered and intensified advertising. Costs of doing business in general, and especially the ratio of fixed to total investment, increase. The third stage also implies a change in the attitude of management. Management loses its innovativeness and is less inclined to take risks. Finally, new competitors with price-based retail concepts enter the market and the process starts all over again. In this way, the Wheel of Retailing revolves continuously (McNair 1958:16).

Other authors have tried to refine McNair's approach. Criticizing a lack of empirical validity, Izraeli (1973) proposed the possibility of market entry on either extreme of the cost – margin continuum, with established retailers filling the middle ranks. The emergence of a new competitor leads to an adaptation of strategies on the side of established players as well as on the side of the innovator. The need for adaptation is due basically to the reaction of the demand side, with preference for a compromise between the old sales concept and the new. The final outcome of this convergence of formats is the continuous opening up of opportunities for new innovators on either side of the continuum.

Hollander (1966) denied the validity of the Wheel of Retailing and proposed instead the analogy of an accordion to describe developments with regard to the scope of assortments. He ascertained that in the history of retail development domination by general line, wide-assortment retailers alternated continuously with domination by specialized, narrow-line merchants. However, he admitted limitations to his own findings by stating that there are always certain retailers that go against the trend and thereby the analogy of an orchestra of accordion players, some extending assortments while others contracted them, would be more appropriate.

Dialectic approaches see retail evolution as a process of interaction that proceeds through the stages of action, reaction and assimilation (Brown 1988:23). The main advocator of this line of thinking was Gist (1968). He understood change in retailing as a succession of steps where each step contrasts the previous (thesis and antithesis) before merging into a synthesis that starts the process all over again.

Critics of cyclical approaches, however, point out that cyclical theories assume the existence of deterministic developments and behaviour, neglecting a thorough analysis of the factors underlying these developments. Nonetheless, it can be stated that cyclical approaches are of a certain importance, since they show possible and empirically quite common development paths for retail institutions.

Environmental approaches developed later than cyclical ones and see institutional innovations in retailing as consequences of changing environmental factors. Innovation takes place or can be successful solely within a favourable environment and only institutions that possess the ability to adapt to their environment can survive (Brown 1988:21). Environmental theories relate thereby to ecological and Darwinist ways of thinking:

We have noticed already a surprising similarity between the retailing format and the biological species. In both cases, the origin can be pointed out rather accurately in time and place. In both instances the 'mutation' in economic science, we would rather speak of 'innovation', is definite and clear-cut. The result in both cases is a species that is consistent in time, although subject to slow and small changes, due to the necessities of a changing ecology. (Dreesman 1968:65)

Environmental approaches are generally more complex in nature than most of the cyclical ones. Markin and Duncan (1981) emphasized the exchange relationships between institutions and their environment. To survive, institutions have to be accepted by their environment and this aspect dominates the behaviour of the institution. Economic and societal change leads to conflict, and this conflict initiates new institutions or changes in existing ones. This view regards not the status quo but continuous change as normal. Consequently, not the institutions that are highly adapted to their environment, but rather those with a tolerance towards change, have the best chances of survival and evolving to the next developmental stage. Taking the biological analogies one step further, the same authors also conceded the existence of parasitic and symbiotic relationships in the retail sector, pointing to the tendency within retail systems to work towards optimization through cooperation and exchange. Environmental approaches adapt the methodology of contingency theories to the distributive trades and thereby also have to share the same criticism. In particular, the low importance given to managerial decision-making was criticized (Hollander 1981:90–1). Markin and Duncan (1981:65), for example, did not take into consideration the scope of choice of management, and only at the end of their article assigned the role of change agents to the management of institutions. Roth and Klein (1993:17) also pointed to the deterministic character of these approaches and emphasized that a given environment can lead to several results. Environmental approaches explain the existence of different institutions in a given situation, but do not explain why in similar environments different retail structures exist.

The final category is made up of integrative theories that, based on the criticism of existing theories, try to present comprehensive frameworks for the explanation of retail change. Brown, in his detailed review of approaches in 1988, concluded that up to then only two approaches succeeded in this regard. Beem and Oxenfeldt (1966) proposed a 'Diversity Theory for Market Processes', with six main hypotheses at its core. The authors derived these hypotheses not from a review of existing approaches in the area but rather from a criticism of classical market theory, as follows:

- Sellers in all markets are diverse and develop strategies built on their individual resources and capabilities and corporate goals.
- Buyers are equally diverse and have individual needs with regard to products and retail formats. Needs of buyers span over several dimensions, and a theory of retail change therefore has to accommodate factors on the demand side like quality, convenience and choice.
- Sellers look for differential advantages with certain relatively homogenous groups of buyers based on their capabilities. Buyers at the fringes of these groups might fall into the targeted group of several sellers, and competition between stores is initiated by activities of sellers to extend their customer base.
- Competitive settings and differential advantages are changing continuously with the main factors driving development being societal and technological changes.
- Competing sellers will be inclined to cooperate when they see no opportunities to differentiate. Sellers will introduce new features only if they see the possibility to recover costs incurred by the new features. Otherwise cooperation in the industry will prevail.
- Competitive advantages are continuously in danger of being eroded owing to activities of competitors but owing also to changes in society and technology.

Overall, the authors stressed that not an equilibrium but continuous change is the main characteristic of retail markets. They related their propositions to the works of Schumpeter and combined them with a life cycle concept of long and short cycles. Long cycles are being initiated by the emergence of new retail institutions. Short cycles are realized by innovations in features and services offered. Differential advantages are continuously being challenged (Beem and Oxenfeld 1966:78).

The other contribution highlighted by Brown (1988) is the one by Agergård *et al.* (1970). The main hypothesis of their approach is a spiral-like upwards movement of the level of retail formats. It shares with many of the cyclical approaches the recognition of a tendency among retailers to increase services and lose price aggressiveness. This allows innovators to reconstruct the original format; however, owing to overall increases in incomes and living standards they will do so on a higher level. The authors pointed to periods with a high degree of external change as being especially favourable for the introduction of new retail formats.

Other integrative articles were published after Brown's review article. Roth and Klein (1993) criticized the onesidedness of previous contributions that dealt with either external environmental factors or individual decision-making. Their own contribution first names factors in the environment (e.g. size and spatial distribution of population, consumer preferences, income and income distribution, technology, and state regulations) that cannot be manipulated by individual decision-makers, though some could be influenced by collective behaviour. It then demands a projection of institutions that could exist in the observed environment, a much more demanding task than explaining the existence and characteristics of institutions already present. The actual structure realized is then mainly a result of the conscious decision-making of corporate actors. For Roth and Klein, observed developments in retailing are thereby the result of an interaction between the environment that determines the boundaries for survival and the individual entrepreneur who decides how to act within these boundaries.

Evans *et al.* (1993) looked at existing retail institutions and based their contribution on system theory by regarding institutions of retailing as open, living, determined systems that are able to interact with other systems in their environment. Systems search their environment for cues that might either pose threats to their existence or are opportunities for development. Action is taken when these cues are regarded as valid. Thereby, the ability to recognize cues and to react becomes the main concern of these authors: 'A degree of social inertia occurs when the system/retail institution becomes so tightly bounded that it is reluctant to validate and respond to a competitive threat' (Evans *et al.* 1993:82). After an overview of existing theories on retail change and different academic modes of inquiry, they concluded that the main problem of retail institutions in managing change is the problem of information collection and processing. The frequently encountered problem of inertia can be then interpreted as a consequence of missing information about new developments in retailing. Again, they stress the role of management:

> [R]etail evolution connotes a change of retail form over time, 'revolution' rather than 'evolution' suggests that change of form is actually the result of a managerial decision at the corporate level and may occur more rapidly as the result of strategic decision-making. (Evans *et al.* 1993:97)

Consequently, the advice to management is to introduce new information systems and also to include a projection of responses by established players into the analysis of innovations.

Glöckner-Holme (1988) devised a complex framework for the analysis of dynamics in retailing, integrating external and internal factors underlying changes in retail formats. In her model, external factors are classified into factors of the general environment and those of the task environment. External factors are complemented further by motivational factors within the company. She combined these factors with a life cycle model showing how the life cycle of a retail format can be influenced by innovative activity. In her comparatively comprehensive set of factors, Glöckner-Holme, more than others, integrated the change in retail institutions with changes of the whole distribution structure by explicitly pointing out the importance of changes in procurement markets.

Brown (1988:30), who as outlined compiled the most comprehensive overview of theories on retail change, was surprisingly brief in his own views on the origins and processes of dynamic changes in retailing. Reiterating many aspects of the integrated approaches he first asserts that some of the assumptions of the Wheel of Retailing could be upheld not only by allowing modes of market entry based on cost competitiveness but also by taking into regard market entry based on any comparative advantage. New formats can emerge when older ones lose acceptance by consumers. Alterations in the strategies of existing institutions can be explained by environmental changes and institutional antagonism.

Brown laxly characterizes his own conclusions as being based on 'common sense'. This statement, however, does not devalue the efforts on theoretical model building. The existing, rich contributions on the mechanisms of retail change, as summarized above, point out what to look for and what pitfalls to avoid when analyzing changes in retailing. Brown (1990:144) stated that while not being of a general character, the Wheel of Retailing is still a developmental path that many important institutions of retailing have passed through. Goldman (1975:54) argued similarly: 'In spite of their many shortcomings, most of these theories contain important insights and have identified some major development patterns in retailing.' Environmental approaches contributed the importance of external factors for retail development, but their deficiencies are also a warning against neglecting the role of the decision-maker. Instead, integrative approaches are arguing on the basis that the environment sets the boundaries for decision-makers to act in. It is therefore dangerous to assert that the existence of a certain constellation in the environment has led necessarily to the formation of a retail institution with certain characteristics. It can, however, be shown how certain factors in the environment have been in favour of or against the introduction of new formats, and this makes a difference to the deterministic views of contingency approaches.

Savitt (1982, 1989) argued that the existing hypotheses regarding the formation and development of formats are too broad, insufficiently empirically validated and also too centred on the American situation to be used as a general framework for analyzing retail change in a different country. Instead, he demands a historical methodology that analyses the development of retail systems in detail and also takes into regard singular events and actors; only after doing so it becomes possible to derive general conclusions. Within this proposed methodology, he regards the theories concerning dynamism in retailing less as an applicable framework for analysis than as milestones and observation points that can initiate analysis and help to understand certain events (Savitt 1982:19–22, 1989:336). This book largely subscribes to this view. Indeed, the findings will show that the development of certain retail formats, for example general superstores, show a lot of resemblance to some of the above cyclical approaches. Other retail formats, however, like the convenience store, do not fit any of these patterns at all. Undertaking the analysis of dynamism in Japanese retailing with one particular theory in mind would therefore limit the scope of analysis from the beginning. In addition, it will be shown that factors that do not receive much attention in the above-described theories, such as government regulations, have been of major importance in Japan.

Arguing against pure contingency approaches, this book will stress the importance of entrepreneurship. Japanese entrepreneurs did enjoy a large degree of freedom in the development of their retail formats and companies. Yoshino, for example, described the early innovators in Japanese distribution as men that regarded mass merchandising not as a mere business technique but a philosophy that they consequently promoted with an 'evangelical fervor' (Yoshino 1971:145), and this mindset can be seen in innovators in Japanese distribution even today. Indeed, one frequent pattern of innovation in Japanese retailing that will be identified is the supply-side-driven, somewhat hasty introduction of new techniques and formats following overseas examples, these often not finding a market ready to accept the innovations. The perseverance of entrepreneurs and the need to adapt the technique to the Japanese market often led to quick pragmatic changes. Sometimes these changes proved to be superior to the original as in the case of convenience stores, in other cases entrepreneurs were later able to return to the original concept as in the case of home centres or DIY stores. Overall, the book will show Japanese entrepreneurs in retailing as being extremely open and pragmatic in their innovative activities.

Structure and sources

In its structure this book largely follows the above-outlined chronological progression from techniques to formats to systems with a major focus on developments in the 1990s. After the introductory part, the second looks at developments from the 1950s to the 1980s while the third deals with the 1990s and the fourth provides a summary and a conclusion of findings. Within the different chapters of the two main parts – II and III – the issues of innovation and entrepreneurship will be treated in different manners. Chapter 3 describes the introduction of retailing techniques and the first steps towards format formation in general, then analyzes these developments in the light of their underlying factors. Chapter 4 identifies government regulation as a main underlying environmental factor for developments from the 1970s onwards, then Chapter 5 goes on to describe developments in relation to different store formats. Chapters 6 to 10 focus on developments in the 1990s. These developments will take up issues in a theme-based manner, focusing on changes in the environment, the effects of deregulation on format development, emergence of new entrepreneurs with new concepts, problems of existing companies and finally the reorganization of the value chain and e-commerce.

This study is based on a variety of sources. Many of these are academic sources but it also makes extensive use of materials like government reports, company histories and articles in industry journals or newspapers. Apart from publications by Japanese government institutions, think tanks and Japanese academics, the use of a number of industry journals has to be explained. Industry journals published for practitioners in the distribution industry like *Shôgyôkai* (Retail Scene), *Hanbai kakushin* (Revolution in Retailing) or *Gekiryû Magazine* (Raging Stream) discuss in some detail the current developments in Japanese retailing. While sometimes overstating current developments and often strictly benchmarking Japanese models against American models they usually provide a good analysis of the situation of Japanese retailing at the time the articles were written. As such they provide an impression about which concepts and ideas were considered as really new and relevant within the industry at the time of their introduction. Being used by the practitioner and academics alike are the articles in *Nihon Keizai shinbun* and especially in the *Nikkei ryûtsû shinbun* (Nikkei Distribution Newspaper), renamed *Nikkei Marketing Journal* in 2001. This newspaper is published three times a week and often provides not only information and opinions on current developments but also conducts regular surveys of the distribution industry. Results are published in a yearly handbook. Finally, especially for newer developments, the internet has proved to be a useful tool, easing acquisition of information on companies as well as government publications.

Note on the transcription of Japanese names

For reasons of consistency and clarity, it was decided to simplify and standardize the transcription of Japanese personal, place and company names. While, in Japan, surnames are usually given first, it was decided to give Japanese personal names in the Western order. For the same reasons it was decided not to indicate long vowels in place names. For companies, names are used as stated on their English home pages or annual reports.

Part II

From Techniques to Formats (1950s–80s)

2
New Techniques and the Emergence of the General Superstore (1950s and 1960s)

The 1950s and 1960s saw the introduction of new retail techniques culminating in the formation of a number of new retail formats and companies that to this day play a dominant role in Japanese retailing. In the following chapter, these developments will be examined in more detail. First, the stage is set by a short overview of innovative retail activities and the state of retailing prior to the period under examination. After this, the main developments during this period are identified and then discussed in regard to a number of underlying factors such as entrepreneurial conduct, transfer of technologies and the situation in consumer and procurement markets.

Not starting from scratch: department stores and other earlier innovations

While the focus of this book is on developments in Japanese retailing in the second half of the twentieth century, this does not mean that innovative activities were not around before the 1950s. Quite the opposite: Japan has a long tradition of strong and independent merchants, who introduced some advanced retail techniques like fixed, customer-independent pricing and systematic product presentation and merchandising well before 1904, when Mitsukoshi opened the first so-called department store, the first major retail format innovation in Japan based on a western model. Mitsukoshi developed its department store through the reorganization of its established dry goods store, systematically adding new product groups (Yoshino 1971:4–8, Satô 1974:69). Other retailers followed this example, and when store buildings had to be rebuilt after the Kantô Great Earthquake of 1923 not only the merchandising principles but also the outward appearance came to resemble those of western counterparts. This trend spread to the provincial capitals where the model of the department store was reproduced on a smaller scale and assortments modified to the needs of rural consumers. In 1929, a third variation of the department store was added when a railway operator opened a store above a railway terminal, a bold move generally regarded as a unique Japanese invention. In contrast to Mitsukoshi, which had modeled its store heavily on London's Harrods, operators of terminal department stores developed independent principles of operation (Satô 1974:71, Miya 1985b, Abe [Yoshifumi] 1993).

The expansion of department store companies during the 1920s and 1930s was so rapid that the government soon faced demands from smaller competitors to curb their activities. After initiatives by the industry to regulate itself had failed, the government finally introduced a Department Store Law in 1937. By doing so it instituted a tradition of regulating the activities of large retail stores that in many ways dominates the discussion on large-store-retailing in Japan to this day.

Innovative initiative was, however, not limited to the department store sector. Seeking to improve the situation of retailers and consumers alike, the so-called public retail market was introduced in 1918. Independent retailers selling food and daily necessities were offered store space in buildings constructed with public funding. Introduced as a reaction to the violent protests of consumers against rising rice prices at that time, this measure served to improve the provision of the growing working class in the cities with basic supplies (Shiraishi 1991:13–14). In another move to strengthen their position, smaller retailers also started to experiment with collaborative procurement of merchandise; however, the first voluntary chain of apparel stores did not succeed owing to the still overwhelming strength of wholesalers (Yahagi 1993e:57).

In regard to the introduction of the management of multiple outlets, a chain of one-price discount stores developed by the department store operator Takashimaya deserves mention. Riding on high consumer acceptance due to the worldwide economic crisis, the company opened 106 stores of this type from 1931 to 1940. Stores averaged 300 square meters in size and the company had more than 2000 employees. The further development of this project and all other innovative activities in Japanese retailing were, however, brought to an end by Japan's war engagement (Satô 1974:72). Retailers lost most of their independence under the impact of rationing and price controls, retail outlets being transformed into pure distribution centres (Pauer 1993:4–5).

After Japan lost the war, the situation of the retail sector was of low importance to those in charge of reconstructing the economy. Priority was given to reconstruction and expansion of the manufacturing sector, and here the state took an active role by drawing up development plans and directing entrepreneurial initiatives through the allocation of capital, control over foreign exchange and import of technologies. In retailing, the prewar dualistic structure remained, with a small number of strong department store companies on one side and a high number of small, family-run stores on the other. These small retailers usually handled only one product group but lacked the depth of assortments to be really classified as specialty stores. A major characteristic of many of these stores was their dependence on wholesalers. The prevalence of these stores well into the twentieth century can be attributed to a number of factors, some of them still valid today (Satô 1974:80–2). Among these are:

- The relatively underdeveloped state of consumer markets. Despite advances in industrialization, household incomes had remained low and most consumers had to spend most of their incomes on daily necessities.
- The preference of Japanese consumers for fresh merchandise, with shopping being done on a daily basis in stores in the neighborhood of homes.
- The fact that not only the retail sector but also the industries manufacturing consumer goods were dominated by small businesses. This nurtured the emergence of a dominant wholesale sector lending support to small retailers and manufacturers alike.
- The relatively underdeveloped infrastructure further strengthened the position of wholesalers.
- The importance of the retail sector as a catchment basin for the labor market, where low capital requirements, the low competitive strength of existing stores and support from wholesalers enabled a comparatively easy entry into this sector.

With price controls and rationing still in place until the year 1950, leeway for individual entrepreneurial initiative in Japanese retailing remained limited. In this situation, some alternative organizational forms like consumer cooperatives recorded strong growth. Yahagi (1993e:58) reports a case of a regional consumer cooperative that at that time expanded its membership base from 700 to 12 000 within only five years.

When restrictions in retailing were finally lifted, department stores managed to resume their strong prewar position. Department stores organized fashion shows, published their own promotional magazines, established mail order subsidiaries and introduced private brands. Growth was even accelerated by the fact that the occupation forces, under their objectives to promote democratization and reduce state control, had abolished the Department Store Law. New department stores were opened in the metropolitan areas and especially terminal department stores enjoyed rapid growth with commuter figures rising quickly. Traditional department store companies went into direct competition with railway operators for commuters by opening stores of their own above or near terminals. In 1953, department stores had recovered their level of prewar sales and were engaged in a fierce battle for market share. In this situation, history repeated itself when the aggressive strategies of retailers and problems of the traditional retail sector were pointed out by the Fair Trade Commission, resulting in the reintroduction of a Department Store Law in 1956 (Miya 1985a:12, Yoshino 1971:9, 31). At about the same time, however, the competitive situation in Japanese retailing began to change with new competitors and new formats entering the stage.

From new techniques to a dominating format

The introduction of superstores in Japan did not happen overnight, but rather should be seen as an evolutionary process including the introduction, combination and adaptation of various retail techniques. Often relying more on trial and error than on systemized format development, Japanese retailers experimented with new retail concepts to appeal to the Japanese consumer. The founding period saw the introduction of elements like self-service, self-choice, and centralized payment in different product categories. Later, organizational techniques like scrambled merchandising, chain management and departmental organization were added. Efforts finally culminated in the firm establishment of an original Japanese retail format as the dominating format in Japanese retailing, the Japanese General Superstore, displaying as its most distinguished element a heavy reliance on food sales apart from carrying a broad assortment of household goods and apparel products.

New retailing techniques received attention on a larger scale for the first time when Japan's so-called first food supermarket, Kinokuniya, was established in 1954 in Tokyo's Aoyama district; the store still exists in the same location. With its small size of just 130 square meters, mostly serving the expatriate community and not pursuing an aggressive pricing policy, its classification as a supermarket has often been questioned; nonetheless the store displayed a combination of innovative elements of self-choice, self-service and departmental separation that was new to Japanese retailing (WSK 1965a:21, Miya 1985a). Other stores in various product areas followed its example by introducing the new techniques of self-choice and self-service to certain degrees, but it took until 1956 for the first food superstore focusing on the domestic consumer to be opened. Located in Kokura, Kyushu, this store sold all its food products in self-service on a sales floor of 336 square meters. Soon, the area became an incubator for the introduction of progressive sales techniques when two nearby stores followed, not just copying the initial example but introducing additional innovations of their own (WSK 1965a:22).

Afterwards, the expansion of superstores accelerated and soon resulted in the initiatives of involved companies to establish themselves as a separate industry within retailing. In 1958, superstore operators in Ehime prefecture (Shikoku) established the first voluntary chain to organize collaborative procurement. The founding of two industry associations at that time is further proof of the gradual establishment of the new retail format. In January 1958, the Association of Japanese Supermarket Chains was instituted, followed by the Self Service Association in March of the same year. The new phenomenon also attracted the attention of the government bureaucracy, with the first extensive surveys being carried out on the situation and economic impact of self-service stores.

Initial signs of the growing impact of superstores were local protests by traditional retailers against the opening of stores. The first protests were launched in 1959 against the opening of a new store in Hamamatsu, against a chain store of the expanding operator Daiei, based in Kobe, and also against the store of another pioneering company, Kansai Supermarket, in Itami (KS 1985:15–17, Miya 1985a:50). With operators trying to repeat the success of their stores in different locations, the principles of chain operation started to become important. Nonetheless, operators were not satisfied with their store formats yet, and when opening additional stores usually did not just copy already-existing stores but added new features. Daiei opened its second store in 1958 and introduced features such as centralized checkouts and a store design that controlled the flow of customers. It also widened the assortment of this store by adding groceries, daily necessities and apparel (Daiee 1992:189). While most superstores up to that point had largely focused on one product group, the activities by Daiei can be seen as a distinctive move towards scrambled merchandising. Retailers began to assemble assortments made up of easy-to-handle and fast-moving articles regardless of the categories of goods handled. Operators thereby combined three independently developed concepts of merchandising: self-service, discounting and chain store operation. Within Japan, general superstores handling wide assortments of merchandise soon became known as *general supermarkets* (*sôgô suupaa*) or *large-volume stores* (*ryôbaiten*) or just GMSs (general merchandising stores). Being the pioneer in this regard, Daiei followed this concept further, adding electric appliances to its assortment in its third store as early as 1960. By 1961, the company operated six superstores, among them Japan's largest store of this format with at that time an impressive 2450 square meters. With success companies became more self-confident, introducing private brands and also developing stores in suburban areas. In 1960, yet another industry organization, the Association of Supermarkets, was founded with a membership of 150 companies (WSK 1965a:23, Miya 1985a:52–3).

The first official large-scale survey that explicitly classified stores based on the new sales concepts was carried out in 1964. It identified 3620 stores that sold by self-service and had a sale floor of 100 square meters and above. By categorizing stores into four large groups, general superstores, food superstores, apparel superstores and other superstores (basically those selling household goods and home furnishing), the survey established a classification of superstores that has remained largely unchanged up until today. In the initial survey, self-service stores accounted for 4.7 per cent of total retail sales, with general super-stores accounting for 1.2 per cent and food superstores for 2.4 per cent. The majority of stores were still small; nonetheless, nearly 500 food superstores with more than 400 square meters out of a total of 2567 stores, and 34 general superstores with more than 1500 square meters out of a total of 292 stores already point towards a trend of enlarging sales floors (TSC 1976:19). It is interesting to note that apparel super-stores initially enjoyed a relatively strong position with 654 stores showing the early introduction of self-service in this field. The survey also found that most of these stores were still relatively simple affairs, operated in wooden structures. The location of stores was predomin-antly in the traditional shopping districts with a slightly higher share of food superstores in residential areas and general superstores near railway stations. The almost total absence of parking spaces owned by superstores points to the fact that the car did not play any role at all in household shopping in Japan in the early 1960s (NKR 1963:136–68). In accordance with the many theories on the introduction of new retail formats, superstores in their early stage were aggressive in their pricing strategies. A survey of 60 product groups showed prices in superstores to be lower than those of general retailers for all but eight groups, supermarkets undercutting prices of general retailers by 5 to 15 per cent (STK 1969:79–97) (Table 2.1).

Having passed through the phases of introduction and formation the superstore format and its operators entered into a period of rapid expansion. This period, which lasted up until the early 1970s, can be characterized by the following developments (Orihashi 1993:99–102).

• Development of new locations, especially in the rapidly expanding dormitory suburbs of Tokyo.
• Expansion of sales floors: new stores opened after 1965 averaged sales floors of more than 1500 square meters; after 1969 this increased to 3000 to 5000 square meters with single stores reaching sizes of up to 7500 square meters.
• Gradual broadening of assortments through the addition of new product lines.
• Construction of shopping centres with superstores as core tenants.

The format that developed most dramatically was the general superstore. With its distinctive characteristics it soon became the flagship of superstore retailing in Japan. While some operators of food supermarkets

Table 2.1 Retail prices for selected products, 1967 (general retail stores = 100)

Product	Supermarket	Department store
Tea	93.9	99.1
Instant coffee	94.6	96.9
Bread	94.6	99.9
Fresh meat	95.9	124.7
Beef	94.1	108.3
Electric appliances	88.4	95.2
Men's apparel	91.4	113.5
Women's apparel	83.9	120.3
Pharmaceuticals	100.1	199.6
Soap	86.5	90.0

Source: Author's compilation based on STK 1969:79–97.

and apparel superstores abandoned their original concepts and concentrated on developing general superstores, others stuck with their formats and these continued to exist as independent formats despite the dominance of the general superstore. Efforts to further advance these formats could be seen; nonetheless, these efforts were limited to a small number of companies. In comparison with the rapid development of general superstores, these formats stagnated in terms of store format development, the number of stores and their share of overall retail sales (Murata and Mimura 1987:123–6).

In the development of the general superstore Daiei continued to play the leading role. In 1964, the company opened a store in Kobe labeled as a Self-Service Discount Department Store. Leaving behind the concept of pure discounting, the company switched to a policy of offering broad assortments that covered the daily needs of consumers (Daiee 1992:77). Featuring 8609 square meters on 7 stories, 6 of them above ground, and elevators and escalators for customer convenience, the store in Kobe adopted features found in traditional department stores. This resemblance could also be seen in the arrangement of departments; the sales floor for fresh foods was located in the basement and restaurants were on the top floors. The store was planned initially as a shopping centre with tenants taking up a considerable proportion of the total sales space. However, problems with the coordination of tenants soon made Daiei operate most of the sales space directly, including the restaurants on the top floor (Daiee 1992:81–2).

The success of its large stores encouraged Daiei to continue with increases in store size when opening new stores. In 1968 the company opened a shopping centre in Osaka with 15 000 square meters. Having learned from previous experience the company was more successful in attracting and managing tenants. The shopping centre thereby hosted 50 specialty stores and also branches of a city bank and a securities broker. A car park with a capacity of 400 cars catered to the needs of the growing number of owners of automobiles in Japan. After having in terms of size already surpassed most regional department stores, Daiei in 1971 even challenged metropolitan department stores by building a store of 28 000 square meters in Fukuoka (Daiee 1992:84–5, 143).

While Daiei often took the centre stage, other companies also contributed to the development of general superstores in Japan. Nagasakiya, Seiyu, Nichii (later Mycal), Izumiya, Ito Yokado and Jusco (later Aeon) also widened assortments in their stores and increased their reach beyond regional boundaries. In broadening their assortments companies arrived at the general superstore from different starting points. While Daiei's origins were in the drugstore business, quite a few other companies had their roots in the textile sector and only started to introduce food into their stores in the second half of the 1960s (Miya 1985a:79–81).

The predominance of general superstores in Japanese retailing was symbolized by the leading business daily *Nihon keizai shinbun* in January 1971, using for the first time the term 'big store' (*biggu sutoa*) to describe the new phenomenon in Japanese retailing. This term, related to the size of stores as well as to the diversity of product lines handled, was used to distinguish the Japanese approach to superstore retailing from its former role model, the American food superstore (Miya 1985a:79–81). The growth of superstores and operating companies reached a new level in the early 1970s. Nichii had 100 stores as early as 1970 and Seiyu and Daiei followed in June and November 1973 respectively. A year earlier, in 1972, Daiei had already claimed the prestigious top spot in Japanese retailing in terms of annual sales from the department store operator Mitsukoshi.

While companies were openly advertising changes in size and assortment another change in strategy came about rather quietly. Consumers, who were attracted initially to the new superstores by their aggressive pricing policies, from the early 1970s began to voice criticism of superstores that had lost their edge in this regard. Operators reacted to this criticism with initiatives to reconsider their pricing policies (Miya 1985a:109–11).

The end of this phase of rapid growth for the superstore sector can be seen in two events. The first was the onset of the first oil shock, in autumn 1973, which led to a recession in the Japanese economy. The second event was the introduction of the *Law to Regulate the Commercial Activities of Retailers in Large Retail Premises* (*Dai kibo ko-uri tenpo ni okeru ko-uri-gyô no jigyô katsudô no chôsei ni kan suru hôritsu* – known as Daitenhô or the Large Store Law) in March 1974.

Looking at developments in Japanese retailing from a quantitative perspective, the number of self-service stores in Japan had risen to over 12 000 outlets by 1974, an increase of over 8500 stores compared with the year 1964 (Table 2.2). Figures show a generally constant growth of all retail formats apart from the apparel superstore. This store format lost much of its significance owing to the described policies of its operators to add product lines and to transform stores to the general superstore format (Murata and Mimura 1987:124). Later the share of this format dropped further until it reached a mere 0.3 per cent in the early 1990s. As outlined, the fastest growing format was the general superstore, with

Table 2.2 Increase in number and market share of superstores by retail format, 1964–74 (market share in parenthesis in per cent)

Retail format	1964	1966	1968	1970	1972	1974
Total	3 620 (4.7)	4 780 (5.4)	7 062 (6.2)	9 403 (7.4)	10 634 (8.7)	12 034 (10.6)
General superstore	292 (1.2)	228 (0.6)	313 (0.7)	587 (1.6)	682 (2.1)	1 046 (4.5)
above 1500 m^2	34 (0.4)	17 (0.2)	53 (0.3)	180 (1.0)	283 (1.5)	627 (3.9)
Apparel superstore	654 (1.0)	665 (1.0)	927 (1.3)	1 077 (1.2)	1 328 (1.4)	1 167 (1.0)
above 400 m^2	171 (0.6)	221 (0.7)	412 (1.0)	509 (1.1)	809 (1.2)	626 (0.9)
Food superstore	2 567 (2.4)	3 743 (3.7)	5 395 (3.8)	7 380 (4.3)	8 069 (4.7)	9 181 (4.7)
above 400 m^2	493 (0.9)	671 (1.7)	1 178 (1.9)	1 756 (2.3)	2 327 (2.7)	2 747 (2.7)
Other superstores	107 (0.1)	154 (0.2)	427 (0.4)	368 (0.3)	555 (0.4)	640 (0.3)
above 400 m^2	16 (0.0)	24 (0.0)	94 (0.3)	74 (0.1)	183 (0.2)	136 (0.1)

The threshold for specialty superstores was later raised to 500 square meters. Based on this definition number and market share for the year 1974 would change to: food superstores 2013 (2.3 per cent), apparel superstores 539 (0.9 per cent), other superstores 36 (0.1 per cent).

Sources: Author's compilation based on TSC (1976:13, 19); (1983:20, 26).

operators managing to nearly quadruple the number of stores as well as their overall market share. The average size of stores in the category 1500 square meters and above averaged 4375 square meters, and the average store employed nearly 140 employees. Characteristics of food superstores changed to a lesser degree; the majority of stores in the group below 500 square meters had a sales area of 235 square meters and the stores in the larger category commanded 853 square meters (TSC 1976, 1983).

The steps towards the introduction and development of superstores in Japan enumerated can be explained by looking at underlying factors and processes. Overall, the following developments need further discussion:

- The processes underlying the adoption of new techniques in Japanese retailing.
- The factors leading to the fast diffusion and acceptance of the new superstore format.
- The reasons underlying the differentiation and adaptation of store formats resulting in the dominating position of the general superstore format.

Usually, single developments cannot be linked to single underlying factors, but were due to the interaction of a combination of factors. An innovation such as the introduction of new retail technologies or even the establishment of a whole new retail format involved risk and uncertainty and therefore required the presence of entrepreneurs willing to cope with these risks. In doing so, entrepreneurs enjoyed certain degrees of latitude, but were also driven by or had to take into consideration conditions in their environment. The most important factors often were the state of consumer markets and the reactions of competitors. However, innovational activities were often initiated or influenced by additional factors such as the situation in procurement markets, government regulations or the availability of appropriate technologies.

Entrepreneurs with a mission adopting new retail techniques

The introduction of new retail techniques and superstores into Japan was undertaken by entrepreneurs who distinguished themselves by being at the frontier of developments, became role models for others and thereby played a leading role in the transformation of Japanese retailing during the 1950s and 1960s. Yoshino, at the beginning of the 1970s, very appropriately characterized these entrepreneurs by stating that

> the concept of mass merchandising to these men is much more than a mere technique of doing business; rather it is their philosophy. In fact, many of these men are promulgating their newly found merchandise doctrine with an evangelical fervor. (Yoshino 1971:145)

Surveys conducted in the early 1960s (NKR 1963:145) demonstrate that the majority of those individuals and companies that operated the new format had previously been engaged in the retail sector. However, differences in the motivations of operators of the different superstore formats can be shown. While owners of food superstores mainly explained their activities with the expectation of expanding sales and rationalizing operations, operators of general superstores most often pointed out that their activities were required by and in line with overall changes in business and society (NKR 1963:144). Often coming from other areas of business and categories, operators of general superstores seemed to be driven by the need to create something radically new.

In line with the previously mentioned statement by Yoshino and the results of the survey, another publication of that time also stresses the role of the entrepreneur. A study conducted by a team of researchers at Waseda University (WSK 1965a) arrived at the conclusion that in contrast to the American situation, where a largely favourable environment promoted the development of superstores, this was not the case for Japan. Entrepreneurs introduced the concept of the superstore into a less than favourable environment. The eventual success of this innovation thereby has to be attributed mostly to the capabilities of entrepreneurs to adjust the originally foreign concept to the conditions of the Japanese market (WSK 1965a:10). The authors thereby developed an argument that would later also be applied to the introduction of other retail formats into Japanese retailing such as the convenience store or home centres.

Representative of the strong role of founders in the development of new store concepts and the way innovations were introduced is the example of Daiei and its founder Isao Nakauchi. Born in 1922 in Osaka the son of a pharmacist, he grew up in Kobe and attended commercial school there. After the war he had his first entrepreneurial experiences on the black market before joining his father's business wholesaling pharmaceutical products for cash at discounted prices (Ôshita 1993:111). His first contact with modern retailing techniques came through promotional materials by the Japanese subsidiary of NCR (National Cash Register Company) that described an American supermarket. After Nakauchi could not convince his father to convert the family business he set up his own company in 1957. With a concentration on pharmaceuticals, the first store reached its sales ceiling after only three days and a further increase of sales seemed possible only through the introduction of new product lines. The company turned for help to the founders of the Maruwa Food Centre; it had earlier introduced pharmaceuticals through the advice of Nakauchi's brother. A director of the Maruwa Food Centre advised the firm to redesign the store and add a food department selling packaged groceries and confectionery. This advice resulted eventually in the conversion to a supermarket and allowed Daiei to overcome competition from two neighboring drugstores. Nakauchi also recognized early the growing importance of beef, believing that this product would soon become a regular element in the Japanese diet, a judgement confirmed by the quick customer acceptance of the new product in his store (Ôshita 1993:130–3). Only five years after Daiei's foundation the company already employed over 1000 people and was going through its first stages of organizational change. Sales and procurement were separated and university graduates were hired to be groomed for management positions (Daiee 1992:292–4).

The example of Daiei shows that companies did not have an overall plan for their development at hand when they began to introduce new elements into their stores. Rather, innovators arrived successively at different combinations of new techniques and in this process reinvented some existing formats or arrived at new distinctive formats. In this process, Nakauchi was of course not the only person who left his mark on the development of Japanese superstore retailing in its initial period. Other pioneers who could be named were Masatoshi Itô of Ito Yokado, Motaya Okada of Jusco and Kôhachi Iwata of Nagasakiya.

In the introduction of new techniques, retailers were influenced heavily by developments in the United States. Here, several agents of change can be identified. Knowledge was being transmitted through manufacturers of retail technology, publishers of industry journals, organizers of training seminars and research trips, and finally academia. The introduction of self-service was heavily influenced through the activities of the manufacturer of cash registers, NCR. While the first cash register had already been introduced into Japan in 1897, the establishment of a Japanese subsidiary of NCR in 1920 sped up the diffusion of cash registers in Japan. Users of the new technology were at first operators of existing retail formats such as department stores and pharmacies.

A magazine, published by the manufacturer since 1923, called *Tôdai* (Lighthouse), actively promoted the modernization of Japanese retailing through the description of concepts used in American retailing. After the war the company resumed the publication of its magazine and among the themes covered were the principles and techniques of self-service, chain operations and category management (HKH/Takayama 1989:295, Maeda 1992:180). To demonstrate the practical applicability of these concepts the company took a leading role in the opening of the previously described first supermarket in Japan in the heart of Tokyo. In addition, it also conducted complementary seminars for potential buyers of its technology. In 1957 NCR started to offer international seminars in the US. One of the first participants in these was the founder of Ito Yokado, Masatoshi Itô. Participants are reported as having suffered a culture shock when they were confronted with the comparatively advanced level of development of American retailing at that time (Morishita 1990:83).

Other agents complemented the activities of NCR. Shôgyô-kai (Retail World), a publisher of trade journals, offered seminars titled 'Supermarket School I and II' and in addition extensively introduced the concept of supermarkets through its magazines. Among the companies consulting Shôgyôkai Publishing were the founders of Kansai Supermarket, a pioneer in the area of food supermarkets in Japan. In a study trip to Tokyo, prior to the opening of their first store, the founders first visited the publisher to inform themselves about suitable stores to visit (KS 1985:9–10). Shôgyôkai Publishing continues to promote the modernization of retailing today, mainly through its publication *Hanbai kakushin* (Revolution in Retailing). Seminars in retail techniques were also offered by other companies such as the Pegasus Group, which provided training in controllership, chain store management and advertising (Atsumi 1976:111–13).

US examples and techniques could, however, not always provide the solutions to overcome problems encountered by Japanese retailers. Operators of food superstores were perplexed initially by the demands of Japanese consumers for a wide variety of fresh merchandise and the unwillingness of consumers to forgo quality and choice for price. In handling fresh merchandise companies struggled with the difficulties caused by Japan's alternating periods of extreme hot and cold weather. In addition, storage and transport of fresh merchandise was difficult owing to a lack of infrastructure. Techniques for preparation of merchandise, sales floor presentation and packaging for self-service were not yet available. Offering consumers fresh merchandise in the required variety and quality could thereby be achieved initially only by accepting on a regular basis a high degree of spoilage and loss of merchandise (HKH/Takayama 1989:53). These problems explain the secondary role that food super-stores were forced to accept in the development of superstore retailing in Japan. Without being able to resort to existing technology, it was well into the 1970s before operators of food superstores could overcome these technical problems and establish a distinctive business model of their own that was well adapted to the conditions of the Japanese market. Academia was also quick to absorb knowledge from the US. Describing the development and growth of new retail formats as a necessary conse-quence of mass production and mass consumption, academics provided political circles and the bureaucracy with the necessary arguments to support the development of new store formats and the modernization of the distribution sector. During the 1960s these academics were convinced that conditions in Japan would eventually come to resemble the American situation. Mimura (1992:68–72) names this stream of thought in academia during the 1960s the 'modernization of distribution' school, whereby modernization was understood almost exclusively as a development following the US example. The strongest advocate of this direction was Shûji Hayashi (see especially Hayashi 1962, 1964). By focusing on the actual problems of the Japanese distribution system and scrutinizing its state of development by international comparison, he provided an alternative to two established approaches that looked at distribution from a highly abstract perspective, namely the Marxist school and the functional school. Hayashi was also a member of policy-related government advisory panels, and, by emphasizing the positive contributions of an efficient distribution system to overall economic growth, contributed to the overall positive viewpoint towards develop-ments in retailing (Tamura [Masanori] 1984:11). The term 'revolution in distribution' (*ryûtsû kakumei*) quickly gained public acceptance as characterizing the ongoing developments of the 1960s. Later, however, this school of thinking lost some of its influence during the 1970s and 1980s with more and more academics arguing for the possibility of an independent development path for Japan, especially in regard to the continued existence of small retailers. Still, the term was rediscovered in the 1990s with observers naming this period the 'second revolution in Japanese distribution' (*dai niji ryûtsû kakumei*).

The introduction of new techniques into Japanese retailing also had an interesting ideological component. While later the opening of new superstores led to frequent conflicts with traditional retailers, and though it is often assumed that a situation of natural conflict between the two sides exists, this had not been the case when supermarket techniques were introduced initially into Japan. On the contrary, new techniques were seen and propagated as a means to strengthen the position of consumers and small and medium retail companies alike in regard to the dominant role of suppliers in procurement markets and department stores in the consumer markets. This position was represented by the *'shufu no mise'* (housewives' store) movement. Heavily involved in the inauguration of this movement was Hideo Yoshida. He had participated in opening the first real Japanese supermarket in Kita Kyushu in 1956 and afterwards conducted talks and seminars throughout the country to promote the new retail techniques. He also presented his experiences at the national convention of retail managers in January 1957. These activities finally resulted in the creation of a voluntary chain of *housewives' stores*. Organized around a central office in Tokyo, this organization supported its members in the opening of new stores on a nationwide basis (Yoshida 1982:22, Okuzumi 1983:81–3).

Among the businesses established following this initiative are a few prominent examples. Akira Aoki was motivated by hearing of Yoshida establishing a company to open a supermarket in Shikoku under the name of Housewives' Store Matsumoto, with a sales floor of 660 square meters as early as November 1957. Later he was engaged in the establishment of the first voluntary chain and it was through the contact of the group at the wholesale market of Osaka that the later founders of Kansai Supermarket were inspired to get involved in the supermarket sector (Okuzumi 1983:86–8, KS 1985:7). Daiei also opened its first branch as a housewives' store. In another incident the movement assisted eight women in becoming entrepreneurs themselves by setting up their own store, after they had been inspired by getting information on the first store of the movement in Ogaki (Okuzumi 1983:95–7). Yoshida himself described the organization he represented as a countermovement of small and medium companies against big capitalism, as well as serving the needs of consumers (cited in Okuzumi 1983:82). While Yoshida basically refers to department stores here, Yahagi notes that besides department stores, consumer cooperatives posed a particular threat to the traditional retail sector and that their activities were a major force driving the traditional sector towards the introduction of new techniques and the establishment of voluntary chains for joint procurement (Yahagi 1993e:54–5).

Formation of responsive consumer markets

In 1952, private consumption reached prewar levels again. It expanded at a pace that let observers speak of a consumption boom. Consumption moved beyond food and daily necessities, and demand for consumer durables such as refrigerators, sewing machines, radios and cameras rose quickly. The steepest increase, however, was seen in apparel. Increases in consumer spending were based on rising household incomes owing to the recovery and growth of the Japanese economy. Fueled by the Korean War, Japan entered into a long period of growth that, while being interrupted by minor downturns, lasted until the oil shocks of the 1970s. Measures taken under the occupation after the war to promote democratization, land reform and the promotion of labor unions enabled the majority of the population to participate in the merits of growth, a prerequisite for the formation of a consumer society (NKS 1963:58, Uchino 1983:73–4).

The final steps towards a full-fledged consumer society were taken at the beginning of the 1960s. Driven by high productivity increases in the manufacturing sector, incomes that had increased continuously suddenly leaped to new heights and initiated a period that came to be known as the second consumption boom of post-war Japan. In particular, demand for consumer durables increased again, with many households upgrading existing products (Yoshino 1971:57–60, Uchino 1983:122).

However, as has been pointed out this development was not uninterrupted. Long periods of growth alternated with short periods of stagnation or lower growth in the years 1958, 1962, 1965 and 1970 (Nakamura 1981:49–54). From a general perspective, the existence of business cycles has been described as favourable for the emergence of new retail institutions by Agergård, Olson and Allpass (1970:59). They conclude that consumers in periods of economic growth concentrate initially on their basic and daily needs before moving on to fulfilling special needs. However, they do so slightly earlier than they can afford and therefore have to save on daily necessities. Customers get more selective in the choice of the stores they frequent and prefer those offering goods at lower prices. For Japan, Yoshino (1971:138) has confirmed this relationship. Consumers were intensively stimulated to buy new products by aggressive marketing campaigns conducted by consumer goods manufacturers. Price became a major element in choosing retail stores and existing retail stores were not able to fulfill the needs of consumers. Miya stresses the relationship between periods of growth and stagnation and concludes that the phase of economic stagnation in the years 1957 and 1958 promoted the establishment of supermarkets. Consumers had to tighten budgets and became more selective, and a general discount war erupted in retailing involving the new superstores, but also department stores and general retailers. The Japanese Fair Trade Commission even criticized sales below procurement prices and demanded that department stores limit rebates granted to consumers. The activities of retailers also caught the attention of manufacturers, who, fearing for the image of their products as well as their margins, began to strive for control over pricing down to the retail level (Miya 1985a:35).

Consumers at that time generally viewed the new retail formats positively with regard to prices and quickly accepted them. Surveys show that overall, local neighbourhood stores were still the favourite place for housewives to do their shopping. This was especially true for fresh merchandise bought on a daily basis. Supermarkets were at that time visited mainly by consumers to shop for processed foodstuffs and products relatively new to the Japanese market, such as meat products or instant coffee. The main reason for shopping in supermarkets was the price, followed by product quality. Consumers appreciated the introduction of self-service, noting that this enabled them to choose products on their own. They were also aware of the fact that this method increased the sum of money they spent at one time. They were split over whether the new type of shopping increased or reduced the time needed for shopping (WSK 1965b:66).

From the 1960s it was sociodemographic developments that not only promoted the growth of new stores but also determined some of their characteristics. One of these trends was a further migration of consumers towards the large metropolitan areas of Osaka and Tokyo. Within metropolitan areas people started to move to suburban areas. Alongside commuter railway lines new residential towns developed on the periphery of the cities. The population of the new suburban areas was relatively homogeneous in age, household size and income. It was made up of white-collar workers and their families, a segment of the population with rapidly growing incomes. The systematic development of the suburban area led to relatively densely populated areas, often in multistory housing complexes. Uchino (1983:107) argues that, while often looked down upon today, these planned housing complexes (*danchi*) of the late 1950s and early 1960s were seen at the time of their construction as the embodiment of modern living. Apartments in these developments were in high demand. Their inhabitants were regarded as the new urban elite that led the way in consumer behaviour, their dwellings being showcases of a new lifestyle. These sociodemographic developments offered the pioneers of the superstore sector the opportunity to transfer their large-scale store concepts to suburban areas. Besides sophisticated and open-minded consumers, these locations also offered lower land prices and an overall underdeveloped retail structure.

The needs of consumers in the new residential areas not only promoted the expansion of stores but also changed their appearance. Assortments of superstores in prior locations, mostly shopping districts, had been complemented by assortments of retailers in the neighbourhood and superstore operators had mostly concentrated on those product lines where they felt they had a competitive edge. The change in location led to the opportunity and the need to expand assortments to fulfill the entire needs of consumers in regard to daily necessities and to a certain degree beyond this. Operators of food supermarkets included apparel and household goods into their assortments, and operators of apparel stores added food departments. Both recognized the opportunity to cater to the demand of newly founded households for consumer durables, furniture and fixtures. Expanding companies that followed consumers to the suburban areas were thereby presented with high incentives to develop their stores towards general superstores (HKH/ Takayama 1989:45–8, Koyama and Togawa 1992:80–2, Mimura 1992:4–5, Orihashi 1993:100, Takaoka 1993:16). For companies these rapid moves towards wider and deeper assortments also brought along changes in their cost structures and they often tried to pass these additional costs on to their customers. As noted earlier, consumers started to criticize superstore operators for loosing their price aggressiveness towards the end of the 1960s. Offering an extensive selection of merchandise and at the same time having to maintain an image of price aggressiveness became an ongoing managerial struggle for operators of general superstores throughout the following decades.

Conflict and harmony in procurement markets

The introduction of mass merchandising concepts in retailing was facilitated by developments in procurement markets. Self-service can be utilized only if products are packaged and offered in the quantities demanded by the final consumer. Self-selection is made easier if products exist that consumers recognize by their brand name and feel confident to choose on their own. In logistics, stores have to be supplied on time and in the demanded quantities. Of course, store operators can take over tasks like packaging, branding or logistics on their own, but this requires time, capital and management capabilities, resources that the entrepreneurs introducing the new store formats often did not possess at all or preferred to use for other purposes.

While many of the above-mentioned prerequisites can be taken for granted today, this was not the case at the time when superstores were introduced into Japan. Before the war, large manufacturers could be found only in the heavy and machinery industries. In contrast, goods for the rather underdeveloped consumer markets were produced mainly by small enterprises; these small manufacturers were often closely affiliated with single wholesalers. Only after the war, with the dissolution of the *zaibatsu*, were large manufacturers forced to switch production to civilian goods and to develop independent marketing capabilities (Yoshino 1971:92, Koch 1998). Manufacturers of consumer electronics, cosmetics, pharmaceuticals, packaged foods and beverages introduced branded articles displaying the manufacturers' names. At the same time, manufacturers started advertising campaigns in the print media and the radio, but also in rapidly developing television. These campaigns were facilitated by the high spatial concentration of consumers as well as the comparatively early commercialization of the media sector (Yoshino 1971:95–109, Partner 1999:125–30).

In particular, the introduction of branded merchandise and nationwide advertising campaigns were important for the development of new retail formats. Without the existence of branded merchandise the store itself had to guarantee the quality of the goods bought, and consumers would frequent either trusted stores near their homes for daily necessities or else department stores with a established reputation for special needs. The reputation of the store itself, however, became of lesser importance with the introduction of branded merchandise and the manufacturers' names guaranteeing the quality of the products. However, retailers introducing new formats at that time could not thoroughly leverage this development owing to the attempts of manufacturers to control all aspects of merchandising, including the price of their products at the retail level. Especially active in this regard was the cosmetics industry (for example, Shiseido), the consumer electrics industry (for example, Matsushita), the pharmaceutical and soap industry (for example, Kao) and finally the automobile industry. Control over the retail sector was established through strong ties with the wholesale sector. Independent wholesalers were gradually integrated into manufacturers' strategies through capital ties, financing and also personnel exchange. In the same way, small retailers were encouraged to exclusively handle the products of one manufacturer. These measures were supported by rebate systems, honoring not the absolute quantity of goods purchased by one customer at one time but rather the length of the relationship, the share of products of a certain manufacturer of overall sales and the accomplishment of previously agreed sales targets (Yoshino 1971:111–19, Itô *et al.* 1991:136, Yahagi 1993a:125).

The attempts of the manufacturing sector to dominate the distribution system became the cause of ongoing conflicts between manufacturers of branded products and operators of new retail stores. On the one hand, the actions of the industry encouraged innovative retailers to introduce their own brands; on the other, the capability to get hold of branded products and sell them at prices below those recommended by manufacturers offered a constant challenge to and opportunity for new retailers to demonstrate their attractiveness to consumers. Conflicts between retailers and manufacturers were often fought out in public and here the strategy of retailers to always argue their points in the interest of consumers greatly contributed to their popularity. In 1964, a conflict between Daiei and Matsushita erupted. Matsushita stopped all supplies to Daiei after Daiei had sold its products below the company's recommend retail prices by about 20 per cent. Other companies like Kao and Shiseido followed the example of Matsushita. This intensified the conflict and even aroused the interest of a committee of parliamentary representatives that visited Daiei to investigate the case. Daiei finally decided to remove all Matsushita products from its shelves (Miya 1985a:74, 81; Katayama 1993:9). Both companies being dominated by strong non-compromising founder personalities, this situation remained unsolved until the early 1990s. It even motivated Daiei at one time to integrate backwards into the production of household electronics by acquiring a stake in a smaller electronics manufacturer. The conflict was eventually solved in the 1990s when the companies had to resume trading with each other after Daiei took over two retail chains that had established dealings with Matsushita (Miya 1985a:110, Yahagi 1993e:133–4).

The relationship of the emerging new retailers with the wholesale sector was equally ambiguous. Although retailers of the traditional sector had at first succeeded in convincing wholesalers to refrain from supplying new competitors – for example forcing Daiei to move into its own beef production in Australia as early as 1964 – wholesalers later became the main supply source for superstore operators. Soon, a situation of interdependence developed. At a time when the new retailers had no access to the capital markets, wholesalers became their major source of finance by providing generous terms of payment. In exchange, new retailers accounted for an increasing share of wholesalers' sales (Atsumi 1993:29).

Conflicts with suppliers were further reduced when large merchandising stores were opened in direct proximity with each other. Operators expanded their selections to give customers greater choice, and in this process introduced products of higher quality and also some foreign articles. In this situation, retailers could no longer afford not to handle the products of leading brand manufacturers. For Daiei this situation arose when the company decided to expand from its home markets in the Kansai region with the cities of Kobe and Osaka to the Kantô area around Tokyo. Here it had to compete with Seiyu, which had engaged itself in conflicts with manufacturers to a lesser extent. While the conflict between Daiei and Matsushita continued, the relationship with other manufacturers like Shiseido and Kao normalized, leading even to the joint development of products (Yahagi 1993a:137–9). Considering these factors, it has to be concluded that the dependence on wholesalers and the keenness and ability of manufacturers to control prices on the retail level limited pricing options of superstore operators from early on. Companies were forced to look for alternative ways to attract customers and often did so by broadening and deepening their assortments and adding new services and amenities.

Retail competition in a period of growth

It has already been pointed out that the aggressive strategies of department stores and also consumer cooperatives had driven some retailers in the traditional sector into actively pursuing innovative strategies, changing to a more price-aggressive approach and also introducing elements like self-service. In their first stages of development, operators of supermarkets could exploit several niches in the retail market. Competing with the traditional local neighbourhood stores, the products handled by supermarkets were initially different. Supermarkets focused on processed groceries and other products for which no clearly established distribution channels in Japan existed at that time. In addition, supermarkets actively developed new locations in areas without an established retail structure. In this sense, the expansion of superstores did not receive much attention at first. While conflicts erupted occasionally on a local level, general requests for a restriction of the activities of supermarket operators were not voiced (Mimura 1992:5).

The only existing large-scale retail format were department stores; however, their expansion was limited by government regulations. The Department Store Law was introduced in 1956 with the aim of sustaining business opportunities for small- and medium-sized retail enterprises (Suzuki 1993:195). The law heavily interfered with the business policy of department store operators and included rules concerning the construction of new department stores, the merger of companies and the expansion of existing stores. The law was applied on a company basis, requiring every firm that operated a store with a sales space of more than 1500 square meters and which offered an assortment composed of apparel, groceries and household articles, to hold a permit. The law also regulated such companies' activities, including opening hours, and required them not to operate their stores for a certain number of days each month. It further prohibited firms from offering certain services such as complimentary transport of customers to their stores. By applying the law on a company basis regulators had, however, unintentionally left loopholes for the introduction of new retail formats and new principles of organizing retail activities (Ishihara [Takemasa] 1993:240). Superstore operators relatively quickly reached the size limits of the Department Store Law, and the same was true for the handling of the three product groups. Operators, however, circumvented the law by sourcing the management of whole product groups to independent companies.

The overall favourable development of the Japanese economy also lessened competitive pressures. Growth in consumer demand allowed growth for the new retail formats without necessarily leading to losses for existing formats. The favourable situation also reduced the importance of aggressive pricing strategies in the introduction of new retail formats. This situation was different from that usually assumed in theories on retail change. In particular, cyclical theories of retail change assume a situation of intense competition and overall saturated markets, with new contenders being able to enter the market only by aggressive pricing of merchandise or other clear competitive advantages, their entry necessarily resulting in losses for existing companies and formats.

Relatively quickly, however, intense competition developed between the new retail formats. General superstores competed with pure food supermarkets and the latter soon had to realize that operators of the former mainly used food products to attract consumers to their stores. General superstores went as far as accepting losses in selling fresh merchandise, since this could usually be compensated by higher margins in their apparel and household goods departments. In addition, operators of general superstores managed earlier than food supermarket operators to gain access to financial markets. This enabled them to concentrate on expansion and sales growth while neglecting aspects of profitability (Yamamoto 1971:121, HKH/Takayama 1989:53).

Early in the 1960s the looming entry of a foreign competitor added to the complexity of the competitive environment faced by Japanese retailers. In 1963, the general trading company Sumitomo revealed plans for an entry into the retail market in collaboration with the US retail giant Safeway. These plans came as a shock to operators of superstores which at that time could look back on only a few years of experience with their new format. This shock is said to have had far-reaching consequences for Japanese retailing. Retail companies began to examine previous strategies critically, and even intensified their own growth strategies. They also increased their efforts to systematically import and implement sophisticated merchandising and management knowledge from the US. Ironically, Safeway, after encountering high losses in its first store opened in 1964 in Tokyo, pulled out of Japan as quickly as it had entered the country, citing the immaturity of Japanese consumer markets for 'real supermarkets' as its reason for withdrawal (Miya 1985a:49, 57). Sumitomo continued its engagement in the retail sector alone and developed the former joint venture into an overall successful but only medium-sized supermarket chain, Summit, a far cry from the overwhelmingly strong competitive challenge that had initially been expected by the Japanese retail industry.

At the end of the 1960s competition between the operators of general superstores added a new element to the competition in retailing. This competition was expressed by bitterly fought battles for new locations and customers. Retailers opened new outlets in the direct vicinity of competitors' stores and usually tried to outshine existing stores in price aggressiveness and comprehensiveness of products and services offered. Examples of local battles include the contest for supremacy in the Itami area where Jusco, Nichii, Nagasakiya and Kansai Supermarket all opened new stores in 1971, or the Fujisawa battle in 1974 where operators kept opening days a secret as long as possible and Daiei managed to beat Ito Yokado in the opening of a new store by just five days (Ôshita 1993:162–4, 173–8). As has been pointed out, the ability to offer new services played a growing importance in these conflicts. While theories of retail change often focus on the conflicts and adaptive behaviour between new and existing formats, in the Japanese case it was the increased competition within one retail format that led to changes in the appearance of retail formats.

3
Retail Policy: A Law for Large Stores

Izumiya in Kyoto

In 1976, Izumiya announced its plans to open a store with a sales floor size of 10 415 square meters in Kyoto. Eighteen months later, the company managed to submit the developer's report as required under the Large Store Law. It took two more years for the local Committee for the Early Regulation of Retail Activities to meet for the first time. The committee took seven years to reach a decision and only then could the official report be prepared and submitted to MITI. The store was finally opened with a sales floor of 8250 square meters in November 1989 (Kusano 1992:56).

Daiei in Kumamoto

In March 1975, Daiei revealed plans to open a store with 44 000 square meters of sales floor in the city of Kumamoto in Kyushu. At this time, the space of large retail stores in the area already amounted to about 10 per cent of total retail space. After Daiei submitted the formal report it met with opposition from the local chamber of commerce, which was formerly in charge of organizing an assessment committee, supervising the necessary hearings and submitting a final report to MITI. It was thereby quite apparent from the beginning that even in the case of a positive outcome of the hearings no positive report would be submitted to MITI. In July 1975, supported by protest rallies of retailers, the commission eventually submitted a report that advised against Daiei opening a store above 1500 square meters, the threshold of the Large Store Law at that time. In the light of this decision, the representative of consumer interest resigned from the commission citing pressure and the impossibility of voicing opinions.

In March 1977, Daiei made a second attempt and applied for a store with 29 000 square meters. This and two further attempts in 1978 failed. In the meantime, Daiei carried the conflict from the local to the national stage and got diet representatives and the retail unions to lobby for its cause. In addition, Daiei announced that it had won over 30 local retailers as tenants but did not reveal their names.

In December 1978, after having received four negative reports from the local assessment committee, the National Advisory Council for Large Retail Stores that handled the final decision on the opening of stores for MITI finally approved of Daiei opening a store of only 13 000 square meters. Last efforts of the local opposition to convince the minister not to follow the advisory council did not succeed and Daiei finally opened its store in April 1980, nearly five years after its first application (Daiee 1992:247–54, Kusano 1992:69–83).

The above examples demonstrate how retail policy became a major factor influencing the development of Japanese retailing during the 1970s and 1980s. The existence of a law regulating the opening of large stores became important not only for the relationship between small and large businesses but also for the competition between operators of large stores. Owing to the importance of these regulations they are discussed in a separate chapter. This discussion will not just introduce the law but will look also at the underlying political economy.

The Large Store Law

The Large Store Law was passed in the Diet (Japanese parliament) on 1 October 1973 and enacted on 1 March 1974. In the first article of the law its objectives are stated as 'providing for adequate business opportunities for small-and medium-sized retailers in the vicinity of large stores by regulating business activities in large retail stores'. Doing so were to be done under the 'continuous consideration of the well-being of consumers'. The law aimed further to 'secure the normal development of the retail sector' and eventually to 'contribute to the healthy development of the Japanese economy.' From the very beginning the ambiguity of these objectives led to further conflict, with none of the parties involved satisfied with the way the law was implemented and the results it produced.

Before going deeper into the details of this law one point should be taken up in advance: the overall importance and thereby the relevance of the whole discussion in itself. The Large Store Law was introduced in the early 1970s, further strengthened during the 1970s and 1980s, gradually liberalized during the 1990s, and finally abandoned and replaced in the late 1990s. While it was still in place, there was an ongoing discussion about its significance for the development of Japanese retailing. Some critics, including those representing foreign interests, perceived the law as clearly hindering the expansion of large retail stores, and thus resulting in a distortion of the natural course of development of Japanese retailing. Others, however, countered this argument by pointing out that empirical proof for the influence of the law was based largely on anecdotal observations, that the Japanese retail scene with a lot of small stores reflected true consumer preferences rather than the impact of the law, and finally that even with the law in effect the number of small stores had decreased and the number of large stores had increased. While controversial at the time, the developments of the 1990s after a substantial liberalization of the law put an end to the discussion. Superstore operators utilized the regulatory changes to expand their store networks to a degree that could not be explained by other factors such as increased mobility and changes in preferences of consumers or lower land prices alone. The number of reports submitted concerning the construction and opening of new large stores soared from an average of yearly 518 reports in the 1980s to an average of 1779 reports in the 1990s (Figure 3.1).

Concerning the actual implementation and effects of the Large Store Law, several points need to be discussed:

- The political economy at the time of the introduction of the law and during the time it was in place. Why was the law implemented and why did its existence receive so much attention not only within Japan but also worldwide?
- The actual implementation of the law and changes in its implementation over time.
- The effects of the law not only in regard to the number of store openings but also in regard to the development of the characteristics of the different store formats.

The political economy of the Large Store Law

The process that led to the enactment of the new law reflects public opinion towards superstores and the companies operating them. As pointed out, small and medium retailers staged protests against the opening of large stores almost immediately after these had first been opened in Japan. Still, it took some time for policy-makers to react to these

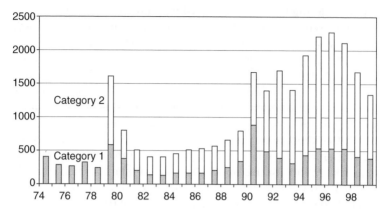

Figure 3.1   Number of reports concerning the opening of large retail stores under the Large Store Law, 1974–99.

Note that figures for 1974 April to 1979 April refer to all stores with more than 1500 square meters (3000 square meters in six designated metropolitan areas). Those for 1979 May to 1991 December subdivide as follows: category 1: all stores with more than 1500 square meters (3000 square meters in six designated metropolitan areas); category 2: all other stores above 500 square meters. Figures for 1992 January to 1999 consist of category 1: all stores with more than 3000 square meters (6000 square meters in six designated metropolitan areas); category 2: all other stores above 500 square meters.

Source: Author's graph based on Keizai Sangyôshô (no date).

protests. Japanese regulators, like regulators in many other countries (Dawson 1979:41–6), had never really regarded the retail sector as a major active driving force of economic development in its own right. The retail sector caught public attention owing mainly to the substantial number of persons it employed.

This tendency can be traced back as far as the 1920s. During the economic crisis following World War I retail trade had become a last resort for people in large cities who had lost their jobs and were encouraged by the overall low requirements with regard to both capital and skills to open retail stores. On a nationwide basis the number of retail stores increased to 1 store to every 20 households; in Tokyo this figure dropped to only 6 households per retail store. To counter this situation, regulators introduced measures for modernization and protection, such as the establishment and promotion of collaborative activities through retailers' associations and the enactment of the first Department Store Law (TS 1980:163). During the war the role of these associations was changed, with associations gaining control over their members in the interest of Japan's war effort (Kawano 1992:123, 136–8).

After the war, regulators were mainly interested in reconstruction and industrialization. Industrial policy focusing on manufacturing and the modernization of the agricultural sector took centre stage, while modernization of the distribution sector was regarded as only a secondary problem (Tatebayashi 1991a:76–7). Again, the retail sector was seen as a pool for unneeded labour and policies for this sector such as the reenactment of the Department Store Law in 1956 were pursued because of social rather than economic considerations (Iwanaga 1988:113–16). Retailers were included, however, in the comprehensive policies to promote small businesses; this was not done in a conscious way but rather because these businesses happened to fulfill the criteria in regard to company size (Yoshino 1971:256).

This view of the retail sector changed during the 1960s when regulators recognized the underdeveloped state of retailing as a future threat for the Japanese economy. Productivity and income gaps between the distributive industries and the manufacturing sector, which could be traced to the low qualifications of people employed in consumer goods distribution, were pointed out. Predictions at that time saw an overall shortage of labour and it was feared that increased labour demand in the manufacturing sector would result in rising income levels in the retail sector, a development that would automatically lead to price increases if not countered by productivity improvements. For the year 1970, demand for workers in the distribution sector was predicted to exceed supply by half a million people, this gap increasing to 2.6 million people by 1975 (TSK 1968:15, TSK 1971). This consideration, which was prominent at the end of the 1960s, helps to explain the reluctance of regulators to introduce measures limiting the expansion of new mass merchandisers at an earlier stage. The situation changed, however, during the 1970s when oil crises and economic stagnation led to restructuring in manufacturing and dampened demand for labour. Suddenly, the distributive sector became again an important catchment basin for unneeded labour and policies for distribution again resumed a protective stance. Besides the overall interest of the government in developments in the retail sector, a wide spectrum of positions existed among the other involved parties. These were department store companies, small- and medium-sized retailers, operators of superstores, political parties, the Deliberation Council for the Distributive Trades and finally the bureaucracy itself.

Since 1956 the activities of department store companies had been regulated tightly under the Department Store Law. Surprisingly, operators of department stores were initially split over the need for regulation in the operation of large stores. Operators of department stores in metropolitan areas could imagine competing with the superstore companies in a totally deregulated environment. Regulations for superstores were, however, demanded by local and regional department store companies that operated comparatively small stores in the prefectural capitals and were already experiencing the negative consequences of the fast expansion of superstore operators (Kusano 1992:97).

From the position of small and medium retailers, theoretically protected from competition by large retail stores through the provisions of the Department Store Law, it seemed to be only natural for these companies to demand the extension of regulations to superstores. However, not all small and medium sized retailers felt threatened by superstores in the same way. Surveys of that time showed that while 40 per cent of stores had indeed suffered through the opening of a new superstore, 30 per cent had not experienced any change in the same situation, while 20 per cent even enjoyed improvements, with new superstores in their neighbourhood drawing additional customers to their stores (Kusano 1992:96). Still, the associations of small and medium businesses demanded strict regulations for all large retail stores and were opposed to any new regulations that might be imposed on their members in the process, as for example the introduction of a general law regulating opening hours that had been proposed by some department store operators.

Political parties, while not agreeing on all points, overall supported the protection of small retailers. This tendency was supported by the general discussion on the conduct and role of large companies in the economy that took place at the beginning of the 1970s. It was felt generally that it had been large companies that had profited most from the fast economic growth of the Japanese economy with other concerns such as the protection of consumers and employees or the environment having not received enough attention. Large retailers were not spared from this criticism, and it was the Communist Party especially that criticized the growing role of large companies in a sector that had up to then been dominated by small businesses. The Communist Party at that time managed to gain influence among small retailers, and its initiative to organize alternative local associations opposing the official chambers of commerce quickly gained popularity.

While generally agreeing that something needed to be done, the issue that divided the political parties most was whether to replace the existing licensing system for department stores with a report system. While the Socialist Party and the Communist Party strongly favoured a licensing system, the Liberal Democratic Party (LDP) overall favoured a report system. However, not all LDP members supported this stance. Some members had a background in retailing themselves, and many Diet members were strongly dependent on the support of local retailers during election campaigns. Under the Japanese election system, politicians of the same party had to compete with each other within one constituency and thereby could not secure their seat in parliament without strong local support. Local retailers often formed the backbone of individual support networks. Politicians were usually highly responsive to demands voiced by their support groups and local initiatives thereby often proved more effective than initiatives of associations on the national level (Tatebayashi 1991a:79, Hayes 1992:114–18, Hayao 1993:131).

Concerning the change from a licensing system to a report system, the LDP finally managed to pacify its representatives with the promise that the difference between the two systems would not be felt much after the implementation of the law. Thus, the complications and delays retailers would encounter after submission of reports as well as the substantial freedom and influence the bureaucracy would enjoy in the implementation of the law were anticipated well before the law was enacted (Kusano 1992:103).

With more than sixty laws having major implications for the retail sector, nearly all Japanese government ministries are in one way or another involved with the retail industry, thus further increasing the complexity of interests (Kubomura, Tajima and Mori 1982:44–7). While normally in Japanese industrial policy-making one ministry takes the lead role in supervising a certain industry, this does not hinder other ministries from contesting this role from time to time (Muramatsu and Krauss 1987:44–7). Overall matters of the distribution sector were under the jurisdiction of the Ministry of International Trade and Industry (MITI). In the process leading to the introduction of the Large Store Law competition between ministries became extremely pronounced. The Ministry of Home Affairs was concerned about the position of prefectures and local communities in the regulatory processes leading to the opening of new stores. The Ministry of Construction saw the new law interfering with its role in land use planning. The Ministry of Transportation was in charge of railway terminals that often housed major shopping complexes. The Economic Planning Agency displayed an early interest in deregulation and liberalization and was worried about an overall increase in regulations. Labour issues were handled by the Ministry of Labour, which saw an intrusion into its regulatory sphere in the attempt to regulate the opening hours of stores. Finally, the Ministry of Agriculture, Forestry and Fisheries argued that supermarkets dealt mainly in foodstuffs and should therefore fall under its jurisdiction (Kusano 1992:106). Indeed, the Ministry of Health and Welfare and the Ministry of Agriculture, Forestry and Fisheries managed to exempt stores run by agricultural and consumer cooperatives from the Large Store Law, an advantage that gave the store operations of these organizations a major boost during the 1970s and 1980s and turned them into serious competitors of commercial retailers (Kunimasa 1985:22–3). Conflict was present, however, not only between ministries but also within MITI itself. The financial and personnel resources of MITI leaned heavily towards the promotion of SMEs with their interest promoted by an agency of its own, the Small-and Medium-Enterprise Agency.

Considering this constellation of interests, it is not surprising that the outcome of the discussion about regulation for large retail stores was a highly controversial law with a lot of leeway given to regulators in implementation. The law led to a lot of conflict even before it was enacted, and many of these conflicts were later continued in the application of the law (Koyama and Togawa 1992:125).

Implementation and functioning of the Large Store Law

The Large Store Law changed the regulations for the opening of new large retail stores. Compared with the former Department Store Law, the object of regulations changed from the company to the single store building (Suzuki [Yasuaki] 1993:196–7, Ishihara 1993:245). After its enactment in 1974, the law was applied initially to all store buildings with a sales floor exceeding 1500 square meters. In specially designated areas, the six major metropolitan areas, a threshold of 3000 square meters was used. The law distinguished between the developer of a store and its tenants and the so-called reporting process went through two stages. In the first stage, the developer had to inform the regulatory authority about his plans. In the second stage, store tenants had to report on the nature of their activities, location, store size and first day of business at least five months before their planned opening date. These reports were examined by MITI. Changes deemed necessary were proposed to the Deliberation Council for Large-Scale Stores. The council's decision was issued as an instruction to the store and building operators. Details examined and regulated were the size of sales floors, opening hours and the yearly number of non-opening days. Before its decision the deliberation council heard the opinions of local chambers of commerce, consumer groups, retailers and their associations (Suzuki [Yasuaki] 1993:200).

After the law's introduction its initial effects were not dramatic, at least not in the pure numbers of newly opened stores. At the time of the implementation of the law, 1846 stores already existed that exceeded thresholds in regard to store size specified by it. After implementation, store operators did not curtail their expansion plans and handed in 1505 reports for the opening of new stores by 1978 (Yasuda 1993:29). Nonetheless, policies of retailers were affected. Companies had to accept substantial reductions both in the sizes of sales floors and in operating days (Table 3.1).

Another indication of the difficulty companies encountered in the process of opening new stores during this time was the increasing number of stores opened that avoided the threshold of the law by keeping store size to just under 1500 square meters. This development soon led to demands for more comprehensive regulations, with some municipalities enacting rules of their own for stores below 1500 square meters. Demands for change in the law were met in October 1978 when the threshold of the law was lowered to just 500 square meters. Stores falling under the previous regulations were called category I large-scale retail stores and for these the regulation process remained under the jurisdiction of MITI. Stores between 500 and 1500 square meters (3000 square meters in metropolitan areas) were called category II large-scale retail stores and the process of regulation for these came under the jurisdiction of the prefectural governments (Suzuki [Yasuaki] 1990:213). Again, this change influenced the activities of retailers. Initially, it led to a large increase in the number of reports submitted for category I stores during 1979, with some companies trying to submit reports before the new law was enacted.

The process of opening new stores became more and more complex. It also became more controversial, since some changes that increased complexity were introduced, based not on changes in legislation but on administrative guidance. Administrative guidance was an instrument commonly used by Japanese regulators in pursuing their objectives, especially in the area of industrial policy. Measures introduced by administrative guidance were usually not backed up by legislation but were based on the strong overall position regulating authorities enjoyed over companies in a certain industry. Companies were asked to comply with advice or practices given to them by the bureaucracy. Though compliance with the advice was voluntary in a legal sense, companies were well aware of the broad influence which the particular bureaucratic

Table 3.1 Results of regulation processes in 1975

Company	Number of reports	Planned sales floor (m²)	Approved sales floor (m²)	Reduction (%)	Planned non-operating days per store	Approved non-operating days per store	Increase (%)
Daiei	19	15 292	9 896	35.3	22	34	54.3
Jusco	14	9 774	6 896	29.5	25	41	61.0
Uny	13	8 960	6 678	23.5	25	40	71.0
Nichii	8	8 014	6 102	23.9	34	39	12.8
Izumiya	4	8 292	6 544	21.1	31	38	21.6
Seiyu	24	8 211	6 488	21.0	21	35	62.8
Nagasakiya	9	7 580	6 165	18.7	27	35	25.9
Ito Yokado	14	9 367	7 678	18.0	15	33	109.8

Source: Author's compilation based on NRS 1976.

institution involved wielded over them and therefore usually complied (Haley 1986:107–8).

In the case of the retail industry, the new rules led to increased influence by local retailers, complicated reporting processes and extended the time needed to handle reports. The first procedure introduced was the need for developers of store buildings to outline their plans to local retailers, chambers of commerce and local administrators even before submitting their reports officially. While it had originally not been intended that involved parties would have to reach consensus on plans at this stage, this became to be expected later. In some cases where consensus could not be reached at this stage plans for openings were withdrawn even before being submitted for official examination (NKS 1990:71). Not only the report of the developer but also the later report of store operators had to be scrutinized before formal submission. For this purpose, in 1979 a Committee for the Early Regulation of Retail Activities was introduced into the process. These committees became heavily dominated by local retailers and soon took over the task of evaluating plans and negotiating changes with the prospective store operators. After the plans were officially submitted the task to be performed by the official committees, which also included academics and consumer representatives, became a mere formality (NKS 1990:75–6, Suzuki [Yasuaki] 1990:212).

The introduction of these two steps created delays owing to conflicts between the different interests involved, but it was not always the expected conflict between small-scale retailers and potential new large store operators that complicated the process. Kusano (1992:26–9) demonstrates that operators of existing superstores or department stores also tried to block new competitors. Other common constellations of conflicting interests included two companies trying to open new stores in the same area at the same time, and small local retailers that expected to profit from a store opening being positioned against other small retailers fearing their demise. The complexity of interests and interest groups could thereby sometimes lead to unusual coalitions. In addition, involved parties competed for the support of local chambers of commerce, municipal bodies, MITI, political parties and even foreign countries.

Activity against the opening of new stores therefore focused heavily on delaying regulatory processes. For companies planning to open new stores this resulted in a heightened degree of uncertainty. Assumptions and conditions under which stores were originally planned changed during the time needed to deliberate reports. In the already highly uncertain economic environment of the 1970s, stores that had been planned during a period of high demand and were opened only years later never reached their projected sales volume. Plans for financing had to be revised frequently and companies had to shoulder high financing costs to compensate for the uncertainties (Miya 1985a:130–1, Kawasaki 1993:61).

The main instrument of regulation remained the control of store size. For example, in the year 1980, companies applied for an average of 13 600 square meters, but succeeded in getting approval only for an average of just under 8000 square meters. While it is not possible to find out about the true intentions of companies submitting applications it can still be stated that the strict application of the Large Store Law practically halted the trend of continuous expansion of store sizes that had taken place over the previous years (Kusano 1992:131).

Still, openings continued with companies moving from the heavily contested metropolitan areas to smaller cities in rural areas. For these towns the situation appeared extremely threatening. Having recognized the high degree of motorization in these rural areas, companies did not open stores in existing shopping districts but developed shopping centres in new locations outside of the cities. Again municipalities started to draw up regulations of their own to counteract this development. Some local town councils even completely froze the opening of new stores for the area under their jurisdiction. Amidst increased demand for the official amendment of the existing law, MITI eased the situation temporarily in October 1981 by demanding that companies restrain their own activities. By January 1982, however, MITI had worked out its own solution which reduced the number of new reports to just 132 in category I and 270 reports in category II for the year 1982. Figures stayed at that low level for the following years.

MITI's way of handling the situation consisted of two measures. First, it had directors of its regional offices suppress the submission of new opening plans for certain municipalities. Following its long tradition of administrative guidance, the criteria for the designation and names of municipalities were not publicized. Reports by the parties involved, however, draw the following picture. Plans for the opening of new large stores were no longer accepted for those municipalities where the number of inhabitants per square meter of sales floor in large stores had fallen below a certain threshold. For municipalities with more than 100 000 inhabitants this threshold was set at 3.4 inhabitants, for those with less than 50 000 inhabitants it was set at 3.9 inhabitants, and for municipalities in between at 3.7. While not being named, it was estimated that 340 municipalities fulfilled these criteria. Reports were only accepted when the municipality was expected to show strong population growth, when the new opening of a store was not expected to have an effect on existing retailers, or when the store was part of a larger project of town development. Apart from these areas, all municipalities with fewer than 30 000 inhabitants were declared off-limits for superstore companies. In total, 80 per cent of Japanese municipalities had thereby been blanked out for the opening of new large stores (NRS 1982:25, NKS 1990:73–4).

The second measure saw MITI assume direct control over large companies. For the years 1982 and 1983 certain companies were designated as 'companies to be individually guided.' These companies had to report to MITI details on their plans concerning the opening of new stores for the following year. Companies were given quotas based on current position in the market. For example, Daiei's expansion was restricted to 60 000 square meters while competitors like Nichii, Jusco, Ito Yokado and Seiyu had to be content with 50 000 square meters. Faced with the overall powerful position of MITI, companies, agreed to these measures and could in return achieve at least some certainty in the allocation of resources (NRS 1982:25, 31, Suzuki [Yasuaki] 1990:13). However, the economic situation of many companies at that time may also have contributed to the willingness of companies to comply with the guidance of MITI. Companies were troubled with declining sales and profit margins. Not only competing with each other for new locations but also feeling the increasing strength of regional food chains and home centres, they were in the process of restructuring internal operations. At the same time they were uncertain about the competitive strength and future of their main format, the general superstore. The blanking out of certain areas and the direct guidance by MITI might therefore have supplied them with a welcome break to reorganize and consolidate operations without having to fear for their position in the market. In this sense, the situation of superstore companies at the beginning of the 1980s was similar to that of department stores at the beginning of the 1930s and the 1950s where a competitive situation that had been perceived as excessive by many involved parties had been ended by the introduction of measures of self-restriction, which in the eyes of the public victimized the companies involved and appeared to solely protect smaller businesses (Abe [Yoshifumi] 1993:40, Azuma 1993:59–61, Kawasaki 1993:63).

Developments surrounding the Large Store Law were thereby highly complex and outcomes not as originally intended. Kawasaki (1993:63), who closely monitored the development of Japanese superstores through his involvement with the industry journal *Hanbai kakushin*, summarized the effects of the Large Store Law as follows:

* The law delayed the modernization of Japanese retailing and thereby led to continuously high consumer prices.
* The law created a feeling of security among small retailers. This led to unwillingness to change. If large stores eventually managed to open, small retailers were caught unprepared and could not stand up to the new competition.
* The law contributed to the reduction of the price aggressiveness of superstores. Because of both high costs for store openings and also internal agreements, operators of large superstores could not and did not pursue price-aggressive strategies in newly opened stores.
* The law protected existing large stores of weaker operators. It kept operators on one level and regulators even provided breaks for restructuring if competition heated up too much.

These developments did not go unnoticed, and during the 1980s slowly led to a reassessment of the activities of large stores. The gradually increasing number of openings of new stores in the second half of the 1980s can be attributed to two developments. First, being faced with increasing foreign pressure the Japanese government took measures to increase domestic demand. These included large-scale projects like the construction of new convention centres, hotels and leisure facilities as well as the revitalization of areas surrounding railway stations. Often such projects would include an upgrading of shopping facilities in the form of shopping centres, with large stores being invited as anchor tenants. Second, relationships between municipalities and large retail companies improved. If municipalities had at first opted against the opening of new large stores, they eventually realized that the lack of large stores reduced their attractiveness, since existing retailers saw no reason to modernize their operations. In rural areas not only did shopping centres create new employment opportunities, but the provision of adequate shopping facilities also prevented the younger population from migrating to larger cities. In their initiatives to increase their attractiveness, municipalities began to actively approach retailers and at the same time did away with some of the regulations introduced earlier to prevent the opening of new stores (NRS 1986:51, HKH/Takayama 1989:68). Municipalities were also confronted with the growing number of companies that had flourished in a niche by opening stores just below the threshold of 500 square meters. Local traditional retailers found the competition of these stores that often opened in their direct neighborhood even tougher than that of superstores and initially succeeded in pressing local governing bodies to enact protective legislation. The number of municipalities with their own regulations for stores below 500 square meters was estimated to have reached nearly a thousand by the end of the 1980s (NRS 1987:409, NRS 1990:44–6, SCC 1993:28).

Overall, the retail environment created by government distribution policy up to the 1990s can be characterized as highly regulated on the one hand and as highly uncertain on the other. It was regulated in the sense that regulations not only limited the opening of large stores but also influenced the characteristics of store formats such as operating hours, store size and closure days, and uncertain in that policies were frequently changed and retailers were left unsure about the length and outcome of application processes before the opening of large stores. Innovative and expansion-oriented retail companies came up with different solutions in the light of this high level of uncertainty. The management of the regulatory environment proved for many companies to be as challenging as dealing with the consumer markets. In general, companies had four different alternatives:

1. Adapt strategies to distribution policies and actively search for opportunities opened up by regulations.
2. Influence policy-makers to change existing regulations and policies.
3. Diversify into different business areas or internationalize.
4. Intensify cooperation with competitors and regulators to make the outcome of the regulation processes more certain.

Companies were of course not at total freedom to choose from these alternatives. While large and established companies had the personnel and financial capabilities to engage in all four alternatives, some of which will be shown in the following chapter, many smaller companies were in a position only to passively adapt their strategies to the environment created by regulators.

4

Diversification of Retail Formats

During the 1970s, the spectrum of retail formats widened further. Several new retail formats were introduced, some gaining considerable prominence within a short period of time. Developments in this period were multifaceted and they will therefore be discussed separately by retail format. Overall, the period saw the continued development of the general superstore with an enlargement of sales floors and the addition of amenities and services. Eventually, these developments led to a situation where some operators denied the relationship of their new stores with the original format of the general superstore. The food supermarket as an already established but not very successful format – being caught in a squeeze between general superstores and the local neighbourhood retailers – underwent a process of refinement that consisted of a strengthening of its operational fundamentals as well as a thorough adjustment to Japanese market conditions. At the same time, new concepts like home centres, discount stores and convenience stores were introduced. While the development of the first two concepts involved only the partial and very pragmatic adoption of concepts from overseas, the introduction of convenience stores can be seen as a systematic attempt to introduce a complex store format with only minor alterations (see Table 4.1).

General merchandisers: growth, diversification and denial

As already pointed out, the opening of new stores continued initially at a high level despite the restriction imposed by the Large Store Law. During the 1970s and 1980s companies continued to develop their store concept. They not only continued to increase sales floor area in

Table 4.1   Development of major retail formats, 1974–91

Format	1974		1982		1991	
	No. of stores	Market share (%)	No. of stores	Market share (%)	No. of stores	Market share (%)
General superstore	627	3.9	1 063	5.0	1 404	5.6
Food superstore	2 013	2.3	4 358	4.4	5 185	4.4
Living-related superstores			531	0.4	1 327	1.0
Convenience store			29 236	3.3	41 847	5.0

A general superstore is a store with more than 1500 square meters selling three product groups. Food/living-related superstores are stores with more than 500 square meters with a focus on one product group, from 1982 onwards this product group must account for more than 50 per cent of total sales.

Source: Author's compilation based on TSC (1976, 1985, 1993).

newly opened stores but also experimented with the introduction of retail brands or non-branded merchandise. Stores were now opened on a regular basis within 'shopping centres' which offered consumers new levels of services and amenities. Towards the end of the 1970s companies also started to develop concepts for the relaunch of older stores. The beginning of the 1980s saw an identity crisis in mass merchandising. Companies registered a general dissatisfaction with their stores. Some companies attempted to change their basic concepts from quantity to quality, from selling products to selling lifestyles, and in this process declared their departure from the format of the general superstore that had been the basis for their success up to then. Together with moves to relaunch older underperforming stores as discount-oriented ones and a localization of sales concepts, these activities led to a differentiation of the general superstore format. In detail, developments were as follows.

The first development was the expansion of sales floor area. Wherever possible, companies put their efforts into building stores with massive sales floors of about 15 000 square meters, the largest stores having more than 20 000 square meters. Representative of this drive was a store with 20 460 square meters opened by Ito Yokado in Narashino in 1977. While for this store and most other stores built at that time the department store design was used, with several floors above ground and one or two floors below ground, some operators started to experiment with alternatives. Uny, for example, opened as early as 1975 a so-called hypermarket with a sales floor of over 17 000 square meters on only two stories and parking facilities for up to 2000 cars (HKH/Takayama 1989:57, SGK 1989:354).

Most stores at that time were integrated into so-called shopping centres. The use of this term needs, however, to be questioned. While being called shopping centres, these shopping complexes were overall relatively small and had only one anchor tenant who heavily dominated the whole complex (Kurahashi 1993:195). While the number of shopping centres thereby had reached a number of 1695 by the end of the year 1992, their average size was only 11 322 square meters, of which the key tenant occupied 4761 square meters and an average of 46 other tenants shared about 3955 square meters (JCSC 1993:174).

Competition between operators of general superstores intensified during the 1970s and companies reacted with attempts to localize policies on price, service and selection. In this process, and also driven by consumers' reactions to the oil crises, companies also rediscovered pricing as a tool to draw customers. Trying to avoid conflicts with manufacturers, companies looked for an alternative in the introduction of non-branded products or private brands. Daiei introduced its own brand called Savings and Ito Yokado followed with products under the Cut Price label. Not all of these attempts were successful. Seiyu initially failed with a product line in cosmetics. Later, however, the same company achieved considerable and lasting success with an assortment of unmarked products (Miya 1985a:133, 136, HKH/Takayama 1989:59). The wish to distinguish themselves from competitors also led to an increase of services. Companies increased sales personnel to cater to costumers and for some products even did away with self-service. They also entered into a core business of department stores, the nationwide home delivery of gifts during the present-giving seasons in summer and at year-end. These moves increasingly blurred the boundaries between general superstores and regional department stores. Seiyu, in 1977, felt confident enough to open and operate a store under the name of its sister company Seibu Department Store. The Seibu Distribution Group (later the Saison Group) thereby consolidated its strategies, leaving the opening of metropolitan department stores to Seibu, and regional and suburban department stores to the superstore operator Seiyu (Doi 1982:32, Miya 1985a:144).

The intensified competition between operators of general superstores and the beginning saturation of certain regional markets also led to intensified efforts to expand the scope of operations. Companies expanded their store networks as far as the relatively remote areas of Northern Japan and Hokkaido. Their efforts were supported by the convergence of consumption patterns in rural and urban areas. While significant differences in lifestyles and incomes between urban and rural areas had existed until the oil crisis, these differences gradually decreased during the 1970s through productivity increases, the government-guaranteed income in agriculture and a slowdown of growth in the secondary industries. Increased prosperity in rural areas led to high ownership rates for cars with increasing mobility, and also Western consumer goods were increasingly introduced into rural areas. From the beginning of the 1970s major retailers started to systematically scout for locations in the more remote prefectural capitals. Often arriving at the same conclusions, the simultaneous opening of several new stores drastically and suddenly changed patterns of competition in some of these towns. As has been outlined in the previous chapter, this development was, however, largely brought to an end by the restrictive measures of MITI introduced in 1982 (Igarashi 1977:118–24, HKH/Takayama 1989:56–7).

At the beginning of the 1980s general superstores entered into a period that in retrospective has been called the Ice Age of large-store retailing (Koyama and Togawa 1992:172) but seems to have largely been forgotten during the even greater turmoil of the 1990s. Store operators had just convinced themselves that they had finally overcome the economic uncertainties of the oil shocks, when consumer spending suddenly dipped again at the beginning of the 1980s. In the majority of stores, sales fell below the level of previous years. Companies that had to cope with a ratio of 40 to 50 per cent of stores with declining sales were still considered lucky, compared with the majority of other companies which had to cope with a ratio of stores with shrinking sales of over 70 per cent (HKH/Takayama 1989:62, Sumiya 1992:20). At the same time, the strengthening of the application of the Large Store Law had made the opening of new stores so difficult that it became impossible for companies to compensate for sales losses by opening new stores. Under these conditions, companies lost faith in the future of their main retail format and Tsutsumi Seiji, the president and founder of Seiyu, was even cited in 1982 as saying: 'The era of the general superstore began in the 1960s and ended in 1981' (Tôda 1982:25). The questions of how to revive non-performing stores and what concepts to use in the opening of new stores thereby became the main issues for retailers in the 1980s. The main reason for the problem of non-performing stores was the increased level of competition. Existing stores faced newer and larger stores being located in superior locations. For example, Daiei alone was operating three stores at that time in the city centre of Okayama within a radius of only a few hundred meters. These stores were challenged by two competitors that had opened large-scale stores on the outskirts of the town (*Hanbai kakushin* April 1980:96, *Hanbai kakushin* April 1981:24). Older retail stores were usually smaller than those opened later by competitors, and were lacking in store design and amenities. Built at a time when most customers would still come by public transport, they were usually located centrally near station buildings. As such, they were difficult to reach by car and lacked parking facilities. The obvious solution would have been to scrap these old stores and to replace them with ones in locations better suited to the needs of retailers and consumers. As has been pointed out, such a policy did, however, conflict with the provisions of the Large Store Law. Regulations were just being tightened at that time, with whole areas being viewed unofficially as saturated and declared off-limits for new openings.

Japanese retailers, like most other Japanese companies at that time, were still largely measuring success in terms of sales growth. Not wanting to lose sales by simply closing down stores, they looked for other solutions and discovered renewed demand for large-scale discount stores, a position once occupied by them, but in the best sense of the Wheel of Retailing vacated by continuous trading-up processes. Daiei again took the lead in exploiting this perceived demand by transforming many of its existing stores to the new concept by thinning out assortments, concentrating on fast-moving articles, and by drastically simplifying the store design and furnishing, copying to a certain degree the warehouse style used by retailers overseas. Initially a drastic departure from the general merchandising store of that time, this concept was however soon to be modified again owing to a less-than-enthusiastic response by consumers who did not want to forgo choice and quality for lower prices. Reductions within assortments were revised and the space allocated to sales of fresh foods increased. Overall, the conversion of non-performing existing stores remained a trial-and-error process, with success often being hampered by the fact that new stores did not get a fresh start in new locations. The new concepts were a compromise in many regards, with cost savings not being fully realized owing to the inadequate store design and locations of the old stores (*Hanbai kakushin* April 1980:90–6, *Hanbai kakushin* April 1981:24, HKH 1993c:58).

For newly opened stores and for some suitable larger stores, the direction of store development took an altogether different approach. Here, companies upgraded assortments, focused on certain target groups, developed lifestyle-oriented concepts and gave sales floors the appearance of being separated into different shops based on the shop-in-the-shop philosophy.

Doing so, operators tried to give their stores an individual outlook that differentiated them from those of competitors. The philosophy behind these new store concepts was characterized by the usage of terms like 'specialty superstores', 'quality superstores' or in its extreme even 'junior department stores'. These new terms contrasted with the term 'mass merchandising superstore' used in the past. From the middle of the 1980s, policies culminated in the opening of extremely large-sized and expensively designed and decorated stores that tried to cater to the individual needs of customers instead of just offering staples to a general audience. Stores were often integrated into complexes characterized by large sales floors, a variety of tenants and a large number of parking spaces, and now justified the usage of the term 'shopping centres'. Aiming to offer customers value beyond the pure shopping experience, these shopping centres also often included restaurant complexes, leisure, sports and cultural facilities (Tôda 1982:24–6, HKH/Takayama 1989:68).

These changes in strategy were based on not only competitive pressures but also on perceived changes in consumer preferences. Over the different phases of their development, mass merchandisers had seen a continuous change in the composition of consumer spending (Table 4.2). Within this process, the proportion of disposable income used to buy material goods declined. In addition, the relative amount of expenditure for food and apparel declined, while the share for household goods remained constant. Expenses for leisure goods showed increases (Table 4.3). In this sense, the changes in assortments of general merchandisers from the 1960s onwards can be interpreted as an adaptation to changes in consumer spending. However, developments seen in the early 1980s seemed to go beyond the pattern of change as described above. During 1980 and 1981 the average household reduced its expenditure for durables and household furnishing by 7.4 per cent compared with the previous year, and spending for apparel dropped by 2.1 per cent. In the light of these developments many observers and also involved players concluded that the era of growing demand for material goods had finally come to an end, and that more sophisticated approaches would be needed to convince consumers to part with their money. This stream of thinking led to the general reassessment of the concept of the general superstore during the beginning of the 1980s (Koyama and Togawa 1992:172, NRS 1983:3).

Indeed, the new concepts introduced by general merchandisers initially proved to be successful, with sales increasing substantially from the middle of the 1980s onwards (Table 4.3). However, these changes

Table 4.2 Change of sales of large-scale superstores, sales per stores and expenses of private households, 1973–91 (change from previous year, per cent)

	Sales of superstores overall		Sales per store		Change in consumer spending	
	Nominal	Real	Nominal	Real	Nominal	Real
1973	38.9	24.4	13.6	1.7	16.7	4.6
1974	31.0	5.2	20.8	−3.0	21.3	−2.6
1975	18.7	6.2	11.8	0.0	16.1	3.8
1976	14.5	4.7	8.7	−0.6	10.6	1.2
1977	17.4	8.7	2.8	−4.8	9.0	0.8
1978	13.2	9.2	7.5	3.7	5.9	2.0
1979	9.8	6.0	3.8	0.2	6.4	2.7
1980	12.3	4.0	4.3	−3.4	7.4	−0.6
1981	9.7	4.6	3.7	−1.2	4.1	−0.8
1982	5.6	2.9	−1.4	−3.9	5.5	2.7
1983	3.9	2.0	1.0	−0.9	2.5	0.6
1984	3.8	1.7	2.0	−0.1	2.6	0.4
1985	2.8	0.8	1.8	−0.2	2.6	0.5
1986	3.6	3.2	1.7	1.3	1.2	0.8
1987	4.2	4.4	3.6	3.8	1.7	1.9
1988	5.8	5.3	5.8	5.3	3.6	3.1
1989	6.3	4.0	6.9	4.6	2.8	0.5
1990	7.1	3.9	6.2	3.0	3.9	0.8
1991	6.3	2.9	4.5	1.2	4.1	1.7

Source: Author's compilation based on Statistics Bureau 1992:530, Statistics Bureau, 1992:118–490, TKS 1991:476.

Table 4.3 Composition of consumption by the average Japanese household by product groups 1955–90 (per cent)

	Foods	Apparel and shoes	Durables	Eating out	Leisure and reading
1955	45.1	11.7	2.2	1.8	5.4
1960	38.9	12.0	4.4	2.7	6.1
1965	35.5	10.1	5.0	2.5	7.1
1970	31.0	9.5	5.0	3.0	9.0
1975	28.7	9.2	5.0	3.3	8.4
1980	25.5	7.9	4.3	3.7	8.5
1985	23.2	7.2	4.3	3.8	8.8
1990	21.4	7.4	4.0	4.0	10.1

Source: Author's compilation based on Statistics Bureau 1988:459–61, 1992:530–1.

have to be seen within the context of the so-called bubble economy that developed in Japan during the second half of the 1980s. In this period of economic growth consumer spending by private households increased again. Reflecting the general optimistic attitude of that time, consumers focused on high-price and high-prestige products in the areas of furnishings and consumer appliances and became more interested in a pleasant shopping experience. Demand for fashion, especially imported goods, also expanded (Koyama and Togawa 1992:173). Department stores in particular, but also newly designed general superstores, could meet these demands in regard to products and the shopping environment. Operators felt reassured and took on additional large-scale projects.

The widening of assortments and upgrading of sales concepts further relaxed tensions between operators of general superstores and their suppliers. Earlier, the oil crisis had already led to a reconsideration of distribution channels by manufacturers. Faced with declining sales and overcapacities, consumer goods manufacturers reacted by finally acknowledging the importance of superstores and supplying them more freely with merchandise. At the same time, brand manufacturers intensified their promotional activities and general merchandising stores tried to participate in these moves by increasing the share of branded products in their stores (Yahagi 1993a:137–9). When introducing new product lines, retailers also increasingly implemented practices that were previously used only by department stores and other established retailers to reduce risk and financial exposure. Superstores started to rent out sales space to manufacturers and wholesalers. Among the product lines introduced into superstores in this way were cameras, watches, fishing equipment, sporting goods and car parts. Manufacturers not only supplied products but also assisted retailers through the deployment of sales personnel. They thereby relieved retailers from the need to train their own personnel to be able to sell these rather specialized products (Ishihara 1977:44). Atsumi (1993:30) regards this method employed by retailers to quickly enlarge assortments as one of the main reasons for a decrease in the overall competitiveness of large superstores during the 1970s. Superstores partly lost control over important aspects of merchandising such as pricing, customer services and configuration of assortments.

Overall, the 1980s led to a strong differentiation between stores that were still all being classified as general superstores in a statistical sense. While some store operators relaunched outlets under different store names, others continued to operate stores of different sizes and concepts that

Table 4.4   Stores operated by Daiei by size, 1994

Size (m^2)	Up to 1 499	1 500– 2 999	3 000– 5 999	6 000– 8 999	9 000– 11 999	12 000– 14 999	15 000– 19 999	Above 20 000
Number of stores	21	32	75	101	78	15	11	2

Source: Author's compilation based on Ôkurashô Insatsukyoku 1995.

did not share much more than the name. Daiei categorized stores into six formats, ranking them by characteristics of assortments and pricing strategies (HKH 1993c:58) (Table 4.4).

Confronted with changes in strategies and facing a variety of stores under the same label, customers, however, felt increasingly uncertain about what to expect from general superstores. Surveys show a diffuse image among the general public. On the one hand, consumers increasingly demanded services from general superstores that resembled those of department stores. On the other hand, their expectations of low prices remained strong. Consumers thereby welcomed the upgraded concepts of the general superstore, but were reluctant to accept higher prices in return. In comparison with general superstores, most other retail formats possessed more consistent images, and consumers more clearly identified them as fulfilling certain needs (Table 4.5) (Meyer-Ohle 1993a:197–9).

Besides developing their core business, diversification into other areas of business increasingly occupied the efforts of superstore companies. Activities in this regard gained a new purpose during the 1970s. During previous periods, diversification had largely supported core businesses, for example the integration of manufacturing steps or logistic operations. In contrast, the move towards horizontal or lateral diversification in the 1970s and 1980s was being pursued under the purpose of expanding overall revenues (Takayama 1982:39–41). The leader in horizontal diversification was again Daiei, which engaged in activities over the whole spectrum of retail formats and was even prepared to do so at the risk of losing money. The overall goal of the company remained the maximization of sales. When expansion in the core business looked more and more uncertain, owing to the strengthening of government regulations, the president and founder of the company, Isao Nakauchi, explicitly refused to abstain from his original plan to grow revenues of the company group to 4 trillion yen by 1985. The company therefore came up with a plan to increase sales in the superstore sector to 2 trillion yen and to supplement these with 1.2 trillion yen revenue from

Table 4.5 Consumer expectations in regard to different store formats

	Requested characteristic										
Format	Deep assortment	Wide assortment	Product quality and safety	Low prices	Spatial convenience	Time convenience	Ease of choice	Amenities	Prestige	Community spaces	Information
Superstore	**	***	**	***	***	**	***	**	*	*	**
Department store	***	***	***	*	*	*	**	**	***	***	***
Normal retailers	**	*	***	**	***	**	***	*	*	*	***
Specialty store	***	*	***	*	*	*	**	**	*	*	***
Convenience store	*	***	*	*	***	***	*	*	*	*	*
Discount store	*	***	*	***	**	*	*	*	*	*	*
Home centre	***	***	*	***	**	*	**	**	*	**	*

*** Strongly demanded. ** Somewhat demanded. * less demanded.
Source: Based on TSS 1989:307.

affiliated companies and 0.8 trillion yen by newly established subsidiaries (HKH 1981b:62, Doi 1982:82). The company largely followed through on this plan and strongly invested in four areas: retail, service, finance and real estate development. In the course of this development it either set up or took over leisure parks, hotels, theatres, a baseball stadium and a baseball team, a construction company and a general real estate developer, a major publishing company, a credit card and consumer finance company and restaurants (Ôsono 1992:48–9).

Daiei's main rival in the area of diversification was the Saison Group. As already pointed out, its founder, Seiji Tsutsumi, had become highly skeptical about the future of conventional mass merchandising in Japan. Consequently, he developed a vision of a sophisticated network of companies that would be able to offer consumers a wide range of lifestyle-related complementary services. In the quest to realize his dream, but also in competition with his brother who reigned over the Seibu railway line, hotels and wide-ranging real estate interests, he began to diversify around his two core companies, Seiyu and department store company Seibu. By the beginning of the 1990s he had built up an empire of his own that consisted not only of a portfolio of different retail formats, the major hotel chain Intercontinental, additional hotels in Japan, resorts, a marina, a life and a risk insurance company, a consumer credit company and restaurants, but also museums, a culture school and various research institutes (Ôsono 1992:50–1).

The determination of companies to diversify and to surround their core businesses with empires of subsidiaries and affiliated companies changed the face of competition in Japanese retailing. The newly created entities were referred to as 'conglo-merchants' (*fukugo ryûtsû kigyô*), and competition in the retail sector evolved into a group competition (Miya 1985a:163–5). With expansion being regulated in their core business of general merchandising stores, these groups engaged in substitute wars on many other fronts. One of these fronts was the smaller store format such as convenience stores, where operators of general superstore managed to assume the leading positions. Another front was an intensified cooperation with regional department stores. After operators of regional department stores had at first tried to establish collaborations with the major metropolitan department store companies, they later turned to general superstore operators for support. Companies collaborated in the area of product supply and superstores took capital stakes in the department store companies. Superstore operators soon found out that cooperation with the resource-weak but very independently minded owners of regional department stores was not without difficulties, but it nonetheless helped them to develop a presence in new locations despite the strict regulations of the Large Store Law (Miya 1985a:139, Koyama and Togawa 1992:138–40). Another area of competition was the growing influence of superstore operators over the joint procurement organizations of Japanese retailing. Through these organizations companies not only strengthened their position in the procurement markets but also gained influence over other mostly smaller members of the joint procurement schemes (Miya 1985a:164–5, DMC 1988:104–5, SGK 1989:1512–13).

The direction of diversification was strongly influenced by the Large Store Law. A survey of 200 large retail stores in 1981 showed the most popular area of diversification to be mail order business or other forms of non-stationary retailing. This was followed by home centres, a retail format with sales floors that exceeded the threshold of the Large Store Law but where plans for the opening of new stores drew less opposition from local retailers, owing to the limited assortments these stores carried. Other formats targeted for diversification like specialty store chains, small-scale food supermarkets and convenience stores did not conflict with government regulations in the first place, though some local governments later tried to extend regulations to these formats (Anonymous 1987).

Diversification, however, proved to be problematic. Superstore operators were often not the first to recognize new business opportunities and therefore usually had to compete with companies that specialized in a certain area. Companies also lost the capability to operate low-cost stores, having built up high organizational overheads and often also using existing store buildings to introduce new store formats. For the introduction of home centres, many of the general merchandising store operators did not even make it beyond the trial stage and in the food supermarket business the situation did not look much better. Companies therefore either forfeited these markets totally to specialized regional chains or tried to intensify collaboration with them (Doi 1982:35, Yui 1991b:157).

The difficulty of companies in operating low-cost stores after having been in the market for some time is a familiar theme in many of the cyclical theories on the internal development of retail companies. For Japan, it was conditions in the wake of the oil crises, the introduction of the Large Store Law and increased competition that led observers to ask the question about the internal competitiveness of companies. In particular, two areas have to be examined in this regard, namely corporate financing and human resource management (Kawasaki 1993:56–7).

Companies arrived in the 1970s with an extremely high dependence on bank financing. While in their first period of expansion wholesalers had played an important role in financing, companies had soon become dependent on financing from banks. The share of equity declined continuously and stood, for the year 1975, at only 6.8 per cent for Seiyu, 13 per cent for Daiei and 18.9 per cent for Jusco; and this was despite the introduction of most of these companies to the stock exchange a few years earlier: Daiei in 1971, Ito Yokado in 1972, Kotobukiya in 1973 and the other major companies Seiyu, Jusco, Nichii and Izumiya all in 1974 (HKH/Takayama 1989:53, Kawasaki 1993:59, Orihashi 1993:107). The high reliance on borrowed funds made companies vulnerable to external shocks such as the oil crisis, when the Japanese government reduced the money supply to curb inflation. Retailers were caught by this development at a time when expansion was most intense. Having committed to high interest payments and faced with a dull economic situation they had to revise plans for amortization of investments (Nakamura 1981:229, Miya 1985a:130). Later, companies diversified corporate financing and started to issue convertible bonds to finance further expansion. However, for the market to pick up these bonds, companies had to give more attention to profitability and cost control. Although they had up to then focused basically on the rapid opening of new stores and sales growth, the profitable operation of existing stores became more important (Kawasaki 1993:61).

Another area that received increased attention was human resources management. Faced with a sudden increase in difficulties and uncertainties in their business environment in the early 1970s, companies suddenly began to realize a lack of specialists capable of coping with these problems. Growing quickly, companies had neglected to nurture specialists in core areas of chain store operations such as merchandising, operating, procurement and controlling, thus leading to organizational deficits (Kawasaki 1993:56–7). Another factor was increasing personnel costs. The ratio of these to sales had been 8.2 per cent in 1976 but had increased to 8.8 per cent in 1982. This was still below that of operators of other retail formats, but the gap had become smaller. Specialty stores became more price-aggressive and even managed to lower the share of personnel costs from 11.8 per cent to 10.2 per cent over the same period. Even consumer cooperatives managed a reduction by 0.3 per cent to 9.5 per cent. The difficulties superstore operators faced in controlling personnel costs are underlined by the fact that cost increases occurred despite an increased use of part-timers. The share of part-time workers increased from 1976 by nearly 14 per cent to 46.2 per cent in 1982 (Anonymous 1987:26, 29).

At the beginning of the 1980s, companies therefore initiated decisive plans to reorganize. However, these plans were followed up to different degrees. The most thorough effort was made by Ito Yokado; other companies followed but could not reach comparable success. The superiority of Ito Yokado in reorganizing might be due to the successful implementation of some of the techniques developed for and by its subsidiary in the convenience store sector Seven-Eleven. Between 1983 and 1989 Ito Yokado increased its gross margin from 25.1 per cent to 29.9 per cent, reduced turnover of stocks from 25.7 days to 15 days and decreased product loss from 6.9 per cent to 4.5 per cent. Effects of the efforts to reorganize led to favourable results for superstore operators when consumer demand picked up again with the onset of the bubble period and profits grew even more than sales (Ogata 1986:23, Koyama and Togawa 1992:186, 190, Sumiya 1992:20, Kojima 1993:67). However, as will be discussed later, this improvement of results proved to be only short-lived, with the 1990s bringing not only the burst of the bubble economy but also an increase in competition due to deregulation and low levels of consumer confidence due to continuous economic stagnation.

Food superstores: finally establishing the right format

Compared with the progressive development of the general superstore, the development of food superstores can be described as lagging behind until the 1970s. When development towards a distinctive format finally took place, change was driven not by large national retail chains but by regional and local retailers. These retailers enlarged their stores, increased the share of fresh merchandise, introduced new preprocessed fresh products and combined these with new ways of presenting the merchandise. They thereby gave their stores a distinctive look that distinguished them from the grocery departments of general superstores, previous food supermarkets and also the traditional, product-line-oriented small neighbourhood retailers.

As has been done for the general superstore, pioneers can also be identified for the food supermarket. One of these pioneers was the company Kansai Supermarket. Changes in merchandising and underlying techniques introduced by this company received constant attention in the retail industry, often through favourable coverage in trade journals. The retail journal *Hanbai kakushin* alone reported on different aspects of this company 54 times in the period 1971–1984 (KS 1985:387–91, HKH/Takayama 1989:270, Orihashi 1993:121–2). An inconspicuous company at first, Kansai Supermarket opened its first store in 1959. During the 1960s only three additional outlets followed. Expansion accelerated during the 1970s, with 16 new stores opened by 1982 (KS 1985:396–407). In developing its store concept Kansai Supermarket progressed through several stages. The first implementation of expert knowledge occurred in 1964 when the company changed the layout of its stores. Disregarding the relationship between customer flow and sales results, the square sales floor had up to then been divided into four areas, with customers not finding their way to the inner areas of the store. The remodeling based on the hot-dog-system and a controlled one-way flow of customers improved results. This was supported by the introduction of open and temperature-controlled showcases for fresh merchandise such as meat, vegetables and fruits. However, the sale of fresh merchandise continued to be handled by sales personnel.

The next decisive development step took place with the opening of the company's fifth store in 1970. The store introduced a number of features that even today in many ways shape the appearance of food superstores in Japan. On a sales floor of 950 square meters, innovations were introduced in the areas of product presentation and temperature-controlled storage, preparation and packaging of fresh merchandise and the arrangement of products within the store to optimize customer flow (KS 1985:101–5). Overall, the store marked the departure of food supermarkets from a focus on offering processed products at aggressive prices. The new concept put central importance on the presentation of a wide and deep range of high-quality fresh merchandise, providing customers with the opportunity to conveniently purchase all foods in one store. Later sales floors were even further expanded and while statistically in 1982 food stores with a sales floor of over 500 square meters averaged only 915 square meters (TSC 1985:296–307), the ideal sales floor of newly built stores was considered to be about 1700 square meters by then (Orihashi 1993).

The development of a holistic model of a Japanese food superstore can be traced through its developmental stages. From today's perspective, the concentration on quality, fresh merchandise and convenience seems only logical when we consider the high share of fresh products consumed by Japanese consumers. However, the actual implementation of such a concept required solutions in three problem areas:

- High costs for personnel engaged in the sales of fresh merchandise, since it seemed to be difficult to sell these products by self-service.

- A high loss of merchandise through spoilage and deterioration of stock. Losses were extremely high due to the climate and the high standards of customers, who would often only consume products bought the same day, with comparatively minimal cooking and preparation.
- Limitations of the traditional distribution system. Traditional wholesalers were either unwilling or unable to guarantee a consistent supply to large retail stores with regard to quality, quantity, price and steadiness of assortments.

The extent of these problems led many operators to shy away from them rather than attempt to solve them. Companies still tried to focus on processed foods and since they could not compete with the local product-line-oriented retailers in regard to location and quality, their only resort was aggressive pricing. Consumers were highly selective in store choice and would often use supermarkets only to buy promotional offers and even then closely compare prices with those offered by general superstores. Thereby, food superstores during their early stage of development were far away from reaching their goal of becoming the main source for grocery shopping for Japanese consumers. A survey conducted in a seminar for retail executives in the early 1970s reinforced this impression by showing that the main perceived reasons for the relative backwardness of food superstores in Japanese retailing were high land prices, low profits, lack of merchandising skills, backwardness in system development, lack of qualified personnel and mistakes of top management in strategy development (Atsumi 1973:255).

Looking deeper into the experiences of Kansai Supermarket demonstrates how problems were finally overcome. After opening its first store, the management of this company soon realized its problems, but unlike other companies, which either continued to operate stores at a low key or diversified into other areas, it actively looked for remedies. In the distribution of fresh merchandise a loss of 20 per cent at each level of the distribution chain was regarded as normal during the 1960s. Not unsurprisingly this became a major issue for the Japanese bureaucracy in its effort to modernize the Japanese distribution system. From the middle of the 1960s trials in the chilled storage and handling of merchandise were conducted by several government agencies, but these were limited to the wholesale sector since retailers usually did not have temperature-controlled storage facilities. Therefore, the introduction of coolers for keeping vegetables and fruit in retailing came only after a visit of the president of Kansai Supermarket to Hawaii where these techniques were already in use. Kansai Supermarket went ahead with its own trials. The prerequisite for this development, however, was to bring the sale of fresh products under direct management in contrast to the usual method of sourcing the sale of these product categories to tenants (KS 1985:48–52, 59–61).

While for other companies human resources management was still of secondary importance, Kansai Supermarket had been sensitized early to potential problems in this area when an ambitious diversification plan into the restaurant sector failed in 1964 because personnel costs could not be brought under control. For its stores, the company decided that the consistent use of self-service would be the best way to reduce personnel costs. However, since fresh merchandise constituted a major share of sales and was not offered prepackaged by suppliers, the introduction of self-service required the packaging of merchandise in a safe but still attractive fashion. Processes such as packaging and preparation of merchandise had to be done in an efficient manner, preferably by part-timers, so as to not simply replace reduced costs for customer service in the sales floor with increased costs for packaging in the back of the store. Another problem to be solved was the stocking and positioning of shelves within the stores (Yamamoto 1971:121–4). To solve these problems Kansai Supermarket and other companies cooperated closely with manufacturers of equipment and packing materials, who developed refrigerated shelves as well as packing machines and materials according to the needs of the companies (KS 1985:191). A major feature of the so-called Japanese food supermarkets became the design of spaces outside the main sales floor. In the initial stage of development, operations here focused mainly on the storage and packaging of fresh merchandise. Later, more and more stages in the preparation of foods were taken over from consumers, these spaces growing in size and their outlay and organization of work processes becoming a major success factor for food superstores (Tamura 1984:45–6). Store areas used for this purpose reached impressive dimensions. The Hiroda store, opened by Kansai Supermarket in 1976, had 736 square meters dedicated to the preparation and storage of merchandise, serving a sales floor of only 1334 square meters.

In the procurement of fresh merchandise, Kansai Supermarket used trial and error to come up with the right system to support its store innovations. Sophisticated techniques in preparation and presentation could be used to their fullest advantage only with a steady supply of required products fulfilling high quality standards. Not satisfied with the capabilities of local wholesalers at first, the company did what is so often proposed by critics of the Japanese wholesaling system, and tried to procure directly from producers. However, with increasing volume and variety needed this proved to be no alternative. Producers themselves were often small-scale, while at the same time buyers at Kansai Supermarket did not possess the necessary market information. Kansai Supermarket reverted back to wholesalers again, but this time used larger suppliers from the regional wholesale market in Osaka that were more capable of complying with the quality standards set by the company. The company continued to experiment in this area, however, and in 1977 managed to procure corn and asparagus directly from producers in Hokkaido, transporting products by air. In 1976, in collaboration with two wholesalers, the retailer began to process fish in a factory in Malaysia (KS 1985:250, 259, 263–9).

Knowledge about the new techniques dispersed throughout the industry owing to the close relationship between food superstore operators. For example, Kansai Supermarket was a member of the AJS (All Japanese Supermarket Association), an organization of initially 15 regional supermarket operators. It not only used its membership in this organization to learn about innovations abroad and in Japan but also actively introduced its own innovative activities. The association organized regular seminars to promote US/Japanese knowledge exchange in Hawaii. From 1967 onwards Kansai Supermarket demonstrated the methods it had developed in handling fruits and vegetables as well as the organization of food processing departments in seminars and store presentations on a regular basis. Other members of AJS like Torisen and Nissho recognized the usefulness of these innovations and closely duplicated Kansai Supermarket's merchandising concept in their own stores (KS 1985:63–4, HKH/Takayama 1989:279, Yahagi 1997). The cooperation between the different companies was made possible by the fact that most companies were comparatively small and operated only on a regional basis. A main concern for these companies at that time was not the competition with other food superstores as such, but rather increasing their competitiveness in comparison with other retail formats such as the general superstore and strengthening their position towards wholesalers and manufacturers (Yahagi 1997). Another source of information was industry journals. For example, *Hanbai kakushin* emphasized strongly the handling of fresh merchandising during the 1970s. Special issues of the magazine in the 1970s extensively featured developments in this regard (for example, *Hanbai kakushin* August 1971, food supermarkets; March 1973, fresh foods and self-service; January 1974, fresh preprepared foods).

However, not all companies concentrated resources on the continuous improvement of their retail formats in the same way. While Kansai Supermarket is sometimes described as having sacrificed growth in the struggle for perfection, other companies focused resources on the opening of new stores (Takahashi 1983:193–5). One of these companies was Maruetsu. Founded in 1954 as a fish shop, it opened its first supermarket in 1965 and expanded quickly afterwards, based on internal and external growth. The company reached 104 outlets in 1977 and increased this number to 145 by 1981. In 1982, Daiei became the dominant shareholder in the company (SGK 1989:1471).

Differences in strategic orientation thereby led initially to differences in knowledge possessed by companies. Later, however, concepts of quality-oriented food superstores gained wide acceptance and were widely imitated not only by food superstore chains but also in the design of food departments of general superstores. Interest in methods of increasing the overall quality of stores and especially food departments rose further in the 1980s after the opening of new stores had been made more difficult by the strengthening of the application of the Large Store Law. Companies had to concentrate efforts on existing stores if they wanted to increase their revenues further.

While most companies improved their food departments one way or another, innovative initiatives were not limited to the upper spectrum of food retailing. In an effort to gain a foothold in the food sector, Daiei in 1979 introduced discount stores following the example of European hard discounters. Stores offered a basic assortment limited to 400 mostly food items on 300 square meters. Seventy-five per cent of the products were private brands, the rest branded merchandise sold at discounts of about 30 per cent. Being in many ways the antithesis to the store concepts described above, it could not capture the attention of consumers and not surprisingly failed to gain support from brand manufacturers. Although 57 stores of that type were opened by 1982, the company abandoned its goal of 200 stores by 1985, opening no new stores after 1983 (Hayashi 1988:144).

During the 1980s, the number of newly opened supermarkets decreased. When new stores could be opened, many operators opted to further increase sales floor area. New stores now were about 2700 square meters in size and much of this space was taken up by the addition of new product groups. Operators experimented with new store concepts called 'combination stores' or 'super-supermarkets', often combining features of food superstores and apparel superstores. With some of these stores reaching sizes between 4000 and 6000 square meters, operators clearly went beyond their original boundaries and advanced in the general superstore sector (HKH/Takayama 1989:246, 258). Developments converged to a certain degree during the early 1990s, when general superstore operators began to experiment with smaller stores concentrating on foods and daily necessities and targeting smaller catchment areas (Arita 1994:62–5).

Discount stores and home centres: developing new locations

The introduction of new retail techniques and superstore retailing in Japan had been driven mostly by companies focusing on foods, drugs or apparel. While these companies had also handled hard goods and household goods to a certain degree, the evolution of distinct formats with an emphasis on these product groups set in only at the beginning of the 1970s, when two new formats were introduced under the labels of discount store and home centre. While both largely handled household goods and could not always be clearly distinguished, the former type was largely price-oriented while the later focused on depth of assortments.

Discount stores can be characterized as stores selling an assortment of articles, all at clearly discounted prices in comparison with other stores. At first, superstores in Japan were also understood as discount stores. However, their operators soon abandoned the concept of general price aggressiveness for the attractiveness of comprehensive assortments and one-stop shopping. This opened the way to the introduction of a new brand of discount stores during the late 1960s and early 1970s, these being recognized as an innovative format by consumers as well as established retailers (Koyama 1993:35).

The appearance of these stores was diverse. While some of them had no focus and just sold a range of products that were available for discounting, other stores focused on certain product groups such as cameras, watches, consumer electronics, spectacles or jewelry. The location of these stores was primarily in the vicinity of terminal stations of commuter lines in metropolitan areas, attracting mainly younger customer groups. Apart from this group, another group of independent discount stores existed. While often overlooked, these stores offered heterogeneous assortments and specialized in items acquired from bankruptcy sales or merchandise discreetly taken off the hands of overstocked wholesalers or manufacturers (Kowata 1993:20, Makita 1993:3–4).

Among these discounters a few made the transformation to large-store retailing at the end of the 1960s. As previously, a few pioneering companies can be identified. Daikuma opened a store in Chigasaki with a sales floor of 1000 square meters in 1968 and gradually enlarged it until 1971 to an impressive 10 000 square meters. The store shared some characteristics with general superstores, having four stories and being situated near a station building. Originally, the store had handled only apparel but the assortment was gradually broadened to include household goods, furniture, car care products, sporting goods and electric appliances. The store sold no food products, a characteristic that clearly distinguished it from most other large retail stores at that time. Later stores were built with smaller sales floors and in less central locations with the focus of products handled being on durables of everyday use (HKH 1980:118).

Articles were sold with considerable discounts from the prices recommended by manufacturers. In contrast to home centres, which emerged at the same time, assortments were not as deep and offered less choice. In particular, the concentration on durables and not apparel (like the dominating product category of discount stores in the US at that time) or food products, in addition to their high reliance on branded merchandise, earned the early discount stores the designation 'Japanese style discount stores' (HKH 1980:119–20). Though accepted by consumers and achieving satisfactory results for their owners, the expansion of these stores progressed rather slowly. Despite the high attention the activities of the company had received initially, Daikuma opened only two new stores per year in the years 1975, 1976 and 1978. After one more opening in the year 1979 no more branches were opened until 1987 (Ishihara 1980:130–2, SGK 1989:1417).

Besides problems with the Large Store Law, which established companies had learned to live with to a certain degree, but were difficult to handle for new, inexperienced companies with less financial strength, the slow expansion of this store format was related mainly to its concentration on consumer durables and household goods. This focus not only required comparatively large and therefore costly sales floors, but also resulted in a low turnover of merchandise, binding the scarce capital available to entrepreneurs in this sector. The procurement of merchandise and especially the focus on branded merchandise proved to be another problematic area. Unlike the general merchandising stores, which had already adapted some of the trade practices of the traditional distribution sector by shifting some of the risk of selling merchandise to manufacturers and wholesalers, the new discount stores usually started out by acquiring all the products displayed in their stores without the possibility of returning unsold merchandise (*Hanbai kakushin* February 1972:49–51).

The early 1970s proved to be a good time for the introduction of discount stores, with the economic stagnation following the oil shock having raised price consciousness on the side of consumers and sales pressures on the side of manufacturers. Manufacturers and wholesalers were overstocked and hard-pressed to sell their products and could therefore be less selective in their choice of distributors. Huge amounts of merchandise found their way at significant discounts to so-called cash wholesalers that would pass them on to retailers in exchange for immediate payment (Ishihara 1980:131, Ôta *et al.* 1977:31–3).

Retail companies soon found out, however, that with increasing expansion the reliance on grey supply channels became more and more problematic. Cash wholesalers could not guarantee the continuous supply of certain products. Operators of discount stores also quickly recognized the limitations of not being able to offer the latest products and therefore gradually began to shift their focus to regular supply channels. A survey conducted in the year 1989, asking for the main supply sources of discount stores, found out that of the major 74 operators of discount stores, 69 per cent named regular wholesalers and distribution subsidiaries of manufacturers as their main supply source. Ranked next with 17 per cent was direct supply from manufacturers, followed by only 10 per cent for cash wholesalers, which had formerly been their major supply source (NRS 1991:450). The strong use of regular supply channels was due also to increased constraints felt by cash wholesalers once the economic situation picked up again. Manufacturers became more careful not to build up oversupplies and also increasingly acknowledged discount stores as a legitimate way of selling merchandise. However, these developments led to increased procurement costs for discount stores that they could not ignore when deciding on their prices. Therefore, price differences between regular retailers and discount stores gradually declined (NRS 1991:450–2). This decline in price aggressiveness was due partly to the fact that discount retailers for a long time did not look for alternative methods to save costs that were already being employed by Western discounters, such as advanced management and information technology, a general reorganization of supply arrangements, or rationalization of assortments (Goldman 2000:52–3).

Discount retailing based on cash procurement, however, revived somewhat during the early 1990s. Again manufacturers and wholesalers found themselves overstocked with merchandise and began to supply goods into the grey channels of Japanese distribution, some of these activities receiving considerable attention as the following examples show:

The King of Discount

Toshio Miyaji earned his title as the King of Discount (*Yasuuri Ô*) more through his glamorous personality and controversial activities than through his business success. Driving around in a Rolls-Royce, openly displaying his suitcase full of money, he was always ready to make cash purchases of merchandise from bankrupt or cash-strapped retailers or wholesalers for his chain of discount retail stores, Jonan Denki. He became a favorite not only of robbers that tried to assault him frequently, but also of the domestic and foreign media (for example, *The Economist* 5 February 1994, *Fortune* 7 February 1994).

Whether it was sending housewives and staff on shopping sprees to Paris to stock his store with designer merchandise, or openly breaking laws by selling rice without having the necessary license, his activities always came in handy to demonstrate the many shortcomings of the Japanese distribution system. In 1996 Toshio Miyaji was able to publish a documentation of newspaper articles on his activities that for the period from 1993 to 1995 filled an astounding 315 pages (Miyaji 1996). At the same time, his business interests never went beyond the relatively low number of six stores with total sales not exceeding 11.3 billion yen per year.

Toshio Miyaji passed away suddenly in May 1998. His company went bankrupt shortly afterwards, leaving behind an accumulated debt of about 8 billion yen. The ongoing stagnation of the market for consumer electronics and the emergence of other discounters with a more stringent sales and expansion policy had made life for his company more and more difficult.

Introduced at the same time and, as seen from today's perspective, more successful than large discount stores were so called home centres or do-it-yourself stores. While these names point to similar concepts in other countries, again development in Japan soon deviated from the original concepts. The first home centre is said to have opened in 1972 under the name DOIT in Yono (Saitama). With 1480 square meters and 20 employees, the results of this store were unsatisfactory, the selection of do-it-yourself articles not being very comprehensive and consumer demand for them being low anyway. The company tried to complement its original assortment with household goods but these could not make up for the shortcomings. It thereby took until 1975 before the company opened its second store, a more impressive undertaking with 3300 square meters. By 1981, the company opened 9 additional outlets; afterwards efforts slowed down and only 8 more stores were opened by1989 (SGK 1989:1429). Keiyo, another pioneer in this sector, opened its first store in 1973 and later concentrated on stores with a comparatively high share of household goods, in contrast to DOIT's focus on do-it-yourself products. Juntendo had also opened its first store in 1972 but it took the company until 1978 to develop its second store. With 498 square meters, just under the threshold of the Large Store Law by 2 square meters, small-scale home centres later became the trademark of this company (Uchiro 1989:1, Ishihara 1985:153).

The sixteenth store opened by DOIT in 1981 in Kawagoe received special attention at the time of its opening. Featuring a sales floor of nearly 4000 square meters on two stories and an open-air space next to the store, the store clearly distinguished itself from others that at that time had only half the sales space and lacked advanced features such as escalators (Hashizume 1982:123, HKH 1982:127). Though this was regarded by observers in the trade magazines as a glimpse into the future of the home centre sector, a general trend towards trading up did not take place soon after, though there is some interesting resemblance with concepts realized in the 1990s after the restrictions of the Large Store Law had been eased.

The official census of commerce did not regard home centres as a separate category. Instead, they were mostly included under the category of 'living-related large retail stores', the census counting 531 of these stores with more than 500 square meters in 1982 (TSC 1985:365). An alternative independent survey estimated the total number of home centres to have increased from 120 to 1050 between 1975 and 1982, accounting for about 0.7 per cent of total retail sales (Munekata 1994:123).

During the 1980s operators of home centres tried to further stabilize their concept. After having expanded assortments in all directions during their founding period they now tried to establish assortments that distinguished their stores from general merchandising stores as well as stores of other home centre operators. Indeed, companies managed to develop individual strategies. Some companies systematically broadened assortments by adding sports, leisure and furnishing products. Others strengthened stores in the area of do-it-yourself or gardening products. In the development of smaller stores, three different approaches were taken. The first was a limitation of assortments, often on do-it-yourself and gardening articles. The second approach was a discount orientation with the aim of making up for the small store sizes by focusing on fast-moving products. Finally, the third strategy proposed the format of 'home convenience stores' with wide and flat assortments (Uchiro 1989:148–9).

Most pioneers in the home centre and large discount store sector were not established retailers but outsiders or even newcomers to the retail sector. What many of them had in common at the beginning of their engagement in this sector was the ownership of plots of land and sometimes buildings in suburban areas next to arterial roads. Their original businesses were often seriously affected by the after-effects of the oil crisis and owners were looking for alternative uses for their assets. Hinode, the company that introduced the DOIT stores had originally been a taxi firm. Keiyo had been an independent medium-sized operator of petrol filling stations that was looking to diversify after having come under more and more pressure from the large petrol chains. Keiyo's first store was converted from a drive-in-restaurant. Finally, Juntendo had managed food supermarkets but had failed to overcome the problems in the handling of fresh merchandise and therefore decided to convert stores after it was introduced to the home centre concept (Ishihara 1985:156, Uchiro 1989:147, Koyama 1993:31).

The main problem these companies had to overcome was consumer acceptance. Companies soon had to realize that in comparison with many other countries where home-centres flourished, Japan had no tradition of 'do-it-yourself.' Repair and renovation work was usually given to craftsmen. Skills in this area and the willingness to spend leisure time on such tasks were not as widespread as in other countries (HKH 1981b:91). In this sense, the introduction of home centres in Japan was based not on clearly perceived consumer demand, but rather on the initiative of owners that were inspired by the fast growth of these stores in the US (Uchiro 1984:68–9). Facing uncertain demand, home centres could still survive, however, though less on the strength of assortments than on other characteristics, such as easy accessibility by car, wide assortments concentrated on fulfilling the growing demand for household goods and finally comparatively attractive prices. Many of these were characteristics they shared with general discount stores that were going through their first development stage at the same time (Uchiro 1984:69, Ishihara 1985:155). Demand for hobby, leisure-related and home improvement articles finally increased from the middle of the 1970s on. This was attributed to a number of trends (HKH 1977:129, Koyama 1993:31), as follows:

- Increased leisure time, especially for office employees, due to the introduction of the five-day work week.

- Disillusionment and search for self-fulfillment after the oil crisis when people looked for alternative challenges outside of their workplaces.
- Stagnating incomes, with increased interest in saving the costs of hired handymen and craftsmen.
- Generally increased interest in creating individual living spaces.
- Increase in books and journals related to home decoration and gardening that provided readers with suggestions and instructions.

These trends eventually allowed home-centre operators to focus their assortments and to establish their concept as an independent retail format. Overall, the Japanese home centre could not, however, free itself entirely from its earlier image of being a low-price format located in places easily accessible by car. Surveys show that for the majority of customers their main demand of home centres was still low prices, followed by the availability of parking spaces. Only when consumers were asked why they frequented a particular home centre did responses change, with the availability of parking ranging first, followed by the quality of assortments and finally low prices (NSK 1993:8).

Convenience stores: from uncertain beginnings to the flagship format of Japanese retailing

Seen from today's perspective, the introduction of convenience stores was maybe the most influential and lasting development in Japanese retailing. The sheer number of stores, their standardized appearance and the apparent suitability of the convenience store concept to any location turned them into a ubiquitous feature of the Japanese landscape. Companies active in this sector were forced to come up with comprehensive and integrated concepts to operate their store networks efficiently. Innovations connected to the introduction of convenience stores reached from methods of procurement, logistics and store design to original combinations of services and products, and even included new patterns of ownership and human resources management. Many of these innovations were later copied and adopted by operators of other retail formats.

This significance later attributed to convenience stores had, however, not been anticipated when first steps were taken towards the introduction of this format in the late 1960s. First initiatives were taken by voluntary chains with the purpose of upgrading the appearance of existing small-scale supermarkets. As already outlined, the formation of voluntary chains had taken place not long after the first supermarkets began to develop in Japan. However, these chains had concentrated on the procurement of merchandise at first. When it became apparent that store owners also needed support in other areas, voluntary chains started to take a more influential role in the store design and merchandising activities of their members. One of these voluntary chains was K-mart, set up in the Osaka area by Hashikata, a wholesaler of candy and confectionary. Hashikata began to work on the concept of a small-scale supermarket with the aim of establishing a foothold in grocery retailing. In 1966, the company opened a trial store with a sales floor area of only 86 square meters. By the early 1970s, after the opening of additional stores by the chain's members and further trials, the company finally arrived at a prototype described as a 'Japanese convenience store'. The store was slightly larger than the original one and focused heavily on fresh merchandise. The chain continued its trials, but whereas 412 retailers utilized its services in the area of procurement, by 1975 only 30 members paid royalties to the chain to operate their stores based on the propagated business model of a convenience store (Koyama 1993:30, Yahagi 1993e:74).

While these stores were regarded as convenience stores in their time (Ogata 1972, Arakawa 1992 [1974]), this view has been challenged in retrospect. Koyama (1993) compares the feature of these early stores with those of stores introduced by other companies later. Based on their overall non-uniform appearance and the high share of fresh merchandise handled, he argues that they should rather have been classified as small-scale supermarkets. Nonetheless, it has to be pointed out that where the internal organization of processes was concerned the chain was far ahead of other voluntary chains of its time. At an early point it had come up with many elements, such as the coding of merchandise, computer-assisted order systems and a financial safety net for members, which would later become typical elements of convenience store chains in Japan (Ogata 1972:115).

Later, it was established large retailers that succeeded in the introduction of convenience stores. The first large company to experiment with convenience stores was Seiyu, the dominating superstore operator in the Kantô region at that time and a member of the Seibu group. After opening two successful stores in 1973, however, the company aborted it trials. As its main reason for this decision, Seiyu cited the strong opposition of associations of small retailers and also politicians towards efforts of large corporations to venture into business domains of small enterprises (HKH 1981d:63, Shimada 1973:44). Therefore, the year 1974 became generally considered the year of the birth of convenience stores in Japan. During that year Ito Yokado opened its first store under the Seven-Eleven brand name and thereby took up the leadership position in this new sector, a role it has not relinquished up until today. Daiei soon followed and opened its first store in 1975 using the Lawson brand name. Eventually, these moves by its competitors led the Seibu group to rethink its reluctant stance on convenience stores, finally reentering the sector under the name FamilyMart in 1977. Other major superstore operators took longer to recognize the potential of this sector and opened first stores in 1980 under the names of MiniStop (Jusco), Circle K (Uny) and Sankus (Nagasakiya). At that time, pioneers like Ito Yokado and Daiei were already commanding impressive chain networks, with the former having exceeded the mark of 1000 stores and the later stepping up its efforts to catch up with the leader (Table 4.6) (HKH 1981a:191, 1981b:61, Nishimuta 1981:194, HKH/Takayama 1989:54, Yahagi 1993e:74).

As already pointed out, the pioneer in the convenience store sector was Ito Yokado. The first store under the Seven-Eleven brand name was a converted liquor store opened in May 1974. Store fittings and furnishings were totally renewed. With no designated storage area all stock was stored on shelves on the sales floor. Though no detailed information on the composition of the assortment is available, one thing that has to be pointed out is the existence of fresh merchandise. Opening hours reflected the company name and were from 7.00 a.m. till 11.00 p.m. and thereby distinctly longer than those of neighboring stores, which mostly opened at 10.00 a.m. and closed at 7 or 8.00 p.m. While the first store was opened in a rather typical Japanese urban neighbourhood, a location that was considered unusual for convenience stores at that time, the second store was opened in a location following the US example, a suburban area beside an arterial road. The company soon opened additional stores in relatively close proximity to its previously opened stores and thereby embarked early on its trademark policy of trying to totally cover and thereby dominate convenience store retailing in particular areas (SIJ 1992:33–4).

While growing its store network the company continuously refined its concepts. As early as 1975 it opened the first store operating around the clock and after favourable responses by customers also adopted this innovation for stores operated by its franchisees. Its growing size also enabled the company to launch commercials with local radio stations. Having to decide on the composition of the assortment, the company did not simply take what was available or copy the assortment carried

Table 4.6 Development of number of stores of selected companies, 1974–99

Affiliation/CVS name	1974	1975	1976	1977	1978	1979	1980	1985	1990	1995	1999
Ito Yokado (Seven-Eleven)	15	69	199	375	591	801	1 040	2 651	4 328	6 373	8 153
Daiei CVS (Lawson, Sun Chain)		10	69	202	327	370	488	1 965	3 770	5 683	7 378
Saison (FamilyMart)				3	13	44	74	767	2 236	3 402	4 555
Yamazaki Pan (Sun Shop)				3	20	50	69	1 819	2 162	2 724	2 616
Uny (Circle K)							9	271	991	1 806	1 895
Nagasakiya (Sankus)							3	235	630	1 273	1 204
Kokubu (Community Store)					21	44	83	441	515	617	663
Maruyo Sakeya (Seiko Mart)				54	65	82	98	206	486	590	888
Kasumi (Hot Spar)					5	23	69	332	451	832	616
Jusco (Mini Stop)							3	118	341	710	1 204

Source: Author's compilation based on SIJ 1992:64, NRS 1998, NRS 2001.

by US convenience stores. Interpreting its role for Japanese consumer as 'providing an extended fridge', the company decided to concentrate on products that were consumed not long after acquisition. The cornerstone of this policy became *bentô*, precooked and prepackaged Japanese lunchboxes that could be warmed up at will by customers in microwave ovens. Changes were also done in the pricing of merchandise. In 1978, the company tried for the first time to change the image of convenience stores as being high-priced by reducing prices for a number of items.

During the 1980s the number of convenience stores grew faster and more companies managed to establish a foothold in the market. In this situation companies increasingly relied on the introduction of additional services to attract customers to their stores. In this regard, while Seven-Eleven was not always the first company to come up with a new service, nonetheless, innovations in this area usually quickly spread from one company to another and by the end of the 1980s the company offered a comprehensive set of services (Table 4.7). In particular, the possibility of paying utility charges proved popular with consumers. With automatic deduction from bank accounts not being widely accepted, the possibility of paying these charges at convenience stores open round the clock was an alternative to waiting at overcrowded bank and post office counters. Gradually the services offered became more sophisticated, with some companies dispensing cash, selling tickets or brokering car rentals and tour packages.

Table 4.7 Services offered by Seven-Eleven

Service	Introduction (year/month)
Film processing	1974/5
Sale of movie tickets	1980/12
Postal package handling	1981/11
Copy machines	1982/4
Telephone cards	1986/12
Payment of utility charges (electricity)	1987/10
Payment of utility charges (town gas)	1988/3
Payment of insurance premiums	1989/2
Payment of charges for TV and Radio	1989/6
Prepaid cards	1989/11
Liability insurance	1990/5
Catalogue sales	1992/1
Payment of telephone charges	1992/4

Source: Based on SIJ (1992:211).

With the introduction of new products and services the reliance of convenience stores on processed foodstuffs gradually declined. Although an average store of the Seven-Eleven network relied for more than half its sales on these products (54.4 per cent in 1978), this share was down to only 40.5 per cent by 1993. Over the same period fast food increased from 6.7 per cent to 21.2 per cent and non-food items from 19.6 per cent to 23.3 per cent (Yahagi 1993d:60).

The development of the convenience store format in Japan having been outlined, the underlying factors and impact of this development need to be analyzed in more detail. As previously, factors of entrepreneurship, patterns of innovation and the acceptance of consumer markets will be discussed.

After the introduction of the superstore during the 1950s and its fast development in the form of the general superstore, the introduction and adaptation of the convenience store during the 1970s can be seen as the second major format innovation in Japanese retailing. As had been the case for other retail formats and new retail techniques prior to their actual introduction in Japan, the development of convenience stores in the United States received attention and a discussion, developed early on whether this retail format would be appropriate for the Japanese market. Different groups with different interests were involved in this discussion, showing again the complexity behind the introduction of new retail formats. As initially with self-service and chain management, Japanese bureaucrats and politicians saw the convenience store as a model to bring existing small retailers up to date and thereby ensure their survival. Bureaucrats were especially concerned about the vast number of rice and liquor retailers that, owing to the government protection of their activities, had not taken the initiative to upgrade their skills and advance their sales concepts. The Small-and-Medium-Sized Enterprise Agency of the Ministry of International Trade and Industry (MITI) in 1972 even published a convenience store guideline that envisioned stores of 300 square meters in residential areas, having longer than usual opening hours, being professionally managed by the owner and utilizing full-time and part-time employees (Atsumi 1971:111, Araya 1973:260, Arakawa 1992:194–5).

Others interested in the concept were business associations. The manufacturer dominated Nihon Nôritsu Kyôkai (Japan Productivity Centre) organized a conference focusing on this new format and the umbrella association of voluntary chains set up a subsection for convenience stores. In a period where the future development of Japanese retailing was generally understood as converging with western models, associations of small retailers also looked to the west for inspirations on how to revive their members' businesses. The only small-scale format growing fast overseas at that time was the convenience store. When the debate took place in Japan, about 19 000 stores of this type already existed in the US, with an increase each year of about 2500. Japanese small retailers faced with rising labour costs saw the convenience store mainly as a model to rationalize labour management, but they were also attracted to this format by another factor: convenience stores appeared to be a store format that was able to prosper in coexistence with superstores (Araya 1973:261).

As already outlined above, the first concepts developed for the Japanese market under the notion of convenience stores deviated from the original American model. Being comparatively large in size, situated in the neighborhood of consumers' homes and handling mostly fresh merchandise, what was demanded in the disguise of convenience stores were in reality small-scale food supermarkets. This relates to the relative backwardness at that time of specialized food supermarkets, which did not cater sufficiently to the needs of consumers in residential neighbourhoods (*Hanbai kakushin* August 1971:135–7, Araya 1973:260–3).

Consequently, plans to introduce a new small-scale retail format attracted criticism (Atsumi 1971:111–15). From the beginning, the ability of existing voluntary chains to set up the complex infrastructure needed for successful convenience store operations was questioned. Voluntary chains, in contrast to leading large retailers, were lacking qualified personnel and most of them had not even taken the obvious next step towards stricter integration of members. Other doubts were raised concerning the acceptance of the new format by consumers. It was argued that Japanese consumers had a different notion entirely of what convenience constituted, not being interested in a fast and hassle-free shopping process but rather demanding comprehensive services and choice in a pleasant shopping environment. It was also pointed out that convenience stores in the US did make a large proportion of profits by selling fast food and petrol and not from their grocery sales.

Contrasting this early criticism with the later development of convenience stores in Japan shows that this criticism was in many regards justified. In fact, the new retail format was introduced successfully by large established mass merchandisers and their success did not rely on the adaptation to the needs of existing consumer segments but rather the cultivation of new segments. Overall, at the beginning of the 1970s no unified view about the concept of a convenience store existed. People were attracted to this format by the possibilities of (1) rationalizing the use of labour and (2) the coexistence of small and large stores; the merchandising concept in itself was however less clear. Later, different types developed, mini-supermarkets with a focus on fresh merchandise, convenience stores closely following the US example and, finally, large-scale food supermarkets closing the gap between large general superstores and the product-line-oriented traditional retail sector.

The main step towards the introduction of convenience stores in today's sense therefore came only when large, established mass merchandisers took the initiative. As already pointed out, the pioneer role fell to Ito Yokado (SIJ 1992:7–17). When Ito Yokado got interested in the concept it was already a comparatively large company in Japanese retailing, being ranked seventeenth among retailers in regard to overall sales and operating 22 general superstores. Still, it was far away from its current leadership position. The company had started to investigate possibilities for diversification and purportedly it was on a trip to the US to conclude an agreement to bring the family restaurant Denny's to Japan that the managers of the company became aware of the Seven-Eleven convenience stores of the Southland group. Getting Southland, at that time a retail giant with a network of 4000 convenience stores and beginning overseas ventures, interested in Japan and convincing the company that Ito Yokado was the right company to be put in charge of expansion there, was not easy. It took the introduction of a general trading company, Itochu, and even then many problems remained to be solved.

Some of these problems concerned the details of the contractual relationships between Ito Yokado and Southland, others the actual adaptation of convenience stores to the Japanese market. Concerning the first point, there were basically four initial demands by Southland that had to be negotiated. Southland had demanded to develop convenience stores in a joint venture to limit the activities of Ito Yokado to east Japan, to open more than 2000 stores within the first eight years and finally to receive franchise royalties of 1 per cent of revenues. Ito Yokado eventually managed to persuade Southland to leave operation of the company totally to itself, to give Ito Yokado the rights to cover all of Japan, to reduce the number of stores to be opened to 1200 and payment to 0.6 per cent of revenues. Based on this agreement, Ito Yokado got hold of management know-how, got the right to use the Seven-Eleven brand name and could also delegate staff to the US to study the management of convenience stores with Seven-Eleven (SIJ 1992:7–17).

The company history of Seven-Eleven reports, however, that the new venture had not been without critics within Ito Yokado. Some argued against the economic sense of the agreement, fearing a loss of face by publicizing apparently overambitions plans to build up a store network of more than a thousand stores in a difficult economic period that rather demanded consolidation of existing activities. Others questioned the appropriateness of the convenience store format for the Japanese market. They based their criticism on the success factors of US convenience stores and asked whether these would apply to Japan. In the US shopping for just a few articles in superstores had become increasingly inconvenient, owing to the distance between the stores and the homes of consumers, huge parking lots, complex and large store outlays and long queues at checkouts. The location of convenience stores was therefore in traffic-wise favourable locations on arterial roads, and stores were often operated in combination with a petrol station. In Japan, the situation was different. The introduction of superstores had not led to the disappearance of local neighbourhood stores. Small stores and restaurants were ubiquitous and often kept close relationships with their customers. Stores were close to places of residence and consumers did most of their shopping not by car but on foot.

The advisers sent from Southland to assist Ito Yokado in setting up its operations in Japan recognized these differences to their home market and therefore recommended that Ito Yokado set up its first store outside the shopping districts to avoid the lack of parking spaces and competition with existing retailers. As in many other cases, Ito Yokado did not follow this advice. Considering the very systematic concept of Seven-Eleven in Japan today, the story of the selection of its first store forms a rather curious episode within the company's history. The store was selected after the company had been approached by the owner of an ailing liquor store in a shopping district in the Koto ward of Tokyo, who had heard about the completion of an agreement between Ito Yokado and Southland. Though it had planned initially to operate its first store directly under its own management, Ito Yokado took up this opportunity. By doing so, it not only developed early knowledge of franchise management but also sent a message to store owners of the traditional retail sector that its intention was not to replace them but rather to provide them with an opportunity to revive their stores.

Recruiting franchisees did not prove unproblematic, however. This was due mainly to Ito Yokado's requirements. While the required sales floor size of 100 square meters appears small from today's perspective, it was far above the average store size in the early 1970s. At the same time, the company attempted to open a network of stores within a certain area to be able to set up an efficient logistics infrastructure to serve these stores. Potential candidates not only were discouraged by having to forgo 45 per cent of gross profits as franchise royalties but also faced stiff opposition from their local wholesalers that feared for their sales. Seven-Eleven also took care to select stores that would be able to sell liquor. Since this license was difficult to obtain, the company targeted liquor store owners to convert their stores. Keeping to this strategy all the way until the 1990s, the largest group of new franchisees of Seven-Eleven in Japan continued to be former operators of liquor stores. For competitors of Seven-Eleven this front runner advantage in terms of profitability as well as customer attractiveness proved to be one of the most difficult to overcome. With the system becoming increasingly sophisticated, Seven-Eleven began to attract not only owners of other stores but also entrepreneurs with no background in the retail sector, such as former salaried workers looking for an independent existence (SIJ 1992:49–53).

While introduced by an already established company and not by a single owner, the management put in charge of the project by Ito Yokado nonetheless displayed a certain degree of missionary zeal that has already also been identified in other entrepreneurs of the Japanese retail sector, such as the founders of general superstores and food super-markets. The aim of founders, of creating a technically perfect system that could provide services and products of a standardized high quality to all customers and franchisees alike, is the theme that echoes strongly throughout its company history, *Seven-Eleven Japan – Never-Ending Innovation*, published after 20 years of its existence. It becomes apparent in extreme strategies such as the use of motorcycles or even planes and helicopters to ensure punctual delivery of merchandise to stores in inaccessible and remote areas (SIJ 1992:102).

Not all convenience store operators have, however, displayed the same diligence as Seven-Eleven in setting up their systems. Looking at the 20 largest convenience store chains in 1991, 10 of these were affiliated with large retailers from the superstore sector, 2 with manufacturers, 4 with wholesalers and 4 were independent. While the chains affiliated with overall leading retailers pursued a close integration of businesses within their network, and often acquired part of their management know-how by international collaboration, for the other chains the relationship between chain headquarters and members was often more distant. This was evident in characteristics such as shorter contract periods, missing social security provisions for operators in case of failure, lower frequency of visits by supervisors to stores, shorter opening hours, more frequent holidays, and a disparate appearance of member businesses in regard to assortments, cleanliness and opening hours. (Yahagi 1993c:55).

The attempt to view the different aspects of convenience store development within the overall pattern of format development in Japan thereby draws quite a different picture from that seen in other countries. The development of superstores in Japan had not resulted in the large-scale replacement of small-sized traditional retailers, initiating the need for a new small-scale format providing the convenience of fast, small-volume shopping near to homes. Therefore, at the time of introduction of the convenience store no direct need for this retail format had been formulated in Japan. The emergence of convenience store development in Japan has to be seen in relationship to existing small stores, activities on the supply side and the overall development of the distribution system; as Momose (1983:20) puts it:

> The convenience store in Japan has grown by skillfully linking strategies of large retailers, manufacturers and wholesalers with the rationalization and modernization of small retailers. Therefore the convenience store in Japan is, unlike in the US, not a retail format that has developed from a need for convenience and dissatisfaction by consumers with large stores, but a format that has evolved as an element of modernization and rationalization of the Japanese distribution system.

The success of convenience stores in Japan can thereby be attributed to the initiative of the supply side, rather than to specific needs on the demand side. Though the convenience store to a certain degree managed to develop a specific segment of consumers, it had overall, to prove its relevance in competition with local traditional retailers. Surveys conducted in the early 1990s showed that small, single-product-line-oriented retailers viewed convenience stores as the main threat to their existence, followed by mini-supermarkets. Food supermarkets or general superstores were not viewed in the same way. This relationship was not reciprocal though, with owners of convenience stores feeling threatened by mini-supermarkets and food supermarkets (Abe 1994:40). The advantages of convenience stores were mainly in the rationalization of processes in product supply and human resource management. This allowed operators to carry wider assortments and offer longer opening hours while at the same time adapting their prices to those of local competitors (Momose 1983:21–4).

While, overall, the development of convenience stores was supply-side-driven, there were, however, some developments on the demand side that at least favoured their establishment. These factors include increasing urbanization, long working hours, and changes in consumption patterns and household sizes (Momose 1983:24). Long working and commuting hours led to the demand for shopping opportunities outside the limited opening hours of supermarkets and the traditional retail sector. The declining importance of food in relation to overall household spending and the lower quantities needed owing to the shrinking size of households resulted in some consumers putting less importance on the pricing of products. Convenience became more important and higher prices were accepted for longer opening hours and broader assortments. While having some relevance for the development of convenience stores where consumers bought only small quantities, the general validity of this assumption has however to be questioned when we take account of the sensitivity of consumers towards changes of food prices and the emergence and popularity of highly discount-oriented stores in the food sector of other countries.

More important than the general acceptance of the convenience store was the popularity the new retail format managed to establish with certain consumer segments that had obviously been less content with what existing retail formats could offer them. Surveys show a high share of single people, students and pupils among convenience store customers. In 1989 over 60 per cent of customers were below 25 years of age, nearly 65 per cent pupils, students or single men and women (Abe [Yukio] 1993:35). Convenience stores thus nurtured a new group of consumers and their preferences are clearly reflected in assortments with a focus on fast food, snacks, accessories and a limited choice of magazines and books. In a way, convenience stores have become meeting points for some of these groups and store operators are encouraged to promote this. It is not uncommon to see people standing in convenience stores during all times of the day and night reading the magazines on display. Leaving them undisturbed is an explicit policy of many convenience store chains aimed at sustaining the popularity of their stores.

The area where the introduction of convenience stores led to the most pronounced changes was the relationship between retailers, wholesalers and manufacturers. At the time of the emergence of superstores in Japan it had been expected that their expansion would lead eventually to the decline of the wholesale sector. Overall, however, this process did not take place. Operators of superstores and later discount stores concentrated on the fast expansion of store networks and were interested mainly in the secure supply of merchandise for their stores.

Utilizing the infrastructure and services of the wholesale sector, they had no need to build up alternative systems.

While serving the needs of existing small retail stores and superstores alike, the existing distribution structure was not appropriate to support the needs of convenience store operators. Realizing this, convenience store operators actively sought to initiate change on the supply side (Yahagi 1992:135). The demands of convenience stores in regard to their suppliers can again be deducted from the characteristics of this retail format. Offering a wide assortment of fast-moving articles on small sales floors, with only very limited storage space, demanded a flexibility from suppliers that they were not able to offer. In particular the organizational relationships between wholesalers and manufacturers proved problematic. Wholesalers were tightly affiliated with certain manufacturers, with agreements not to handle products of competing companies or giving wholesalers the exclusive right to handle products in a certain area. In addition, the majority of wholesalers carried only a limited number of product lines; general wholesalers were nearly non-existent. If retailers wanted to carry general assortments they had to maintain relationships with a high number of wholesalers. Early convenience store operators had to deal with more than eighty different wholesalers for procurement of merchandise. This continuous interaction with wholesalers and store deliveries disturbed the customer flow and kept sales personnel and store owners occupied with administrative tasks (SIJ 1992:73–4).

When Ito Yokado as the pioneer in this area presented its plans to introduce convenience stores to its wholesalers it met with more resistance than enthusiasm. Ito Yokado demanded that its suppliers be continuously prepared to deliver small quantities, something that suppliers feared would lead to high additional costs. Among the supply standards demanded by Ito Yokado were the following (SIJ 1992:73–4):

- The acceptance of daily orders and the daily supply of merchandise, if necessary even on holidays. For bread, Ito Yokado even insisted on fresh merchandise on New Year's Day, the most important Japanese holiday and the only holiday when nearly all businesses were closed.
- The delivery of merchandise in quantities below the smallest packaging sizes of manufacturers.
- The guarantee to deliver not only on particular days but also exactly on time, preferably at times when the storeowner was present, this enabling the storeowner to leave the running of the store to less qualified part-timers at other times.

- The delivery of exactly the merchandise ordered in items of quantities and specifications in order to reduce sales losses. Ito Yokado, pressured by Southland, introduced penalties for late deliveries, a first in Japanese distribution. In addition, suppliers were asked to store merchandise for Ito Yokado separately. Later, after Ito Yokado had frequently taken up all supplies of certain products during promotional periods this demand was extended to the provision of exclusive storage spaces for Seven-Eleven.
- The exact compliance to quality standards formulated by Seven-Eleven. Ito Yokado did not want the overall image of the company endangered by the failures of single suppliers.
- The waiving of the right to set prices independently. At that time, distinct regional difference between wholesale prices existed. Ito Yokado, however, wanted equal treatment for all its franchised stores, resulting in similar prices in all its stores. Since it could not legally interfere in the relationship between franchised stores and suppliers, Ito Yokado in collaboration with manufacturers instituted recommended wholesale prices for participating wholesalers.

For wholesalers, the acceptance of these standards drawn up by Seven-Eleven Japan and thereafter supplying convenience stores resulted in losses during the first two or three years of the system. Nonetheless, most wholesalers continued to deal with Seven-Eleven owing to initial capital investments they had made and also because they feared for their existing business with the superstores of Ito Yokado (SIJ 1992:86). The situation of participating wholesalers improved, however, when the number of stores grew. Seven-Eleven utilized its increased leverage to initiate substantial changes with the aim of changing the heavily manufacturer-oriented distribution system to one operating more in the interest of the retail sector. The number of wholesalers required to stock one store could be reduced to about 53 in 1976 after some competing manufacturers could be convinced to supply merchandise through the same wholesaler. Where this was not possible, or the reluctance of manufacturers too strong, Seven-Eleven at least initiated the establishment of joint distribution centres by wholesalers. The joint distribution of products to stores substantially reduced the number of deliveries to be handled by one store. First trials were made with fresh merchandise, then dairy products of different manufacturers followed in 1980 before the system was widened to beef (1982), household goods (1984) and cosmetics and soap (1985). In 1982, the delivery of merchandise was also systemized according to cooling requirements.

Apart from taking a larger role in the physical distribution of goods, Seven-Eleven also took an interest in the manufacturing processes of products to be sold in its stores. This started with *bentô* (boxed precooked meals), where storeowners were initially given the freedom to select suppliers of their own locally. However, this resulted in grave differences in the quality of products offered, leading to fears on the side of the chain management that this might hurt the overall image of the stores. The company therefore drew up detailed quality guidelines for manufacturers; later it even established the joint procurement for raw materials used by its *bentô* suppliers for products sold in the Seven-Eleven stores (SIJ 1992:114–20).

Although this was an overall success story, not everything went smoothly for the company. Fresh produce was initially part of assortments; however, owing to problems with quality control and product procurement, vegetables and fruits were taken off the shelves of Seven-Eleven stores in 1980. Fast food, today one of the most successful products of convenience stores, also proved to be problematic. Products that sold well in the US stores did not appeal to customers of the Japanese Seven-Eleven stores. American fast food was just being introduced into Japan at that time; the first McDonald's store had only been opened in Japan in 1971. After the failure with American fast food the company eventually had more success with products developed to the Japanese taste (SIJ 1992:109–12).

The growth of convenience stores in Japan thereby required extensive changes in the existing distribution system, which ranged from distribution channel strategies of manufacturers and wholesalers to details in the manufacturing processes of products. This made the introduction of convenience stores a difficult task for newcomers and explains the alliances formed by established Japanese retailers and US companies. The knowledge about the Japanese retail markets, the distribution system and the established relationship with suppliers made the large superstore operators attractive partners for US companies. Apart from Ito Yokado's collaboration with Southland, Daiei cooperated with Consolidated Foods, which owned the Lawson brand, and Uny was supported by Circle K. Only Seiyu developed a system of its own from scratch and therefore only relatively late reached a level of sophistication that could compete with those of the other chains (HKH 1980:63, 1981a:191).

To offer advanced services to consumers and to overall manage their franchised stores efficiently, Japanese convenience chain operators invested heavily in information technology and in this regard became pioneers in Japanese retailing. The central issue regarding the management of convenience stores was how to offer comprehensive assortments in comparatively small spaces. To do so efficiently, they had continuously to fine-tune assortments to consumer preferences, and to keep stores neither over- or understocked with certain items; product loss had also to be kept at a minimum. Achieving these objectives required close and constant communication with franchisees, especially in the form of information systems that constantly monitored sales at stores, processed this information and provided storeowners with purchasing recommendations. Seven-Eleven started in 1981 with the development of POS-systems. From 1983 onwards, this system was introduced into stores and thereafter used not only to record sales data but also to provide the customer services described above. Not only product information was recorded but also customer details. Cash registers at Seven-Eleven require staff to record the gender and estimate the age group of customers at the time of purchase (SIJ 1992:185–96, Katayama 1993:13). The sophistication some Japanese companies reached in managing their store networks became known to the larger public when Ito Yokado and Seven-Eleven Japan managed to take over the American company Southland, the firm from which Ito Yokado had acquired the franchise rights originally – a rare case of a franchisee taking over the franchisor (Koyama 1993:30, Sparks 1995).

Part III
Development of Systems (1990s)

5
The 1990s: A Radically Different Environment

The 1990s proved to be a period of change and uncertainty for the Japanese economy and its players. Low growth rates, rising unemployment and a growing number of bankruptcies characterized a prolonged period of structural change that after the turn of the millennium was still ongoing. During this period no element of the Japanese economic system remained unquestioned, and many of the distinct features of Japanese political economy, industrial organization and company management that were once regarded as cornerstones of Japan's success became the target of reinterpretation. For example, close ties between companies that had once been mainly interpreted as enhancing communication and collaboration were suddenly blamed for serious flaws in corporate financing and governance. Similarly, collaboration between business and government was reinterpreted as blocking structural change and necessary deregulation, and the once-hailed human resources management system was recognized as a threat to creativity and cost competitiveness. In addition, consumers who were once praised for their fast acceptance of new products, appreciation of good services and preference for quality over price were described as having redefined their priorities by having become more price-conscious.

For the distribution sector it has to be noted that many of the above elements had never been evaluated in the same positive way as had been the case for manufacturing, the financial sector or the large trading companies in the first place. This had been due to the low international exposure of the leading mass merchandisers and also to their relatively late rise to prominence. With the exception of department stores, large

Japanese retailers had only emerged as important players in the late 1960s and while sharing some characteristics with companies from other sectors, such as a general growth focus or a dependence on bank financing, they had neither gained entrance into the large horizontal business groupings nor received explicit support from the government.

Nonetheless, companies were affected by changes in the 1990s such as deregulation, stagnating consumer demand, internationalization and an unstable financial system. Many of the players who dominated up till then were apparently unprepared for these developments. Looking for ways to regain competitiveness, they finally realized the necessity to come up with strong comprehensive systems that ensured not only growth of revenue but at the same time profitability. In an environment of open price competition and greatly reduced support by stable shareholders and lenders, companies of the distribution sector could no longer afford to forgo profitability for growth targets.

Retail companies that proved to be successful during the 1990s possessed all-round strengths and in many ways point to the future of Japanese retailing. Foreign companies such as Toys 'R' Us entered the Japanese market and insisted on implementing their usual standards in dealing with suppliers. Domestic newcomers such as Fast Retailing came up with new ways of combining international product design and procurement with unique sales concepts. Convenience store companies, who had over the years patiently worked on the development of comprehensive systems, found themselves in a favourable position in the development of Japan's e-commerce industry.

In analyzing the developments in Japanese retailing during the 1990s up until the turn of the millennium, two factors will be singled out in this chapter as the major forces driving the development of Japanese retailing and distribution during the 1990s: consumer behaviour and deregulation. The impact of these two factors on format development in Japanese retailing is then demonstrated in a case study in Chapter 6 that analyzes the changing retail situation in a suburban area of Tokyo. Chapter 7 deals with newcomers in Japanese retailing during the 1990s. It shows that the emergence of foreign companies and the rapid rise to prominence of certain domestic companies with innovative concepts was in one way a consequence of the factors described above, but in another way has become a major driving force for changing of established retail companies itself. Consequently Chapter 8 gives an overview of the problems of formerly dominating retail companies and their efforts to restructure. An important area in the overall quest to build comprehensive systems is the changing relationship with suppliers

(Chapter 9). While facing rapid change in their core businesses retailers had at the same time to deal with an additional challenge, e-commerce based on the emergence of the internet. Chapter 10 will therefore look at some of the strategies Japanese retailers have developed in this regard, especially those advocated by convenience store companies.

As already pointed out, the Japanese business environment changed drastically during the 1990s. For their overall importance in regard to retailing, two factors, consumer conduct and state regulations, can be singled out. Developments in other areas (for example, changes in the financial sector or trade practices) are closely related to activities of certain players and will therefore be taken up in the later chapters.

Consumer behaviour in a stagnating economy

After the end of the bubble economy consumers adjusted their spending to the new realities of lower disposable incomes (Figure 5.1; Tables 5.1 and 5.2). Changes in household income and expenditure that still showed a positive development during the first half of the 1990s turned negative in the second half of that decade. In the year 2000, the overall

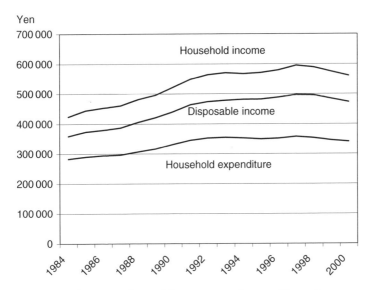

Figure 5.1 Development of monthly income and expenditure of an average worker's household, 1984–99.
Source: Author's figure based on Statistics Bureau (2002).

Table 5.1 Living expenditure for selected product groups, 1975–2000

Year	Total monthly living expenditure in yen	Food		Furniture and household utensils		Clothes and footwear		Reading and recreation	
		A	B	A	B	A	B	A	B
1975	166 032	30.0		5.0		9.0		8.5	
1980	238 126	27.8	32.9	4.2	22.4	7.5	20.0	8.5	43.0
1985	289 489	25.7	12.3	4.2	20.7	7.0	12.6	8.7	25.5
1990	331 595	24.1	7.6	4.0	7.6	7.2	18.5	9.6	25.7
1995	349 663	22.6	−1.3	3.7	−0.5	6.0	−11.8	9.5	4.6
2000	340 977	22.0	−5.1	3.3	−14.0	5.0	−18.5	9.9	−4.1

A = share of product group in percentage of total expenditure, B = change in expenditure to previous year, given in per cent.
Source: Author's compilation based on Statistics Bureau (2002).

Table 5.2   Savings and liabilities of Japanese households, 1975–99 (in million yen)

	Yearly income	Total savings	Liabilities
1975	3.0	3.2	0.85
1980	4.6	5.8	1.8
1985	5.6	8.5	2.7
1990	6.8	13.5	3.6
1995	7.6	16.0	4.6
1999	7.5	17.4	5.8

Average household based on sample survey of 10 000 households.
Source: Author's compilation based on Statistics Bureau (2002).

level of income and spending was back to the level of the year 1991. Overall, the willingness of consumers to spend dropped. While the propensity to consume stood at a relatively stable level of around 77 per cent from 1975 till 1985, it dropped to 73.3 per cent in 1990 and further to 72.1 per cent in 2000. This development has been attributed to a number of factors, the most important one being the rising uncertainty concerning the security of employment and provision for retirement.

Consumers, whether in their roles as employees or employers, fell victim to the economic restructuring of companies. Though many households did not not necessarily experience unemployment themselves, the threat of unemployment still loomed large over them. The rise of unemployment was a new phenomenon for Japanese society. Even throughout both oil crises Japan had managed to keep it low, but the unemployment rate steadily increased from only 2.1 per cent in 1990 to 5.6 per cent at the end of the year 2001. With bankruptcy becoming a reality for even established large security houses and insurance companies, not only blue-collar workers but also the so far relatively sheltered white-collar elite of Japanese corporations could no longer feel secure. In addition, the reorganization of personnel policies of large companies added to the uncertainties of employees. Companies began to introduce performance-based remuneration schemes and thereby changed the system of advancement in rank and pay by seniority that had so well fitted the life cycles of Japanese households by providing them with adequate funds at the time they were needed. Instead of being allowed to develop steadily with their companies as their older colleagues had been able to do, many employees that entered companies in the 1990s underwent a quite different experience of continuous reorganization, sudden job transfers and increased competitive pressure at the workplace (Nitto and Shiozaki 2001:6).

Another factor adding to the uncertainty of consumers was the ongoing discussion on the future of the social security system. The Japanese population is among the fastest aging among highly developed industrial nations with the share of people 65 years or older expected to increase from 14.6 per cent in 1995 to 22 per cent in 2010. Realizing that the population was aging at a record pace, the Japanese government started a comprehensive nationwide awareness campaign. The government, not being able to provide for the social security needs of its citizens alone – nor being trusted by its citizens to do so – propagated a model of social security based on the three pillars of government welfare, company welfare and self-provision. While during the 1980s all three pillars appeared stable, this changed during the 1990s. Government debt increased at a record pace, companies had to admit shortcomings in pension reserves and some of the financial institutions which consumers had invested their money in appeared to be on the brink of bankruptcy.

For these reasons consumers have become reluctant to consume during the 1990s and since, and have overall become more price-sensitive (Ishikawa and Yashima 2001, Nitto and Shiozaki 2001). Pointing to the considerable length of time consumer spending has remained stagnant, observers have stated that changes in consumer behaviour can hardly be described as merely recession-related and cyclical any longer, but should be viewed rather as permanent changes in consumption patterns and consumer behaviour (Masuda 2000:43). Masuda (2000:43–5) argues that consumer patterns of the past can be summarized under the keywords of pleasant or festive consumption (*ukare shôhi*), characterized by the spread of luxury consumption to the masses, consumption based on the accumulation of assets, and the simultaneous progression of diverse reciprocal needs. In contrast, he describes the consumption behaviour of the 1990s as wise consumption (*kashikoi shôhi*) characterized by price sensitivity, saving and simplicity. Nakamoto (1995:198) looks at developments from a long-term perspective and argues that the patterns of consumption in the 1990s should not be viewed as totally new and disruptive but rather as a continuation of trends initiated after the two oil shocks and the difficult economic situation of the early 1980s. In retrospect, the period of the bubble economy can thereby be seen as an exceptional temporary return to patterns of a mass consumer society characterized by a very materialistic lifestyle.

Konishi (2001) has analyzed changes in the spending pattern of households in relation to different life stages over the period between 1994 and 1999. She shows that spending for unmarried persons in single households remained comparatively stable, with the increases in income this group enjoyed during this period being used mostly for communication and computer devices. Unmarried couples without children reduced their monthly spending by 1.9 per cent and overall consume only 72.4 per cent of their disposable income, down from 77.2 per cent five years ago. Konishi explains this shift by the considerable increase in homeownership of this group promoted by government initiatives, lower land prices and low interest rates. Other groups have reduced the amount they spent from their disposable income to a lesser degree, but decreases of over 3 per cent within a period of five years are still significant. For these households, the recorded increase in monthly disposable income was due mainly to the reduction of taxes by the government. In accordance with the sources already cited, Konishi argues that the reluctance to spend additional available income is due mainly to the insecurity of these groups about provision for old age and health- and nursery-related costs.

A look at the development of consumer prices, however, puts the developments outlined above into a slightly different perspective. The official consumer price index shows an increase from 93.5 for the year 1990 to 101.5 for the year 2000 (base year 1995). Within this overall development some product groups show decreases (for example, furniture and household utensils to 91.7); others like clothing and food, however, remain largely stable (Statistics Bureau 2002). The official consumer price index thereby seems to be in strong contradiction to the numerous reports of price destruction (*kakaku hakai*) or a pricing revolution (*kakaku kakumei*) in Japan (e.g. Miyazawa 1995, Takaya 1994). This problem can be resolved, however, if we consider that the official consumer price index does not take into account promotional prices by retailers and, being based on a given basket of products, does not adapt to changes in consumer preferences. In particular, the first point appears to be critical within the competitive environment of the 1990s where many products were constantly sold at promotional and campaign prices. Recognizing these problems, the Saison Research Institute (Sezon Sôgô Kenkyûjo 2000) has come up with an alternative index based on the actual POS-data of large general superstores in Tokyo (Table 5.3). This index shows significant decreases in prices for all product groups, especially from the year 1998 onwards, with the indices for clothing and furniture and appliances being down to 83.4 and 84.2 respectively.

Based on these findings the current attitude of Japanese consumers can be interpreted as an unwillingness to spend, but it has to be questioned

Table 5.3 Comparison of the POS-Price Index (POS PI) and the official Consumer Price Index for Tokyo (Tokyo CPI), 1995 to 2000

Year	Total		Food		Clothing		Furniture and appliances	
	Tokyo CPI	POS PI	Tokyo CPI	POS PI	Tokyo CPI	POS PI	Tokyo CPI	POS PI
1995	100	100	100	100	–	–	100	100
1996	99.4	99.4	98.8	100.4	–	–	96.7	93.8
1997	100.1	99.4	100.8	100.8	–	–	95.3	91.7
1998	101.4	97.4	102.8	98.0	106.1	106.2	93.1	89.6
1999	100.1	94.0	101.5	96.0	104.7	96.8	91.9	87.0
2000	97.9	90.0	98.9	93.9	104.3	83.4	89.5	84.2

Source: Author's compilation based on Sezon Sōgō Kenkyūjo (2000).

whether the drop in absolute consumer spending and store sales is really a reflection of consumers foregoing consumption. The falling prices are a result of consumers having become more price-sensitive but also of an increased competition in the retail sector after the deregulation of the Large Store Law. Japanese retailing has thereby entered into a vicious cycle where companies try to attract consumers by lower prices, but consumers do not utilize savings for additional consumption, preferring rather to save to prepare for uncertainties.

Another important development in the shopping patterns of consumers is increased mobility, which has allowed consumers to become more selective in their store choice. An increase of roughly 10 million normal-sized passenger cars from 1990 to 2000 alone means that today nearly 90 per cent of Japanese households own a car (Naikakufu 2001). Motorization has thereby increased and shopping attitudes seem to be converging with conditions in other advanced countries. In a survey by the Management and Coordination Agency (Sorifu 1997), 41.7 per cent of consumers answered that they do all their shopping by car. This compares with 24.5 per cent who do not use a car for their shopping at all. Asked for their reasons, consumers responded that the car was convenient for the transport of goods (53.5 per cent) and also allowed them to buy larger quantities (39.3 per cent). In addition, respondents enjoyed the mobility (50.6 per cent) or answered simply that they always used their car when leaving their homes (36.5 per cent). The availability of the car and the preference for using it is one factor to explain the fact that the frequency of consumers using large stores has surpassed the frequency of consumers using traditional shopping districts (Table 5.4). Besides preferring the comprehensive selections of large stores, consumers also point to the existence of parking lots as an advantage of large stores over the traditional shopping districts.

In viewing these developments, the current problems of the majority of Japanese retailers should not, however, be blamed totally on fears of Japanese consumers about an uncertain future. Many among Japan's manufacturers and distributors alike could not provide the kind of products demanded by consumers in response to the stagnating economy. Japan's economy is still described as driven largely by manufacturers. Manufacturers took a leading role in product development and for a long time heavily relied on traditional methods of market segmentation and mass marketing (Katô 1995). In this sense, control over distribution channels, heavy advertising and a high frequency of new product introductions were more important to manufacturers than the

Table 5.4 Frequency of the usage of large stores and stores in shopping districts

	Large stores (above 500 square meters), usage (%)	Stores in shopping districts, usage (%)
Every day	14.6	5.7
2 or 3 times a week	27.3	13.8
Once a week	23.8	15.4
1 to 3 times a month	20.2	21.8
Do not use at all	13.6	42.6
Other	0.3	0.2
Do not know	0.2	0.5

Source: Sorifu (1993).

creation of lasting value for consumers by responding to individual needs. Overall, retailers and wholesalers did not challenge the position of manufacturers. This was in contrast to other countries where retailers early on assumed an independent position. The example of a number of Japanese retailers (see Chapter 7) who, based on their departure from established trade practices, prospered during the 1990s will further reinforce this argument.

Deregulation and liberalization

In Part II of this book regulations for large retail stores have been described as a major factor underlying retail development during the 1970s and 1980s, regulations for large stores gradually being strengthened during this period. During the 1980s, however, a gradual reassessment of the activities of large stores and regulations to limit their activities occurred. This led eventually to the liberalization of the Large Store Law at the beginning of the 1990s and finally its repeal in 2000.

An early step in this direction was the publication of the *Vision for the Distribution Industry of the 1980s* by MITI's Deliberation Council for Distribution (TSCK 1984). The role of these deliberation councils in the political economy of Japan has been a subject of much discussion. Onlookers point out that it is difficult to detect whose views are represented in officially published reports – those of council members, representatives from business, interest groups, the press and academia, or those of the bureaucracy that provides background information and drafts the reports (Schwartz 1998:86). Nonetheless, the content of the report issued by the Deliberation Council for Distribution in 1984 was regarded as being of such a controversial nature that in consideration of an upcoming election its publication was postponed for six months (Kusano 1992:152). The report's main message was that the diversifying needs of consumers should be reflected by a wide portfolio of retail formats. Different retail formats were analyzed and each attributed to fulfilling certain needs for consumers. This line of argument culminated in the conclusion that it was possible for different retail formats to coexist and co-prosper. Consequently, the report criticized the application of the Large Store Law and demanded that municipalities come up with systematic plans for the development of the retail sector within their jurisdiction (TSCK 1984:89, 92–5, Kusano 1992:152–3). While this report met with heavy criticism from the associations that represented the interests of small retailers, the subsequent *Vision for Distribution in the 1990s* was received with even more contempt. It demanded substantial changes to the application of the Large Store Law and also included a projection that saw the aggregated market shares of traditional retail stores decrease by more than 30 per cent by the year 2000 (TSS 1989:181, 328; see also Table 5.5).

Contrary to some popular views, Japanese political circles and the administration were thereby well aware of the problems of the retail sector and the need for a change in regulations even before foreign pressure for change mounted (Kusano 1992:4). Foreign governments brought up the issue of the Large Store Law towards the end of the 1980s. The existence of regulations for large retail stores having already been mentioned earlier in reports by the OECD and the European

Table 5.5 Projected and real development of market share of major retail formats, 1985–2000 (percentage market share)

Year	1985 real	1990 projected	1991 real	2000 projected	1999 real*
General retailers	62.8	55.2	60.5	36.0	60.2
Department stores	8.7	8.4	10.1	9.0	6.7
General superstores	8.0	8.4	7.3	13.8	6.2
Food superstores	5.8	6.8	5.5	12.8	11.6
Household goods superstores	0.7	1.2	1.2	2.0	4.0
Other superstores	9.7	13.0	9.1	17.8	6.7
Convenience stores	4.2	5.8	6.3	8.4	4.3

*Sales without sales of car dealerships, gasoline stations and sales in restaurants of department stores and general superstores. Classification changed for 1999 for all formats apart from general retailers, department stores and general superstores.
Source: Author's compilation based on TSS (1989), TSC (1993, 2000).

Union, the US introduced it as a major issue during the Structural Impediments Initiative in February 1990. While the law was seen as a barrier to the entry of US retailers into the Japanese market, overall the US side was more interested in a general increase in the market share of large retail companies and large retail stores in Japan, since large retail stores were seen as more capable of handling imported merchandise than smaller stores. After intense negotiations (for the process see Schoppa 1997:146–80), both sides finally agreed on a gradual liberalization of the regulations for large-scale retail stores. First amendments were made as early as in May 1990 and included the following points (NKK 1990:68–71, SCC 1993:29):

- Shortening of the time span between submission of reports and acceptance of plans to 18 months.
- Expansion of existing sales floors for the sale of imported goods by 100 square meters without additional application.
- Expansion of sales floors without application for increases below 10 per cent of overall sales floors and below a total of 50 square meters.
- Extension of operating hours until 7 p.m. and reduction of closure days per year to 44 days without additional application.
- Instructions to local municipalities to amend their own regulations in accordance with the objectives of the law.

In particular, the shortening of the application process reduced the uncertainties for retailers substantially. At the same time, MITI abandoned the praxis of simply not accepting reports in certain designated areas. Overall, these changes led to a substantial increase in the opening of new stores (Figure 3.1). The formal revision of the law took place only 18 months later and went even further. The categories for store size were amended, with the threshold for stores in category I raised to 6000 square meters in metropolitan areas and 3000 square meters in the rest of the country. The threshold of 500 square meters for smaller stores remained unchanged; however, authorities practically guaranteed approval for stores below 1000 square meters that complied with certain minimum restrictions in regard to opening hours and closure days. The process was shortened further to a maximum period of one year and large retailers were also allowed to open until 8 p.m. and a reduction of yearly closure days to 24 days without further application. The change of the law also explicitly ruled out individual regulations by local governing bodies. Together with the revision of the Large Store Law, other laws were introduced and revised, with the aim of modernizing small retail stores and, among other measures, providing subsidies for the upgrading of infrastructure and facilities in the traditional shopping districts. Finally in June 2000, the law was completely abolished. It was replaced by a set of laws specifically, a revised City Planning Law, a Law Concerning the Location of Large-Scale Retail Stores and a Law for the Revitalization of Shopping Districts. The new rules raised the power of local community councils to influence retail development in the areas under their jurisdiction, especially in regards to aspects of traffic and pollution control. While the previous Large Store Law aimed explicitly at the protection of small retailers, the new Law Concerning the Location of Large Stores no longer includes this objective. Instead, it focuses on the environmental effects of new large retail stores and includes provisions for the handling of waste, traffic and noise that accompany the operation of large stores. Small and traditional enterprises were compensated for the change by a set of provisions to upgrade and modernize shopping districts (NRS 2000:146–56). By formerly separating regulations for large retail stores and the issue of promotion of small retailers Japan has consciously moved closer to the example of Western countries.

Still, the retail industry and many observers felt that the new laws at least had the potential to regulate the activities beyond their original scope. The retail industry therefore reacted and despite the economic stagnation tried to obtain approval for as many stores as possible while the old regulations were still in place. Looking at the new regulations, retailers anticipated a substantial increase in costs for the opening and operation of new stores.

The first community to propose new regulations even before the laws were formerly changed was the Arakawa ward of Tokyo. The ward came up with the following points to be taken into regard for new store openings (*Nikkei ryûtsû shinbun* 7 January 1999):

- Planned parking lots and measures to regulate traffic in the neighborhood of stores.
- Details of operation of car park (operating hours, estimated demand during peak periods, and methods of traffic control).
- Situation of roads in the area (traffic volume and traffic regulations in regard to pedestrians, cyclists, cars).
- Estimation of customer traffic and effects on the neighborhood.
- Estimation of traffic by suppliers and other service providers (type and size of vehicles used by suppliers and waste disposal companies, number of vehicles at different hours of the day and map of routes).

- Measures to secure safety of pedestrians.
- Overview of situations at other existing stores of the company resembling the planned store.
- Planned trees and lawns.
- Measures for handling of waste and recycling.
- Measures to assist elderly and handicapped persons.

In many regards these rules became part of the later legislation. Since the first company that applied for the opening of a new large store in the Arakawa ward after the new rules were introduced did not manage to get approval, other retail companies studied these rules closely. Pointing to drastically increased costs (an increase of up to 50 per cent) for the opening of new stores and complicated regulation processes they revised their expansion plans for the following years downwards (*Nikkei ryûtsû shinbun* 7 January 1999).

Uncertainty about the new policies also affected the stance of companies towards existing stores. While other factors such as sluggish consumer demand and problems in securing financing might well have also influenced decisions, companies revised the scrap-and-build policies they had just started in the second half of the 1990s. As has been pointed out, owing to the Large Store Law companies had been very reluctant to close existing stores before, mismatches in store design and location largely contributing to continuously decreasing sales during the 1990s (Table 5.6). Under the new circumstances Seiyu, which had originally planned to close 30 small and unprofitable stores per year from 1998 on, reduced this number to only 15 and announced that it would focus its attention on the modernization of existing stores (*Nikkei ryûtsû shinbun* 15 October 1998). Life, which operated about 150 stores in 1998, had expected originally to expand its network to 250 stores till the end of the fiscal year 2001 but reduced its expectations to only 200 stores. Like Seiyu, Life refocused its attention on existing smaller stores and instead of scrapping these, studied alternatives to raise their attractiveness (*Nikkei ryûtsû shinbun* 23 July 1998).

Consumer conduct and the aspects of the regulation of the retail industry were brought together in a survey of 3000 consumers (valid responses 71.3 per cent) commissioned by the Management and Coordination Agency in June 1997 (Sorifu Kôhoshitsu 1997). The survey asked consumers about their opinions on different retail formats and also large- and small-scale stores. Asked for their impression of changes in the retail industry over the 1990s, 73.2 per cent of consumers responded that shopping had become more convenient. The main

Table 5.6 Distribution of existing superstores by company and opening years (percentage share)

	Absolute no. of stores	Less than 5 years ago	6–10 years ago	11–15 years ago	16–20 years ago	21–25 years ago	26 years ago and older
Ito Yokado	169	20	11	12	20	21	16
Jusco	278	44	14	11	14	9	8
Seiyu	189	11	7	9	17	21	35
Daiei	389	14	10	11	17	21	27
Nagasakiya	98	12	10	10	20	15	33

Source: Based on Atsumi (2000:20).

reasons for this change were seen in the increased number of large stores (51.5 per cent) but also in the increase in the number of convenience stores (39.0 per cent), the extension of opening hours (39.2 per cent) and a general improvement of assortments in terms of breadth (37.0 per cent). Only 5.1 per cent answered that shopping had become less convenient and gave as their main reasons the decreased number of small stores in their neighbourhood (26.4 per cent) but also the closure of familiar large stores (26.4 per cent). Consumers therefore seemed basically to have profited from the changes in retail regulations. At the same time, consumers supported the shift to new regulations. Asked for their concerns about the opening of additional large stores they mainly pointed to traffic problems (51.4 per cent), and pollution through noise (26 per cent) and garbage (23.3 per cent). Only 18.8 per cent expressed concern about the situation of small retailers in their neighbourhood and 27.3 per cent had no special concerns at all.

6

Changes in Retail Formats in a Deregulated Environment: A Case Study

Driven by deregulation, changes in consumer behaviour and additional developments, Japanese retailing underwent significant change during the 1990s. This chapter will analyze these changes in regard to retail formats. In doing so, it will take an approach different from that adopted for the previous periods. Developments will first be described in quantitative terms based on the latest available retail statistics. To put the quantitative developments into perspective and to incorporate qualitative developments a case study of a suburban area of Tokyo will be employed. More than the quantitative overview, this case study will show the dramatic changes that occurred within a very short time in the Japanese retail landscape and that not only affected the level and quality of competition but also the overall appearance of Japanese towns. Within this larger case, smaller cases of store development will demonstrate how companies positioned new formats during the 1990s, how existing stores had to revamp their strategies to survive and also the failure of a foreign company to enter the Japanese retail market.

Development of retail formats

In quantitative terms large stores and other so-called modern retail formats such as convenience stores gained in overall importance during the 1990s (Table 6.1). Growth, however, did not extend to all large-scale formats. Department stores lost in terms of market share and general superstores, the dominating format of the 1970s and 1980s, largely stagnated. It thereby became specialty superstores that managed to expand their market share considerably during the 1990s. Overall, their

Table 6.1   Market share of major retail formats, 1991–9 (per cent)

	1991	1994	1997	1999
Department stores	8.0	7.4	7.2	6.7
General superstores	6.0	6.5	6.7	6.2
Food superstores	7.9	9.2	10	11.6
Apparel superstores	0.6	0.6	0.8	0.9
Household superstores	1.4	2.1	3.1	4.0
Convenience stores	2.2	2.8	3.5	4.3
Other self-service stores	5.1	5.8	6.8	5.9
Specialty stores	47.2	42.6	40.4	43.5
Other stores	21.7	22.5	21.5	17.0

Source: Author's compilation based on TSC (2000).

share increased from a market share of 9.9 per cent to 16.4 per cent from 1991 to 1999. Food and household goods superstores increased their shares by about 3 per cent respectively and even apparel superstores staged a slow but constant comeback. Another retail format that showed growth was the convenience store, which nearly doubled its market share from 2.2 per cent to 4.3 per cent over the same period.

However, the changes in market shares between the different formats seem to be surprisingly moderate when compared with the drastic increases in the number of large stores, employees and sales floors (Table 6.2). Operators of general superstores increased the number of employees and the size of their sales floors by 38 per cent and 40 per cent respectively but could record an increase in sales of only around 4 per cent. Operators of food superstores managed sales growth of 48.3 per cent, but to do so had to increase the number of employees by nearly 86 per cent and expand sales floors by 78 per cent. The average sales floor of a food supermarket increased from 593 square meters to 832 square meters within only eight years (Table 6.3). Developments for apparel and household superstores show similar patterns. Only the convenience store shows a more balanced pattern of development. This overall imbalance in development points to a drastically changed retail environment in the 1990s.

Decreasing real estate costs certainly contributed to the expansion of sales floors and the increase in employees is to a certain extent due to the strategy of companies to substitute qualified, full-time employees with lower-paid, less qualified part-timers. It will be shown later, however, that sales increases of companies and formats were due mainly to the opening of new stores, with existing stores experiencing continuous

Table 6.2 Development of retail formats, 1991–9.

Format	Stores		Sales		Employees		Sales floor	
	1999	Change 1991 (%)	1999 billion yen	Change 1991 (%)	1999	Change 1991 (%)	1999 million m²	Change 1991 (%)
Total	1 406 884	-12.4	143 833	1.1	8 029 000	14.5	133.9	21.8
Department stores	394	-17.6	9 705	-14.5	168 000	-18.5	7.3	8.3
General superstores	1 888	12.2	8 850	4.2	320 000	38.1	13.4	40.6
Food superstores	18 707	26.7	16 748	48.3	743 000	85.8	15.6	78.0
Apparel superstores	4 780	113.7	1 271	61.5	53 000	92.1	3.3	117.0
Household superstores	12 044	214.5	5 711	188.3	225 000	288.0	11.0	297.7
Convenience stores	39 628	66.2	6 135	96.3	537 000	183.2	4.1	82.7
Other self-service stores	86 367	19.9	8 440	16.5	496 000	47.3	9.5	36.9
Specialty stores	920 277	-8.8	62 598	-6.7	4 184 000	7.1	47.2	6.5
Other stores	319 685	-30.7	24 003	-17.4	1 285 000	-18.1	22.2	-17.6

Source: Author's compilation based on TSC (2000).

Table 6.3 Change in store characteristics, 1991–9

Format	Sales area per store			Employees per store		
	1991 (m²)	1999 (m²)	Change (%)	1991	1999	Change (%)
Total	68	95	39.0	4.6	5.7	24.6
Department stores	14 086	18 503	31.4	432.1	427.3	–1.1
General superstores	5 659	7 094	25.3	137.9	169.7	23.1
Food superstores	593	832	40.4	27.1	39.7	46.6
Apparel superstores	673	683	1.5	12.3	11.0	–10.1
Household superstores	722	913	26.4	15.2	18.7	23.4
Convenience stores	94	103	9.9	8.0	13.5	70.3
Other self-service stores	97	110	14.2	4.7	5.7	22.9
Specialty stores	44	51	16.7	3.9	4.5	17.4
Other stores	58	69	18.9	3.4	4.0	18.1

Source: Author's compilation based on TSC 2000.

Table 6.4 Changes in store concepts and formats

Characteristics	1970s and 1980s	1990s
Competition	Small stores and general superstores	General super-stores and specialty superstores/category killers and franchise systems of smaller stores
Catchment area	Small	Large
Location;	Customer-oriented	Cost-oriented
Store architecture	Attractive, amenities	Simple, cost-oriented
Size	Small or extremely large	Medium-sized
Pricing	Inactive	Active
Assortments	Wide and deep	Category-based
Opening hours	Short – regulated	Long, flexible

Source: Author's compilation.

declines in sales. Already, the total failure of some companies or conscious scrap-and-build policies by others have led to an increase in the number of closures of large stores and this trend might well continue in the future leading to an overall consolidation of the industry. Current statistics thereby reflect the state of Japanese retailing in a period of rapid transition, and a more stable picture of Japanese retailing in quantitative terms might emerge only in future statistics.

Companies did, however, not just increase the number of their stores and expand their store sizes. With new companies entering the market and established companies developing their formats, further paradigm changes in the design of formats took place that cannot properly be covered by just pointing to quantitative statistics (Table 6.4). To show these changes and to give a more illustrative account of the changes during the 1990s a case study approach will be employed. This case study will show not only developments in formats but also how aggregated changes led to changes in the appearance of Japanese communities.

Retail development in a suburban area of Tokyo

The communities of Shiki, Niiza, Asaka and Wako are situated on the northwestern border of Tokyo in the southwest of Saitama prefecture and occupy an area of about 61 square kilometers. Though they are separate municipalities, no clear boundaries between territories exist. People

Table 6.5   Development of population, 1960–2000

	1960	1970	1980	1990	1995	2000
Asaka	24 182	67 941	90 088	103 617	110 793	119 660
Niiza	14 401	77 704	119 309	138 919	144 735	150 260
Shiki	12 259	31 809	50 925	63 491	64 430	65 341
Wako	17 242	39 513	49 713	56 890	62 590	68 453
Total	68 084	216 967	310 035	362 917	382 548	403 714

Source: Author's compilation based on years 1960–95: Population Census in (Statistics Bureau: different years), year 2000: Saitama Statistics Division at www.pref.saitama.jp.

living in the four communities share public and private facilities such as railway stations, parks, shopping and education facilities. Since 1998 the four cities have been negotiating a possible merger to formalize this situation. The number of inhabitants has grown continuously from 68 000 in 1960 to 404 000 in 2000 (Table 6.5).

Due to their convenient location for central Tokyo and good public transportation the communities have developed into dormitory suburbs of Tokyo. It takes about 40 minutes by train and subway to get into the central districts of Tokyo. Beginning in the early 1970s, retail companies not only developed this area systematically but also used it continuously as a testing ground for new types of retail formats. Today, the area is described as one of the areas in the Tokyo region with the toughest competition between retail formats and the opening of new stores within it has been covered on a regular basis in professional journals and newspapers (for example, *Nihon keizai shinbun* 31 March 1994, *Nikkei ryûtsû shinbun* 16 May 1995, Tamura 1995, *Nihon shokuryô shinbun* 24 February 1997, *Nikkei ryûtsû shinbun* 15 July 1997, Nishikawa 1997, *Nikkei ryûtsû shinbun* 6 October 1998, *Nikkei ryûtsû shinbun* 23 July 1999, *Nihon shokuryô shinbun* 22 September 2000).

Retail development until the 1990s – locations and retail formats

The change of retail locations is no new phenomenon in the area. Till the construction of the railway line (Tobu Tôjô line) in 1914, the river Shingashi and the old trade route of the Kawagoe Road were the main traffic routes. Consequently, city centres were located along these routes. The construction of the Tobu Tôjô line brought some change; however, the final relocation of city centres did not happen till the 1960s, when commuters who used the railway to get to work in Tokyo moved into the area and the population increased rapidly. As a result the first large retail stores were built close to the railway stations (Figure 6.1)

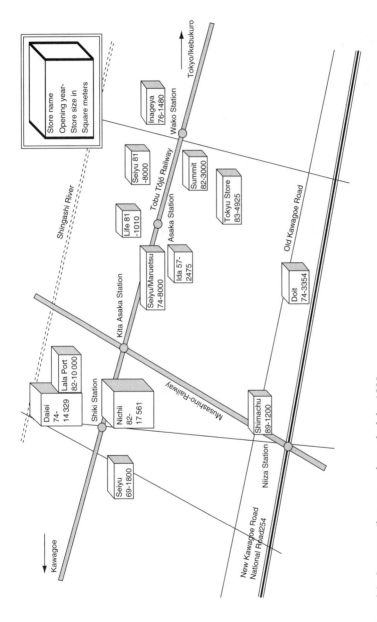

Figure 6.1 Large retail stores at the end of the 1980s.
Source: Author's figure based on Toyo Keizai (2001).

Figure 6.2   Daiei store in Shiki.

Seiyu opened a store with a sales floor of 1800 square meters on one side of Shiki Station in 1969. Daiei followed in 1974 with a store on the other side that, with its size of over 14 000 square meters, ranked prominently among the largest self-service stores in Japan at the time of its opening (Figure 6.2). In 1976 Nichii (now Mycal) opened a smaller store on the eastern side of Shiki Station that was replaced in 1980 by a larger store with a sales floor of 12 000 square meters. The area around the station became the new centre in terms of shopping facilities.

However, this process of relocation has not ended yet. In an area near the river Shingashi, which still operates under the name 'main shopping street', some traditional small shops for Japanese clothing, basketwork or household goods can still be found (Figure 6.3). The architecture of some buildings continues to reflect the style of the Meiji period. Still, over the last years the number of vacant stores has increased. While some attempts have been made to revitalize this area, many owners of stores seem to have lost interest in modernizing their stores and in preserving this shopping district.

Around the other railway stations development was slower. In 1974 Seiyu opened an outlet with 8000 square meters in Asaka. After a second wave of openings of smaller stores in the early 1980s, mainly in Wako

Figure 6.3 Traditional shops in Shiki.

and Asaka, the activities of retailers in the observed area largely stagnated despite an ongoing increase in population. The main reason for this stagnation was the Large Store Law. The fruitless efforts of the retailer Life – the company had tried for ten years to open a store in Shiki – were even brought up by the US as an example in the Structural Impediments Initiative negotiations with Japan and were covered in detail in the Japanese press in the early 1990s. The medium-sized company Life argued that the Large Store Law protected not only small traditional stores, but also existing large retail stores, whose operators thereby enjoyed an unfair competitive advantage that could not be equalized (*Nihon keizai shinbun* 12 April 1990, 16 April 1990).

Some companies limited their floor sizes to just below 500 square meters, the threshold of the Large Store Law. Store sizes of 495 square meters, for example of the discount store Jason that opened in Wako in 1984, can only be interpreted in this way. Relatively small-category killers for formal menswear, electric household appliances, DIY goods, sporting goods or even books opened in roadside locations mainly along the new Kawagoe Road (National Road 254) in the 1980s (Figure 6.4). The location away from stations also shows the rising importance of the car for the purpose of shopping. Owing to their small size some other modern retail concepts – especially convenience stores – were not affected by regulations

Figure 6.4   Stores along National Road 254.

at all and managed strong growth. From 1985 till 1990 the number of convenience stores in the area more than doubled from 23 stores to 51. Overall, convenience stores proved to be the fastest-growing retail format in the 1980s.

At the beginning of the 1990s the area's retail landscape could therefore be summarized as follows. A small number of dominating large general superstores that were built in the 1970s and located close to stations were supplemented by a growing number of rather small-sized category killers and convenience stores. Small retail stores had their location in the traditional shopping districts but could also be found in the direct vicinity of larger stores, either handling products that large stores could not handle because of the licensing system for liquor and rice or competing with larger stores on price by concentrating on very limited assortments and freshness of merchandise offered. Nearly absent were medium-sized or large food supermarkets and medium-sized category killers.

Change in the 1990s

The 1990s saw significant change in the observed area (Figure 6.5). The total floor space of stores with a sales floor of over 500 square meters

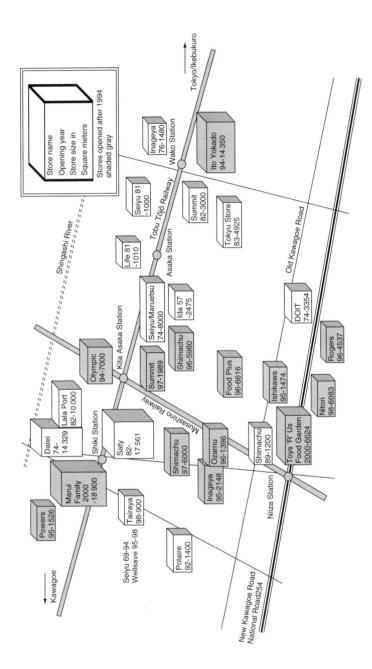

Figure 6.5 New large retail stores in the 1990s.
Source: Author's figure based on Toyo Keizai (2001)

opened by 1991 amounted to about 90 000 square meters. By March 2000 this space had more than doubled to around 204 000 square meters (Shûkan Tôyô Keizai 1991, 2001). Among the major openings in the area during the 1990s was Ito Yokado, which opened a general superstore with 14 350 square meters next to Wako Station in 1994. In the same year Olympic opened a store with 7000 square meters next to Kita Asaka Station that can be described as a combination of a food superstore and a strongly discount-oriented non-food store. The conversion of the former Seiyu store near Shiki station into a heavy-discount-oriented food store called Wellsave marked the arrival of foreign companies in the area. This store concept was not successful, however, and by 1998 an outlet of a regional food supermarket chain had replaced the Wellsave store. In 1996 Seiyu opened a new, mainly food-oriented store, Food Plus, with 6616 square meters in Niiza in a location slightly off National Road 254. In the same year Rogers opened a general discount store of nearly equal size not far away.

Two major companies came to the area to target the demand for furniture, interior, home improvement and household goods. In November 1997 Shimachu opened a home centre of nearly 6000 square meters in a location between Shiki Station and National Road 254. Nitori followed in October 1998 with a store of 6000 square meters in a roadside location along National Road 254. In terms of size, width and depth of assortments as well as store design, these stores are a clear departure from the somewhat eclectic concepts to be found in this area previously. Finally, the retail scene became even more diversified in the year 2000 when Marui opened a family-oriented department store with a sales floor of 19 000 square meters next to the station in Shiki (Figure 6.6). The construction of this store was part of a larger redevelopment plan for the area adjacent to the station on the Shiki side and overall totally changed the appearance of that part of the city. The store focuses on young families and younger consumer groups in general and carries a full line of goods. It has the added attractiveness of a number of specialty stores, among them international retailers such as Virgin Megastore and The Gap (*Ryûtsû saabisu shinbun* 8 February 2000). In September of the same year a new shopping complex was opened in a location along National Road 254 and near Niiza railway station that not only houses another food supermarket but also a 3700-square-meter branch of Toys 'R' Us.

These examples of large-store development were supplemented by a number of openings of smaller stores focusing on certain categories. Besides a number of food superstores by companies such as Inageya,

Figure 6.6 Marui store and Shiki station area.

Summit and Life, these include stores for apparel (for example, Aoki, Fast Retailing), and computer and household electronics (for example, Case Denki, Kojima) or sports (Alpen). Overall, the area thereby saw a significant widening of the retail spectrum which can be discussed under different aspects: competition, store design and sales concepts, and location.

Competition

As already pointed out, the rise in real estate prices and the gradual intensification of the Large Store Law during the 1980s had been especially hard to cope with for smaller and thereby less experienced and resource-rich companies. This situation changed during the 1990s. As a result of deregulation and falling land prices many existing stores lost their *de facto* protection and it was often the less-established companies that were contesting their position. For example, Hokushin Shôji, the company operating the Rogers store, had originally been viewed as a promising addition to Japan's retail scene after it had opened its first stores in the early 1970s. However, the company had not developed as expected and the store opened in Niiza in 1996 became its first new opening after a stagnation of 17 years (*Nikkei ryûtsû shinbun* 29 August 1996:11). Another company, Inageya, had opened three food superstores in the area in the 1970s, but in spite of a growing population and the ongoing development of residential areas had added no new stores in the 1980s. After the relaxation of the Large Store Law in the 1990s it opened new stores in 1995 and 1997 and enlarged its store in Wako. Overall, retail competition thereby reached a new level. This was especially true for food superstores. Fourteen new stores with dedicated sales floors for foods were opened during the 1990s, often within close proximity to other stores. Competition thereby heated up and, as has been outlined for the national level, the massive increases in employees and sales floor space have not led to comparable increases in sales. On the contrary, sales dropped from 1991 to 1994 and from 1997 to 1999 (Table 6.6). Nonetheless, when looking at these figures one has to take into consideration that store operators had greatly reduced costs for real estate and could calculate their profits differently. In the area real estate prices reached a peak in 1991 and have been falling ever since. In 1991, land for retail use sold at 1.6 million yen per square meter in Asaka and 3.7 million yen in Niiza. By the year 2000 prices had dropped drastically to 515 000 yen per square meter in Asaka and 650 000 yen in Niiza (Shûkan Tôyô Keizai 1992, 2002).

The number of small stores continued to decrease quickly in the 1990s (Table 6.7). However, the developments in the area show that the decrease in small stores was not a new phenomenon of the 1990s, but had started in the 1980s when competition from large retail formats was not so severe. To explain this development one has to take factors apart from the strong regulation into account, such as changes in shopping behaviour, the lack of successors in small family-owned businesses and the availability of other income opportunities. The rising land prices of the second half of the 1980s motivated many owners of small stores to sell their stores or to redevelop their land for office or residential use. At the same time, abundant employment opportunities existed, making it difficult to motivate children to take over family businesses. In contrast, competition increased during the 1990s, but storeowners have still been reluctant to close their stores in a period of falling land prices, because of the difficulty of finding alternative employment or not wanting to lose the preferential tax treatment that is granted to owners of small businesses in Japan. These factors delay the real effects of the increase in large stores in the area in statistical terms. For example, the number of stores selling rice fell only by 12.5 per cent between 1994 and 1997, but their sales decreased by 39 per cent (Figure 6.7). While this is the most drastic example and clearly due to the abolition of the licensing system for rice sellers, other product groups show a similar tendency.

Table 6.6 Development of sales floor, sales and employees 1972–99 (change in per cent)

Year	72/4	74/6	76/9	79/82	82/5	85/8	88/91	91/4	94/7	97/9
Sales floor space	30.8	19.3	8.5	19.2	8.6	0.3	10.1	16.3	13.4	6.4
Sales	65.8	54.1	33.0	35.3	14.1	18.4	25.4	–3.6	8.4	–3.4
Employees	20.1	13.2	9.2	10.2	9.7	8.5	3.0	11.2	7.7	5.5
No. of stores	11.9	5.1	–1.7	3.5	–3.7	–0.2	–4.7	–9.0	–4.3	–7.9

Figures are for Shiki, Niiza, Asaka and Wako. Figures for all Japan 1991–4: sales floor 10.7 per cent, sales 0.7 per cent, employees 5.5 per cent; for 94–97: sales floor 12.2 per cent, sales 3.1 per cent, employees–0.4 per cent.
Source: Up to 1997 TSC (a) (pertinent years); for 1999 Saitama Statistics Division at www.pref.saitama.jp.

Table 6.7 Change in the number of specialty food stores, 1974–99 (per cent)

Year	74/6	76/9	79/82	82/5	85/8	88/91	91/4	94/7	97/9
Fish	4.2	–3.0	–4.2	–6.5	–15.1	–6.8	–23.5	–30.8	5.6
Vegetables/fruits	–4.6	0.0	–4.8	–1.9	–14.9	–6.1	–21.1	–17.5	–8.8
Bread	13.7	5.7	–3.1	–9.9	–14.5	–18.7	–14.0	–14.4	–4.0
Rice	10.9	7.0	–3.9	0.0	5.5	–7.8	–9.9	–12.5	–3.6
Meat	1.6	4.0	–1.5	–10.9	–7.0	–22.4	–6.0	–19.2	–1.6

Source: Author's compilation based on TSC: pertinent years.

The intensified competition affected not only small stores of the traditional sector, but also established stores of the large companies, like Daiei, Mycal and Ito Yokado. General merchandisers with their broad assortments and no particular strength were feeling the increased competition from price-oriented category-based stores (Table 6.8). Daiei's sales fell over 42 per cent from 1991 to 2000, back to the level of 1977. Mycal's Saty store, which initially showed favourable results after a general revamp in the early 1990s, still suffered an overall decrease in sales of 40 per cent (NRS, pertinent years). The opening of Marui's department store further increased the complexity of the situation, putting general merchandisers in a squeeze by not exclusively targeting mature up-market needs like the traditional metropolitan department stores, but rather focusing on the needs of families and younger consumers.

A format that proved to be largely immune to the fast growth of large stores was the convenience store (Figure 6.8). The number of convenience stores increased from 51 in 1990 to 87 in 1997. As already pointed out,

Table 6.8 Sales and floor space of major stores

	Daiei Shiki	Saty Niiza	Ito Yokado Wako	Food Plus Niiza	Rogers Niiza	Olympic Asakadai
Format	General superstore	General superstore	General superstore	Food superstore	General discount store	Food superstore and hard goods discount store
Floor space (m^2)	14 339	13 151	12 977	6 616	4 537	6 697
Sales 1991*	13 612	14 534	–	–	–	–
Sales 1997*	9 412	11 202	12 393	3 438	9 863	6 656
Sales 2000	7 863	8 612	11 832	–	9 601	–

* Fiscal year in million yen.
Source: Author's compilation based on NRS (pertinent years).

Figure 6.7 Rice vending machines in Shiki.

convenience stores managed to coexist with large stores by attracting a distinct customer segment. Some convenience stores are located very close to large stores. Convenience stores, however, have increasingly to compete within their retail format. For example, 14 convenience stores operate within a radius of only one kilometer around Shiki Station, among them four by Seven-Eleven and three by FamilyMart alone.

Locations

As already pointed out, the car has continuously gained importance as a means of transport in Japan. In the past, companies had to build their stores in locations with high natural customer traffic or locations near customers' homes. In this situation cost considerations played a secondary role. In the 1990s, with consumers being more mobile, companies could attach higher priority to cost considerations when choosing store sites. Car ownership has been increasing further during the 1990s. By the year 2000, 80 per cent of households owned a car, up from 68 per cent in the year 1990 (Shûkan Tôyô Keizai 1991, 2001). Large food supermarkets and general discount store operators built stores in locations that were no longer within walking distance of a railway station. Seiyu closed its old branch with its insufficient sales floor and parking near the station and opened a new store in a location with good access for car

Figure 6.8   FamilyMart store in Wako.

traffic, but two kilometers away from the nearest station. Though its concept focused on customers living within a radius of 2 kilometers of the store, it offered 370 parking spaces. Rogers opened alongside National Road 254 with more than 600 parking spaces. While the road-side locations around Road 254 saw spectacular development and now form a continuous stretch of retail stores and restaurants, the areas around the station were able to sustain a high level of attractiveness, as the opening of the department store by Marui near the Shiki station and the development of additional stores near the Niiza and Kita Asaka stations demonstrate. Despite the increase in car ownership the train continued to be the main means of transport for commuters and com-muter lines were being improved continuously to shorten travel time and to reduce overcrowding of trains. Locations near stations thereby continued to provide stores with a stable customer flow, especially on weekdays. In addition, car ownership and use among younger con-sumer groups such as students and unmarried women, groups with a lot of discretionary spending power, is still low and will probably remain so.

Store design and sales concepts

Store designs and sales concepts of stores newly opened in the 1990s were distinctly different from those opened earlier on. The most striking feature was store architecture. Stores built earlier normally had four to seven stories, large sales floors of over 10 000 square meters and offered only a limited number of parking spaces in multi-storied parking garages. Newer stores were designed smaller but occupy relatively more space by having no more than two stories and large parking lots, often on vacant plots next to or on the roof of stores. Retailers saved considerably on initial costs through the use of cheaper locations and on construction through the need for fewer elevators and escalators and by having to comply with less strict safety regulations. Operating costs proved to be lower as the transportation of goods and the restocking of shelves became easier. While operators of multi-storied stores had never solved the problem of how to attract customers on a regular basis to the upper floors, companies were now able to control the movement of customers on the sales floors more efficiently. In addition, customers found the use of shopping trolleys made more convenient and store layouts easier to comprehend.

Looking at the store structures, most of the stores opened during the 1990s seem to have been built for a much shorter life span than was expected from store buildings in the past, enabling companies to pursue scrap-and-build policies in the future. Most operators clearly see the outward appearance of a store as not being of major importance for drawing customers: alternatively, a simple store building might even symbolize the price aggressiveness of the operator.

While still carrying a wide range of product lines compared with formats in other countries, the assortments of new stores tend to be more focused. In new stores, companies limited assortments to a single product category or a combination of selected ones such as foods, DIY goods and household goods, or furniture. Pricing became a major instrument of competition. Prices for groceries in the area have been going down in the 1990s. Retail prices in Asaka are monitored on a regular basis in the official retail price census. Out of approximately 120 food items monitored, about 30 per cent were priced lower in 1990 than in 1988. In 1992, only 18 per cent were at a lower level than two years before. However, in 1995 nearly 60 per cent of items showed lower prices than two years before, and in 1996 this figure was 47 per cent (Sômuchô Tôkeikyoku 1989, 1991, 1993, 1995, 1996, 1997). In competing on prices companies did not pursue an 'everyday low price' policy but rather stuck to the old concept of promoting certain articles and heavily advertising these. In addition, most stores introduced a weekly campaign day with discounts on a wide range of products. However, as has already been pointed out, owing to the quality consciousness of

Japanese consumers lower prices could usually not be realized by offering lower quality or less choice, but had to be based on savings in initial and operational costs.

Another feature of large-store retailing in the 1990s became extended hours of operation. Before, opening hours had been regulated through the Large Store Law, and most stores in the area had been allowed to operate in the evening only till 7 p.m. In 1990, the latest closing time that did not require formal approval under the rules of the Large Store Law was changed from 6 p.m. to 7 p.m. and in 1994 from 7 p.m. to 8 p.m. Today most stores in the area are at least operating from 10 a.m. to 8 p.m.; some of the large stores like Seiyu, Saty and Daiei open even longer till 9 p.m. and during the summer period even till 9:30 p.m.

Owners of existing stores were forced to rethink their strategies. Compared with today's situation their past method for success had been rather simple. Very large stores with a broad selection of daily foods and necessities in central locations had focused on wide catchment areas and had offered consumers and especially families the possibility of one-stop shopping. While the original concept of the general super-store as developed in the 1960s had contained a discount element, companies had gradually traded up in the 1970s and especially in the late 1980s by offering broader and deeper assortments and additional services. Discount policies had become less important. In comparison with the very limited competitive strength of local stores of the traditional sector these strategies had proven to be sufficient. However, in the 1990s this competitive advantage was lost through the opening of additional stores, which often offered a wider and deeper selection in their respective product categories and at the same time were more price-aggressive than the traditional general superstore. Existing operators started looking for original and unique concepts to revitalize their stores. Daiei opted initially for a discount strategy with reduced service. To do so, it centralized operations and standardized assortments on a national level. An important part of this strategy was the reduction of regular employees on the shop floors. In Shiki, Daiei reduced rapidly the number of regular employees from 124 in 1989 to 86 in 1995 and further to only 56 in 1997. Mycal, the operator of the Saty store, focused on service, deepened assortments and moved in the direction of department stores, a strategy that was initially successful, but problematic in terms of cost control and undermined later when Marui opened a real department store in the same area. Daiei eventually abandoned its discount strategy when the company realized that consumers would, for a low price, make only small concessions in regard to service and depth of assortments. It split its centralized company into seven regional operations and increased the independence of its store buyers with the goal of adapting stores and especially their food sections to the needs of local communities (*Nikkei ryûtsû shinbun* 2 June 1998). Later, Daiei started to strengthen certain categories such as men's suits and unisex clothing in its stores. In doing so, it was closely modeling strategies of upcoming companies like Fast Retailing or Shimamura that based their success on the introduction of original products at low prices produced under their own control in China. In a sense, the company is thereby aiming to follow the example of Wal-Mart – which has been described as a 'killer of category killers' – by reaching comparable strength in most of the different categories it offers under one roof.

The quality of food assortment continued to be a major concern of all companies. Compared with demand for other product groups, that for food remained relatively stable even throughout the period of economic stagnation of the 1990s. Many Japanese households still buy fresh food on a nearly daily basis, and therefore food remained an extremely important category in Japanese retailing for attracting customers to stores. As will be shown in the following example, most store assortments include fresh foods, and generally consumers do not accept reductions in quality of merchandise and product choice. Even stores that do not offer food themselves take care to have one offering food within the same building or in close proximity.

Examples of store developments

The points raised above can be illustrated with more detailed examples of store development in the area. The example of Wellsave shows the failed attempt to introduce a food discount store, a store concept which had been very successful in other countries. Rogers stands for the pragmatic stance many Japanese retailers take in operating their stores and especially in combining lines of merchandise. Seiyu introduced Food Plus as a new concept focusing on cuts in initial and operating costs while still adapting strongly to consumers' needs. Finally, the case of Saty shows how a company reacted to developments in the characteristics of its location and achieved initial success in revitalizing an existing old store.

Wellsave

The store named Wellsave was opened in May 1995 in the former premises of Seiyu near Shiki Station (Figure 6.9). It was the first store opened by

Figure 6.9   Closed Wellsave store in Niiza.

a company called DFI Seiyu, a joint venture in which Seiyu held a share of 40 per cent and foreign retailer Dairy Farm 60 per cent. The company had been set up with the objective of opening relatively small-scale discount supermarkets for foods and daily necessities based on the know-how that Dairy Farm possessed through the operation of similar stores in Britain, Australia, Hong Kong and Taiwan. The company planned to open 70 stores within 5 years, reaching 150 within 10 years.

For Japanese food retailing the concept was a novelty in many aspects. Compared with the average Japanese store the company saved about 50 per cent on initial costs on store design and furnishings. Shopping carts and cash registers were imported. Merchandise was stored in high simple shelves within the sales floor. The company concentrated on staple merchandise – around 4000 articles by brand manufacturers – and offered these at a discount of about 15 to 20 per cent compared with normal prices. Only a limited assortment of fresh groceries was offered. The attitude of the company was described as aggressive. The company did engage in direct price comparison with competitors, a strategy that was not common in Japanese retailing up to then. Within this strategy the company even displayed in its stores shopping carts with merchandise bought at rival shops in the neighbourhood (Nishikawa 1997).

However, sluggish sales forced the company to remodel its shop after only two years. The sales area for fresh food was moved from the back to the entrance area, and the space given to fresh groceries increased from 35 to 50 per cent. Management had to admit that it had initially not realized that in selecting stores Japanese consumers prefer choice and quality of fresh merchandise over low prices of processed merchandise. To satisfy consumers in this regard the management of fresh groceries was transferred to specialized tenants. At the same time, the company reduced minimum package sizes and offered more products in the price range of 200 to 300 yen because, owing to the location of the store in the vicinity of Shiki Station, a large share of its customers were single people shopping on their way home after work (*Nikkei ryûtsû shinbun* 15 May 1997).

After having deviated so far from its original concept anyway, the Wellsave venture finally came to an end in spring 1998, when Seiyu, engaged in widespread restructuring efforts, pulled out of the joint venture. The company argued that pursuing a pure discount strategy made it difficult to operate profitably within the current Japanese distribution structure. In addition, its stores had lost most of their price advantages after other supermarkets had also reduced their prices. Nonetheless, some tenants pointed out that the company had not made enough effort to offer Japanese consumers sufficient choice and that even after remodeling the store the area designated to fresh articles had still not been large enough (*Nihon shokuryô shinbun* 9 February 1998, *Asahi shinbun* 7 April 1998). The Wellsave store in Shiki was closed in April 1998. However, this did not bring retail activity there to an end. Wellsave sold the store to Tairaya, an expanding operator of small food supermarkets. Tairaya had through a strong regional store network not only built up a deep knowledge of local consumer needs but also maintained strong ties with distributors at local wholesale markets for fresh merchandise, qualities that enabled it to become a serious competitor of large national chains (*Nikkei ryûtsû shinbun* 10 September 1998).

Rogers

As already pointed out the Rogers store was opened as a general discount store by the company Hokushin Shôji in September 1996. The store is located adjacent to Road 254 and has a sales floor of 4500 square meters (Figure 6.10). It offers a broad selection of clothing, household goods, consumer electronics, sporting goods and some fresh and processed foods. For the procurement of goods the company does not sustain continuous

Figure 6.10   Rogers store in Niiza.

relationships with manufacturers and other suppliers but rather utilizes imports and the grey markets for excess inventories. Location, presentation of merchandise and store furnishing are clearly discount-oriented (*Nikkei ryûtsû shinbun* 29 August 1996). From the outside the building appears like a warehouse and this impression is reinforced by its interior, which lacks elevators and escalators to connect sales floors and displayed cracks in the flooring only five years after completion of the building. The development of this store concept over time demonstrates once more the importance of fresh foods in Japanese distribution as well as the pragmatic attitude of many Japanese retailers when it comes to putting together assortments. In May 1997, the company added 490 square meters to its store and designated this area for fresh foods products. The company did so to increase the frequency of consumers' visits to its store (*Nikkei ryûtsû shinbun* 20 May 1997).

While the whole concept appears to be rather unsophisticated – especially compared with concepts of discount stores in other countries – it seemed to meet the demands of Japanese consumers during the 1990s. Sales in fiscal 1997 even topped those of the much larger Daiei store. In summary, the Rogers store seems to be a good example for Goldman's (2000) assessment of the Japanese discount store sector. He points to a general lack of sophistication of systems in regard to procurement, supply chain management and product development in comparison with discount store systems developed by companies in other countries. Having increased the number of stores from four to nine between 1996 and 2000 the company has, however, been making efforts to upgrade its operations. While the appearance of the stores has not been changed, the company has reorganized its logistics. Taking logistics under its own management, it set up four distribution centres for different product groups and also introduced electronic data exchange with manufacturers and wholesalers (*Nikkei ryûtsû shinbun* 19 October 2000).

Food Plus/Seiyu

At the time of its opening in Niiza at the end of 1996, the Food Plus store was only the second branch Seiyu had opened under this name, but the firm had publicized plans to open 100 stores of this type by the year 2000 (Figure 6.11). The store concept differed significantly from earlier stores opened by Seiyu, which were either medium-scale food supermarkets or large general superstores.

With the Food Plus concept Seiyu aimed at combining three formats under one roof, all of which showed fast growth in the Japanese market at that time – food supermarkets, home centres and drug stores. In the store, foods and non-foods were clearly separated and store design was kept at a basic level. While general superstores and many other large formats of the past focused on a large catchment area and did not target specific consumer segments, the concept of the Food Plus store was more focused. With a sales floor size of just over 6000 square meters it was designed to be smaller than the traditional general superstore and as such was supposed to target only consumers within a radius of two kilometers around the store. About 58 000 people live in that area and the management defined its main target group as housewives aged around forty.

As with other stores, the Niiza store has already undergone a number of changes since its opening in 1996, pointing to the high degree of uncertainty the management of retail companies have faced during and since the 1990s. In the beginning, the food assortment of the store had consisted of only 3200 articles but this was gradually increased to 5000 articles after it had become clear that customers regarded the original assortment as not satisfactory. The foods assortment was brought onto the same or even a higher level than that of general superstores, and some upper market products were added in view of the

Figure 6.11   Seiyu store in Niiza.

relatively high average income of the targeted customer group. Nonetheless, the store overall pursued a price-aggressive concept. Non-food
items had originally numbered 50 000 and had included a wide range of
products such as gardening supplies, general household goods, office
supplies and electric appliances. However, the company had soon to
recognize that within the area competition in the home centre segment
was already too strong and it had to reduce the number of DIY goods
and other non-food items significantly (*Nikkei ryûtsû shinbun* 15 July
1997:5, Nishikawa 1997).

As of the end of the year 2001 the Food Plus sign had been replaced
with the normal Seiyu logo. In line with the decision of Seiyu to concentrate on the development of its food business the store displayed a strong
assortment in this area. How to best utilize the remaining space not taken
up by food items seemed, however, to be a largely unresolved issue. It
remains to be seen whether the capital engagement of Wal-Mart in the
Seiyu group will result in a strengthening of the non-food business of
Seiyu or might even lead to a complete redesign of store concepts.

Mycal

Mycal, then still under its old name Nichii, began as early as 1990 to
redesign its stores and to adapt to a changed competitive situation.

At a time when many operators of large stores were still undecided on which direction to develop their stores – options were to concentrate on discount strategies, to trade up or to just stick to the concept of the general superstore – Mycal decided to trade up and develop its stores into so-called department stores for everyday life. The store in Niiza near Shiki station was remodeled at the end of 1993 (Figure 6.12). Assortments were strengthened and products added that before were previously handled only by department stores. Facing sluggish sales, brand manufacturers had to give up their former reluctance to supply companies other than department stores. Mycal thereby reduced the share of products for everyday use from above 80 per cent to around 60 per cent. Inside the store the company introduced the shop-in-the-shop system. It set up a number of new subsidiaries so as to develop a whole range of independent shop-in-the-shop concepts. As soon as June 1997 the store in Shiki was again remodelled. The company strengthened the groceries sales floor, reduced self-service and introduced counters for the sale of individualized portions of fresh foods. The company reacted to the price competition in the area by inviting independent tenants to operate additional sales areas for fruit and vegetables, meat and fish (*Nikkei ryûtsû shinbun* 15 July 1997:5).

Figure 6.12   Mycal store in Niiza.

Initially, the company's concept proved to be a successful solution to the repositioning of large stores in the neighbourhood of railway stations. Through the growth in population, many areas around the railway stations in the suburbs developed into new city centres, with shoppers expecting shopping facilities of a higher standard. However, this had been realized not only by Saty but also by department store operators such as Marui, which opened a store near the Shiki station and with its expertise in the management of department stores heavily challenged the upgraded stores of general superstore operators. At the same time, Saty experienced difficulties with the way it organized its new stores. The creation of a number of separate companies to operate the different smaller shops within its stores led to problems in responsibilities and cost control. Many of the subsidiaries did not reach profitability and were eliminated when the company began to experience financial difficulties at the end of the 1990s. On 22 November 2001 Mycal finally had to file for protection from its creditors under the Corporate Rehabilitation Law. When visited in December 2001, the Saty store in Niiza displayed a message to customers asking for their continued support, pointing to the help of the Aeon group in the restructuring of the company. While the company closed 19 stores during the year 2002 with a total sales space of 189 368 sq.m. and plans to close another 10 stores with a total sales space of 80 766 sq.m. till July 2003 the store in Niiza has not been included in this list (company information at www.mycal.co.jp). It will be interesting to see whether and how a store of this size and location can be repositioned in a competitive environment where, through the intense addition of new store formats during the 1990s, most spots seem to be filled already.

Development of towns

The observation of the area demonstrates the significant effects the developments of the 1990s have on the appearance of towns. The regulation of large retail stores caused conflicts between politicians and bureaucrats on the local and national level. On the national level the developments in retailing in the 1990s were welcomed and used to demonstrate to the doubting Japanese public and representatives of foreign countries the success of Japan's efforts to deregulate (see for example Sômuchô 1995). While deregulation in other areas of the Japanese economy produced no instant success, the highly visible developments after the revision of the Large Store Law became a symbol of deregulation.

On the local level, the opening of new stores often led to drastic changes in the appearance of cities. As most communities did not pursue consistent town planning policies in the past, commercial, industrial and residential areas were not clearly separated. At the same time, the traffic infrastructure was often not prepared for the opening of new stores. Therefore new stores frequently became the cause for pollution and traffic congestion.

After the revision of the Large Store Law in 1992, the power of local community councils and chambers of commerce to influence the opening of new stores was largely reduced. Under the old law local governments forced retailers into cooperation by delaying or speeding up approval processes and could thereby negotiate benefits for their communities. Owners of local shops were often given the opportunity to operate as tenants in newly opened large stores. Carefully planned and well-furnished shopping centres could even boost the attractiveness of townships (HKH/Takayama 1989:68–9). However, as the examples of store development in the area show, new stores in the 1990s are clearly planned under cost and traffic considerations, offer no space to tenants and thus do not contribute much to the visual attractiveness of towns, nor offer business opportunities for local companies. Other than the department store opened by Marui in the direct vicinity of Shiki Station no project seems to be integrated into the efforts of town councils to plan and redevelop their communities. Instead, available plots are utilized and structures used or erected by store operators are not very pleasant to look at and many appear to be of a rather provisional nature. With its agglomeration of stores the area has also become a major attraction for shoppers who do no reside locally; at the same time more and more people who live in the area are using cars. The traffic situation has become a major problem; parking capacities of stores are insufficient, with queues of cars reaching back far on the main roads. These developments give some credibility to the fact that the Large Store Law was not simply abandoned but rather was replaced with one focusing on the environmental consequences of new store openings.

Together with the new law concerning the location of large stores a set of laws were introduced focusing on the revitalization of the traditional shopping districts. The town of Shiki used this opportunity to come up with a comprehensive plan for redevelopment (Midori no Machizukurika 2001 *Basic Plan for the Revitalization of the Central District*). The rationale underlying these activities is stated as follows and leads back to the beginning of this case study:

> Due to the completion of a net of traffic bypasses that resulted in the opening of roadside stores, and deregulation that enabled the opening

of large stores in locations outside of towns, the hollowing out of the central district has further progressed. Our town is in a situation where the central district that up to now housed various city functions in regard to housing, trade, public services and others, and that played a leading role for the development of business and culture has lost much of its vitality.

The aim of the ambitious plan is to revitalize the whole area between the Shingashi River and Shiki Station and turn it into an area that firstly can fulfill the complex future needs in regard to Japan's shrinking and aging population, that secondly will provide an advanced information infrastructure to help existing businesses and attract new ones, and that thirdly also will ensure the effective use of public resources and the protection of historical and natural resources. The plan proposes a variety of measures that also include propositions on how to utilize vacant stores for community development, incorporation of the associations representing the different shopping districts in the area, training of store owners, and the development and promotion of products related to the long history of the area as a centre for trade along the Shingashi River. With most of these proposed activities still to be realized, it remains to be seen whether small shops and with them traditional shopping districts really can find a new span of life within the highly competitive retail environment that developed in the area observed during the 1990s.

7
Newcomers in Japanese Retailing

While the Japanese retail climate during the 1990s has been described overall as rough and highly challenging, eventually even leading to the downfall of prominent retailers, this period has not been equally disappointing for all companies alike. Some retailers have even managed to achieve surprising growth and have thereby established themselves as major players in Japanese retailing. These retailers have been doing so not only by responding to changes in consumer needs with adequate store formats and sales concepts but also by coming up with innovations along the whole value chain from product design to procurement, logistics and merchandising. Overall, the systematic approach they pursued in the development of their operations has become the trademark of successful Japanese retail companies of the 1990s and beyond.

In the following, this approach will first be illustrated by outlining the business models of some of these companies in more detail (Table 7.1). The first two firms, Fast Retailing and Shimamura, have achieved their success in apparel retailing, a field where consumer spending has overall been decreasing and established general superstores as well as department stores suffered their most painful declines in sales. Other companies, Toys 'R' Us, Yamada Denki and Matsumotokiyoshi, have succeeded by proposing alternative business models in areas that until the 1990s were characterized by large numbers of small-and-medium sized retail companies, these often being under the control of manufacturers or wholesalers. Finally, Daiso Sangyo and Ryohin Keikaku developed wide and unique assortments under one common theme, one-price and non-branded products respectively, that in both cases proved strong enough to allow the companies a high degree of flexibility to adapt stores to the requirements of different store sizes and different locations.

Table 7.1 Fast-growing companies, 1995–2000

Company	Sales (bn yen)		Sales rank		No. of stores	
	1995	2000	1995	2000	1995	2000
Fast Retailing	48.5	229.0	192	36	176	486*
Shimamura	128.6	227.0	54	37	368	506*
Yamada Denki	87.9	471.2	95	15	90	131
Matsumotokiyoshi	112.0	231.7	68	35	232	532*
Japan Toys 'R' Us	57.6	154.0	162	56	37	111
Daiso Sangyo	23.3	202.0	375	43	n.a.	2000
Ryohin Keikaku	47.9	115.5	195	83	222	251

* Year 2001.
Sources: Author's compilation based on NRS; pertinent years and company information from company web pages.

While the illustrations given below largely pronounce the importance of entrepreneurship – this being due partly to the fact that information for the case study was derived from company information and newspaper articles – the following discussion will show that as previously the success of companies was based on a variety of factors, among them entrepreneurial spirit and capabilities as well as favourable factors in the external environment. Overall, the environment for entrepreneurship during the 1990s proved to be quite different from that experienced by the earlier entrepreneurs of the 1960s and 1970s. This fact is significant as such and might also be of major importance for the future development of these companies.

Examples of retail success during the 1990s

Fast Retailing

The roots of Fast Retailing lie in a local Men's apparel shop founded in 1959 in Yamaguchi Prefecture. It was incorporated under the name of Ogori Shôji in 1963. However, it took the company until 1984 to come up with the concept of a retail chain store for unisex casual wear under the name of 'UNIQLO' that eventually became the basis of the company's success (Figure 7.1). In 1991, the company name was changed to Fast Retailing Co. Ltd (company information at www.uniqlo.co.jp). As has been the case with many retail companies, success has been associated with the leadership of one individual – in the case of Fast Retailing, Tadashi Yanai. After graduation he began his career with Jusco but after just one

Figure 7.1 Fast Retailing Store in Niiza.

year joined the then Ogori Shôji in 1973 and became its managing director within a year. He has been president of the company since 1984 and is currently also its largest shareholder, owning about 30 per cent of issued stock (HKH 2000b).

Over the last decade the company has been growing rapidly. Having reached 50 stores in April 1992, it took the company five years till 1997 to reach 150 stores and then only another two years to double this figure. By March 2001, the company was managing nearly 500 stores. Growth of sales was equally stunning. Annual sales reached 132 billion yen in August 2000, an increase of 18 per cent over the previous year. Yearly sales growth in previous periods had frequently been even higher, averaging 40 per cent between the years 1991 and 2000 (company information at www.uniqlo.co.jp).

However, growth did not occur in a consistent pattern. In 1998, sales increased by 10 per cent, owing only to the opening of new stores. Existing stores suffered decreases in sales averaging 7.5 per cent. This led to a comprehensive turnaround of the company that proved to be so successful that existing stores reported average sales increases of 18.9 per cent for the following year. More than the previous growth, this successful turnaround of a large network of stores earned the company a high degree of recognition not only from the press and investors but also from competitors (Tsuki 2000a). The company was promoted to the first section of the Tokyo Stock Exchange in February 1999. The success of the chain has been related to its systematic approach of organizing activities along the value chain. Here, the company has reached a higher integration than most other Japanese companies by assuming a leading role not only in the development of its store concept but also in product design, procurement of raw materials, logistics and the production of goods. Growth during the first stage of development of Fast Retailing was based on four factors: the mass procurement of private label products from overseas, the opening of standardized stores in cost-saving locations, a high degree of centralization of store management through detailed manuals, and relatively narrow assort-ments that still appealed to the needs of a broad range of consumers in relatively small catchment areas. Initially, this strategy appeared to secure sustainable success. However, with increasing growth and regional scope the disadvantages of centralization – not being able to react quickly to consumer needs and regional differences – became more apparent and threatened the future development of the company. Stressing the necessity of communication and expertise, the company, in a move considered highly unusual within Japan's corporate environ-ment, exchanged its existing top management team for a team of experts recruited from other companies. It ended up with one of the youngest management teams in the industry with an average age of just below forty (Tsuki 2000a).

After this move, the autonomy of outlets was increased, with stores being regarded as profit centres. Utilizing its POS data very efficiently and closely monitoring its stocks, the approach of the company in many ways resembles systems successfully introduced by Japanese convenience store chains. In addition, the company further integrated production and merchandising by moving from bulk procurement to contract production based on consumer response and sales projections. To become more flexible, the company tightened its relationships with selected manufacturers, reducing the number of contract manufacturers from over 140 to just 40 (Tsuki 2000a, Hata 2000).

At the same time, Fast Retailing followed successful Western examples by beginning to pursue a product focus. It aims to sell large quantities of certain articles to achieve various economies of scale along the whole value chain. To do so, all attention and resources are focused on a selected relatively low-priced article. This article is massively promoted in the press and in television commercials, with the company trying to reach every second household at least weekly with its newspaper advertisements.

The high popularity of the company with the public led to a tie-up with several magazines that actively feature UNIQLO products in their articles. The symbol of this strategy became the sale of fleece pullovers, the company managing to sell 2 million pieces of one product within only one season. Customers queued in front of the UNIQLO stores to get hold of the product in one of its 15 colors and 5 sizes (Ikeda 2000). The high popularity built up with consumers also enabled the company to diversify the location of its stores. It began to supplement its freestanding stores in suburban roadside locations with stores in central locations, in shopping centres and even in some department stores. Some of these branches now occupy very prominent retail locations in the fashion districts of Tokyo.

Shimamura

Like Fast Retailing, Shimamura also managed to succeed in the apparel sector, however with quite a different concept. Founded in 1924 and incorporated in 1953, the company introduced the principles of self-service and chain operations early on. The development of an original business model started in 1975 with the introduction of information systems for stock management. Stores were connected in an information network as early as 1981. By 1984, the company managed 50 stores. It was promoted to the first section of the Tokyo Stock Exchange in 1991. During the 1990s the company expanded its store network rapidly from 100 stores in 1989 to 300 stores in 1994, 500 stores in 1998 and finally 816 stores in 2002. It plans to increase its network to 1000 stores in the near future. In the tough environment of the 1990s the company has overall managed to increase or at least sustain sales in its existing stores (company information at www.shimamura.gr.jp, HKH 1999).

Shimamura's main format is a store of 1000 to 1300 square meters that carries around 40 000 items of apparel. It caters to about 5000 to 8000 households and targets housewives aged between 25 and 45 as its main customers. The company is price-aggressive, with the average price per item being a low 855 yen and the average shopper just spending around 2800 yen. In addition to its basic format the company is experimenting with other formats. It wants to develop a chain of currently only 21 men's apparel stores into 500 stores eventually. For two other formats, one for maternity clothing and children's apparel, another for accessories and household goods targeting young women, growth plans are equally ambitious with projections of 300 and 500 outlets respectively. The new formats are to contribute to Shimamura's objective of becoming a dominant player in the industry, its stores making up for a third of consumer spending on apparel in their respective catchment areas (company information at www.shimamura.gr.jp).

The company regards and promotes itself as an innovator of retail technology. Aiming to sustain true low-cost operations, it wants to realize the principles of standardization, specialization, simplification and systematization. Based on these principles, the company has developed a detailed set of manuals for its employees to follow. Still, it remains open to suggestions by employees for improvements, reporting that it receives more than 10 000 of these every year (company information at www.shimamura.gr.jp/).

To support its operations, the company set up its own logistics network. The 450 suppliers of the company deliver the merchandise into six distribution centres. From there products are delivered to the store network at night, following strict rules for delivery times. Assortments and stocks are controlled on an item-by-item base. Automated ordering systems exist for non-season and non-fashion items that account for around 60 per cent of all items handled. This set-up, which in many ways resembles the principles of lean production applied in Japan's manufacturing industries, has made Shimamura one of the companies with the highest sales margins in the industry, despite handling relatively low-price items (Tsuki 2000b).

Yamada Denki

Yamada Denki began to sell electric appliances in the early 1970s but entered into chain development only in the 1980s. By the year 2000 the company was operating 131 stores, divided into four store formats: a large-scale general appliances and computer store format, and separate smaller formats for software, personal computers and Apple computers. The number of stores does not in itself tell the full story, however, since the company pursues a strict scrap-and-build policy – one described in the previous chapters as highly unusual for Japan where most companies have prioritized sales volume over profits. In the year 2000 Yamada Denki opened 37 stores and closed 15. The stores scrapped were mostly smaller than 500 square meters and were replaced with large-sized ones of an average size of nearly 4000 square meters. Increasing its sales by over 138 per cent in just one year, the company is leading a group of very dynamic retailers of electric appliances. While 18 out of 20 of the largest electric appliances chains managed to double their revenues for the fiscal year 2000, the fact that Yamada Denki has not sacrificed profitability in this process makes it stand out among its competitors. On contrary, the company managed to continuously increase the ratio of ordinary profits to net sales from 2.6 per cent in 1995 to 3.5 per cent in 2001, compared with figures of 3.0 per cent to 0.7 per cent recorded by its major competitors for the same years (Yamada Denki Co. Ltd 2001:3). The company aims to achieve low costs not by reducing services to customers but rather by rationalizing overall operations. Unusually for a Japanese discount store, it provides consumers with additional aftercare packages at nominal prices, allows consumers to test products within the store and has also led the industry with a guaranteed price and return policy. The company opened its first distribution centre in 1984 and has since then continuously upgraded its logistics network. It introduced a comprehensive POS system as early as 1984 to gather customer and finance-related data. The company was thereby in a good position when electronics manufacturers in the 1990s decided to change their trade practices by extending substantial rebates to companies that were willing to buy products at bulk, did not insist on the traditional right to be allowed to return unsold merchandise and could take over logistics on their own. One of the companies that started to distinguish between retailers with supply chain management and those without was Matsushita Electric, and a newspaper report has concluded that this 'move has effectively put an end to traditional practices where give-and-take and personal connections held wide sway' (*Nikkei Weekly* 14 May 2001). To control all aspects of its business model, Yamada Denki has also revised its earlier franchise strategy and is now aiming to manage all of its stores directly. Overall, the success of the company is thereby credited to its speedy decision-making processes and efficient backup operations (Okamura 2001).

Recently, the company increased its efforts to develop its store network nationwide. The industry leaders are no longer respecting each other's territories. Newspaper reports indicate that 'the members of the Nippon Electric Big-Stores Association reportedly had a tacit agreement of not breaking into the sales territories of other firms' (*Nikkei Weekly* 18 June 2001) but are increasingly competing directly with each other, and that in this quest Yamada Denki is aiming for 10 per cent of the total market and is participating in the reorganization of the industry by collaborating with smaller chains that cannot withstand the pressures of the highly intensified competition in this sector (*Nikkei Weekly* 11 June 2001, *Nihon keizai shinbun* 14 September 2001).

Daiso Sangyo – 100 Yen Plaza

Visiting the website of Daiso Sangyo (www.daiso-sangyo.co.jp), the operator of one-price stores (Figure 7.2) under the name of '100 Yen Plaza', one is immediately bombarded with figures and statements put up to impress: '202 billion yen sales, 2000 stores in Japan, 80 per cent original products, brand power of 60 000 items, 1 million shoppers per day, a logistics system without comparison'. Indeed, the development of the company has been stunning in most regards. Having been incorporated only in 1977 by its founder Hirotake Yano, the company started out in the one-price business by organizing 100-yen sales in event halls. Realizing the dissatisfaction of consumers with the quality and choice of the goods sold, the company began to expand assortments and also altered its principles of calculation. The company changed from an item-based calculation to one based on overall returns and costs and this allowed for the inclusion of additional products with low margins. Daiso Sangyo started expanding its business around 1987 and has been growing continuously ever since. During the 1990s the company achieved annual growth rates between 38 and 75 per cent. In the year 2000, the company was opening

Figure 7.2   Dasio Sangyo store in Bizen.

new stores at a pace of 60 stores per month. One of the factors underlying the fast growth of the company was its capability to adopt its concept to different store sizes and different locations. While some of the older stores are still operating on sales floor sizes as small as 50 square meters, the company in April 2000 opened a store with a floor size of 6600 square meters. Looking for buildings in good locations, the company claims to have opened that store without any prior market assessment (HKH 1998, 2000a, NKR Guruupu 2000, Kruger and Fuyuno 2001).

The following additional points can be brought up to explain the success of the company: Daiso Sangyo is procuring goods in large quantities; half of these goods are bought overseas. The sourcing of products has been diversified and while China and Korea still account for a large share of products, products are now also sourced from Italy, Portugal, India and Southeast Asia. Every month the company is processing 1700 twenty-foot containers of merchandise and to do so has set up a network of distribution centres. The development of new products is continuous and Daiso Sangyo claims that 80 per cent of products currently handled are original articles. The number of articles increased rapidly from 15 000 in the middle of 1998 to 60 000 in the middle of the year 2001. This includes a variety of 1300 food products, 1500 cosmetics products, 2000 different kinds of plastic containers, 2500 products of glassware and 200 different ties (NKR Guruupu 2000).

Overall, the company therefore does not see its stores as places where goods of low quality and low value are sold. Based on its strength of buying large volume, it wants rather to provide its customers with an experience that is enjoyable overall, constantly surprising with products that are deemed too high in value to be sold at the fixed price of only 100 yen. In this quest the company has come up with an electric toothbrush and hand massage sticks, and has also widened its selection of watches to 180 articles. The company regards this philosophy as a key to long-term success, especially in the time after the Japanese economy recovers, when consumer behaviour may change again.

Matsumotokiyoshi

Matsumotokiyoshi's history as a company selling drugs and cosmetics goes as far back as 1932 and it is thereby among the older companies discussed here. While the main business of the company is drugstores (Figure 7.3), it also diversified into food supermarkets in 1977, convenience stores in 1980 and home centres in 1988. It withdrew from the convenience store business in 1996, but in 2001 still operated 23 supermarkets and 8 home centres besides its 501 drugstores. In its core business the company

Figure 7.3   Matsumotokiyoshi in Tokyo's Harajuku area.

has expanded decisively over recent years, opening new branches at the rate of about 60 a year (Matsumotokiyoshi Co. Ltd 2001).

Matsumotokiyoshi clinched the top spot in the drugstore industry by its aggressive marketing strategies including heavy advertising and substantial discounting:

> Matsumotokiyoshi is different from traditional drugstores. Its shops are crowded with a jungle of products and placards highlighting discount prices. In each of its two-story outlets, around 10 000 items – from cosmetics and medicine to toiletries – are stacked everywhere, even on the staircase, to fully utilize available space. The shops have no front doors and bright lights are used to attract the attention of passers-by, especially teenagers. (*Nikkei Weekly* 27 November 2000)

Until March 2000 the company concentrated its efforts on the Tokyo area, operating stores in highly frequented locations. Since then, it has started to open stores in other areas. While in the past the company had relied heavily on its high name value (Kane 1999), during the mid-1990s the company name created much the same enthusiasm among consumers as Fast Retailing and 100 Yen Plaza did among consumers at the turn of the millennium, the company has realized that it needs to strengthen its overall capabilities to create a stable customer basis. It has therefore collaborated with manufacturers in the development of private brands and is also trying to strengthen its sales of pharmaceutical products (*Hanbai kakushin* January 2001, *Nikkei Weekly* 20 August 2001). The company has ambitious plans for future development, striving for a market share of 25 per cent in the Tokyo area and a total of 1000 stores by building and expanding its store network throughout Japan. In its aim of expanding nationwide it has also started to pursue business tie-ups with or acquisitions of smaller regional retailers. The management of the company regards growth as a way to further strengthen its position towards wholesalers, to enable it to introduce private brands and to improve the productivity of its distribution centres (*Hanbai kakushin* January 2001).

Ryohin Keikaku

The Muji Stores operated by Ryohin Keikaku developed out of an initiative by Seiyu in the 1980s to develop a new product line. In its company brochure 'Ryohin Keikaku 2000' the company attributes this initiative to the market conditions of the early 1980s that in many ways resembled the conditions of the 1990s:

> In this growing trend towards lower prices, the age of 'consumption as a virtue' came to an end. Consumers were becoming much more critical in examining the balance between quality and price, carefully selecting only products suitable for their own lifestyles. (Ryohin Keikaku Company 2001a)

Products are developed and internationally procured with the aim of providing products of high quality at lower prices. At the same time products are recognizable in their avoidance of unnecessary functions, over-decoration or excess packaging. Having started with 40 products initially, the company today sells a range of 4000 items consisting of household goods, apparel, food products and recently even cars. The expansion of the product line also made it possible for Seiyu to set up separate stores for the Muji products. In 1989 the company became independent, being introduced to the over-the-counter market in 1995 and to the second section of the Tokyo Stock Exchange in 1998. Products are sold through a variety of channels, mainly in directly managed stores, licensed stores, Seibu department stores and Seiyu supermarkets.

Throughout the 1990s, the company achieved substantial growth in sales and profits. Though its number of stores did not increase as much as those of the other companies described so far, the opening of larger stores increased the sales floor space significantly from a total of only 44 500 square meters in 1996 to nearly 140 000 square meters in the year 2000 (Ryohin Keikaku, Company 2001b). This rapid growth in sales space and expansion of assortments did not, however, lead to equivalent results in sales and profits, and the company has entered a period of consolidation of activities (*Nikkei Weekly* 22 October 2001).

Still, in view of the difficult consumption climate of Japan during the 1990s the company can be considered as very successful. Its product concept, developed to counter the economic problems of the early 1980s, was already in place when consumers finally started to demand more value for money in the 1990s. Some of its problems at the end of the 1990s result from the fact that other companies have caught up, thereby forcing Ryohin Keikaku to cut its prices for many products. The success of the company is also due to strong overall operations. The company has been procuring internationally since its beginnings and currently procures 54 per cent of its merchandise outside Japan. The overseas procurement ratio for apparels rose dramatically from 47 per cent in the financial year 1996 to 84 per cent in the fiscal year 2000. Taking full risk for the sales of self-designed and procured goods, the company has also developed sophisticated information systems to keep inventories low, besides taking care of its own logistics (Ryohin Keikaku, Company 2001b).

Toys 'R' Us

Toys 'R' Us opened its first store in Japan in December 1991. Less than ten years later in November 2000 it opened its hundredth store and has become Japan's largest toy retailer. As of early 2003 the company was operating 133 stores (Figure 7.4). It plans to continue its steady growth and hopes to reach 200 stores by the year 2010. Japan Toys 'R' Us was set up as a joint venture between Toys 'R' Us, US, and McDonald's Japan in 1989. When the company entered Japan it saw its main obstacle and opportunity in the complex distribution structure of Japan. The president of Toys 'R' Us was quoted as saying: 'I hate the Japanese wholesale system. By the time we have opened our thirtieth store the Japanese system will have changed towards the American system' (NRS 1992:76). The main objective of the company had thus been to convince manufacturers to distribute to the company directly and the company has recorded considerable success in this regard. Today the company describes direct dealings with manufacturers as being the foundation of its success in Japan. Manufacturers deliver directly to the two distribution centres of the company. From there products are delivered to the stores. Cutting out wholesalers not only reduced costs but also ensured a speedy and simple flow of merchandise constantly monitored through advanced information systems (Toys 'R' Us Company Overview at www.toysrus.co.jp).

Overall, the company thereby seems to be successful, but its growth so far was driven mainly by the opening of new stores. In existing stores the company has just managed to keep sales stable on a yearly basis, a fact that it itself rated as a major success under the tough market conditions in Japan (Toys 'R' Us Japan Ltd 2002). The company has reacted, though, and has changed its philosophy of doing business in Japan substantially. Having so far opened large stores of about 3000 square meters largely based on the price-aggressive American model, the company has introduced its own 'Concept Japan' in 1999. Stores are now clearly divided into 12 categories based on certain themes or customer segments. The store outlay was changed to shorter and lower shelves with controlled walkways. Separate in-store shop concepts were developed for infants, educational articles, gaming and electronics, and accessories

Figure 7.4   Toys 'R' Us store in Okinawa.

for elementary and middle-school girls (Hasa 2000). To distinguish itself further from competitors the company also began to increase the number of exclusively handled or private brand products. At beginning of the year 2002 these products accounted for 11 per cent of all products, and the company aims to raise this figure to 20 per cent over the medium term (*Nikkei Weekly* 4 November 2002). Here, the company is also working together with established manufacturers. For example, together with FT-Shiseido it has introduced a sun blocker and this collaboration might result in a whole new line of children's cosmetics in the future. From the middle of the year 2001 on, the company went one step further and introduced additional customer service personnel into its shop floors. The company admits that this is a move away from its original concept, which highlighted efficiency and low prices, to a store concept that offers toys in a friendly atmosphere. This move has been interpreted as a convergence with traditional Japanese selling techniques. In a newspaper article the chief merchandising manager of the company is cited as saying 'You cannot gain consumers' interest just with a wide variety of products or better prices any more' (*Nikkei Weekly* 26 November 2001).

Since April 2000 shares of Toys 'R' Us Japan have been publicly traded and the company is making efforts to turn its customers into shareholders of the company by promising to honor their engagement as shareholders with the regular distribution of shopping vouchers. Besides developing its store business Toys 'R' Us Japan also set up a subsidiary for e-commerce in December 2000, in collaboration with Softbank, Japan's leading company in this area.

Success factors and a different corporate environment

The above illustrations have shown the fast growth of a number of companies within the difficult Japanese retail climate of the 1990s and the early years of the new millennium. Regarding the factors underlying the growth and success of these companies, the case studies show that the companies themselves stress their own genuine advancements in sales concepts and overall system design. Nonetheless, a number of factors in the environment did exist that promoted the growth of companies in Japan in general and new companies during the 1990s in particular. Highlighting these factors seems to be especially important, since recent difficulties experienced by some of the companies examined here point to the fact that their systems and internal strengths might not yet be as stable as is generally believed.

If we look at genuine advancement in store concepts and system design, the quickly growing companies of the 1990s have certainly managed to differentiate themselves from existing concepts. In merchandising and sales companies have come up with concepts that not only offer products at low prices but also at the same time offer the shopper genuine shopping experiences. This seems to be especially important for success during the 1990s where consumers want to spend less money but at the same time want to express some individuality in shopping, still one of the major leisure time activities in Japan. The other major success factor seems to be the high emphasis of companies, from the outset, on the development of strengths in the area of procurement and support systems. In contrast to predecessors that relied heavily on wholesalers and manufacturers to configure their assortments, companies now control their own merchandising. They often possess genuine knowledge of the product groups they handle and even develop many of their products on their own. This knowledge enables retailers to take over risks and responsibilities independently of relationships with manufacturers and wholesalers. In addition, companies have often set up their own logistics, further emancipating themselves from the restrictions of the traditional distribution system. In this sense they distinguish themselves from past companies that have been heavily criticized for their unsystematic approaches (see for example Goldman 2000).

At the same time, however, companies that grew during the 1990s could make full use of a number of positive developments within their environment that were not fully available to established firms, which were deeply entrenched in traditional ways of doing business. Here, the following factors can be singled out:

Overall, the number of positive cases of corporate growth was extremely limited during the 1990s. This was the case not for retailing alone but for all Japanese industries. The few promising companies had thereby no problems financing their expansion. While it had been difficult for young companies in the past to finance themselves in a system characterized by close relationships between established companies, this has changed during the 1990s and since. The growing retail companies were highly welcomed by national and international investors. Some of the new companies have even attracted a surprisingly high share of foreign ownership. The willingness of investors to finance these companies was enhanced by the fact that these companies were not burdened with failed investment projects of the past that often made the assessment of the risk attached to investments highly complex.

Companies became not only popular with investors but also with the media. Consumers enthusiastically welcomed the new shopping alternatives and through heavy media coverage frequenting these stores and buying certain items became a fashion in itself.

At the same time companies had a choice of locations. Not only did prices for land drop significantly; at the same time some retail companies (also banks and brokerage houses) abandoned branches that thereby became available to other retailers. Shopping centre developers also discovered the popularity of these new stores with consumers and often a combination of stores of the above-described companies can be found in one place. The same is true for established department stores that began to invite popular companies to become tenants in their store buildings.

Another factor was the increased willingness of manufacturers to reward retail companies that developed their own capabilities in supply chain management and logistics. In the past manufacturers used to favor affiliated companies and basically controlled the distribution of margins on the different levels of the distribution chain. In doing so they were disregarding the fact that different companies had developed different capabilities or that the distribution of functions along the value chain could differ with different business models.

Finally, the emergence of China as a procurement market for products played a major role. In the eyes of Japanese consumers the image of products procured from abroad changed and companies have profited from this or have even themselves contributed to changing the image of products from overseas. Fast Retailing is said to have played a major part in convincing Japanese consumers that products procured in China can be not only low-priced but also of high quality. It has thereby opened the floodgates for a number of other companies that are also increasingly looking to China for the procurement of merchandise.

These points become of special importance in explaining a change in the mood towards the development of these companies at the end of the year 2001. Companies like Ryohin Keikaku and Fast Retailing had to announce drastic decreases in sales or even losses during that year. The question was promptly raised whether these companies were really so different from those cited as examples of success in earlier periods, which initially had also achieved strong growth but did not manage to become stable in the long run, a point that will be taken up in more detail in the next chapter. Comments by the founder of Daiso Sangyo, like 'We have no planning, we have no budget, we have no objectives or quarterly forecasts' (Kruger and Fuyuno 2001:34) certainly echo these sentiments.

However, it has to be pointed out that companies are acting overall in a corporate environment quite different from that of their predecessors, and this might be the real difference when the development of companies in the past and today are to be compared. As a sign of this different corporate environment, where criticism surfaces at an early point, companies are constantly forced to rethink strategies, and to improve their concepts and management structures. Companies have been financing themselves over the stock exchange and as has been pointed out quite a few of them have a high proportion of international investors that demand transparency and frequent updates on results and activities. For example, the ratio of foreign investors for Yamada Denki stood at nearly 48 per cent, for Fast Retailing at 25.8 per cent (Investor information on company homepages). In 2001, Ryohin Keikaku listed two major foreign institutional investors among its larger shareholders, Chase Manhattan Bank with 3.14 per cent and State Street Bank and Trust Company with 3.12 per cent (Ryohin Keikaku Company 2001b). The influence of foreign investors is increasingly being felt and they do not content themselves with a passive role as many of the stable Japanese institutional investors had done in the past, with even banks intervening only in an actual situation of crisis. In the case of Ryohin Keikaku, a US pension fund voted against the election of two external auditors that were seen as not independent because of having worked previously for the former parent company Seiyu (*Nikkei Weekly* 5 November 2001). Shares of companies are intensively traded and investors react immediately to changes in company results. Shares of Fast Retailing were traded at about 350 yen throughout the year 1998 before they gained value with increasing speed to peak at 13 300 yen in April 2001. They were down to 3200 yen by March 2002. Shares by Ryohin Keikaku were traded at around 24 000 yen at their peak in November 1999 and came down to around 2700 yen in March 2002.

The way Fast Retailing itself explains its sudden fall from grace adds another piece to the complex puzzle that Japanese distribution presents to the observes at the beginning of the new millennium. After problems began to occur, the company reinterpreted the sales results of previous years as extraordinary and the drop of 35 per cent in sales and 27 per cent in customers as a return to normality. Initially, Fast Retailing had succeeded in creating a totally new market for fleece apparel at low prices. As has been pointed out, among shoppers, wearing these products became not only a matter of sensible shopping and dressing but also a fashion statement in itself. The company did not fully realize this development and expected consumers to take up its products year after year. However, during the year 2002 Fast Retailing fell out of fashion with younger consumers and many older consumers who stayed loyal to the company were not willing to replace items bought just a year ago, and only continued to use the stores to shop for smaller items. This left the company with a huge amount of ordered stock that threatened to overflow its warehouses. Having ordered the merchandise already the company did not want to cancel contracts with its manufacturers in China since it wanted to continue its close collaboration with them. In response to this situation the company has been strengthening its product development capabilities. Despite the high acclaim it had originally received from investors and the media for the sophistication of its systems, the company's president has admitted that Fast Retailing has reached its objective of becoming a full-fledged specialty retailer dealing in private label apparel only to an extent of 30 to 40 per cent (*Nikkei Marketing Journal* 15 January 2002).

The situation of Fast Retailing has been made more complex by its focus on casual clothing, an area that operators of general superstores regard as their original core domain and are therefore not willing to give up without a fight. They have flooded the market with products of their own and have in the process closely duplicated the concepts of Fast Retailing in their own sales floors (*Nihon keizai shinbun* 14 September 2001).

The situation has been quite different in other categories where companies have also been growing quickly, like toys, electric appliances or drugs and cosmetics. Here companies mainly gained market share from the traditional sector that had collaborated closely with manufacturers and wholesalers. On the one hand, retailers themselves, as in the toy sector, drove change. Toys 'R' Us succeeded in reorganizing a market that was characterized as a managed market where retail sales were handled mainly by small stores and department stores under the control of strong manufacturers and wholesalers that suppressed competition on prices. General superstores also handled toys, but did not regard this category as an area of high importance that would justify the allocation of substantial resources or efforts. Toys 'R' Us managed to break down the traditional three-tier structure and offered Japanese consumers a new experience: toy discounting (Takayama 2001). On the other hand, change was supported to a large degree by changes in the manufacturing sector. Manufacturers themselves recognized that their current distribution strategies were cost-inefficient within the changing economic environment of Japan and no longer fulfilled consumer needs. They therefore became more open in dealing with larger chains and more forthcoming in rewarding companies for initiatives in creating efficient logistics solutions and fulfilling consumer demands in regard to price and locations.

Finally, the overall situation of these new companies after their first stage of expansion can be compared to those of the general superstore companies at the beginning of the 1970s. As pointed out in previous chapters and is to be further indicated in the next, these companies had arrived in the 1970s with a high dependence on bank financing, depleted of self-capital and problems in management and organizational structures. Still, they had been able to enter into large-scale diversification plans, largely foregoing profitability for ambitious growth plans. The situation of the companies outlined above seems to be highly different. Relying heavily on the stock markets for financing, they come out of their first phase of expansion with a strong capital basis that for Yamada Denki stood at 51.5 per cent, for Fast Retailing at 47.4 per cent, for Shimamura at 54.5 per cent and for Ryohin Keikaku at 72.6 per cent (finance information at http://quote.yahoo.co.jp/). Some companies were even strong enough to buy back their own shares from the stock market. While the development of share prices and the media hype surrounding the development of these companies might have blurred the view of some investors, shareholders and the financial industry are still monitoring these companies more strictly than retailers in the past and are looking not only for future growth but at current financial results. As the case of Fast Retailing has shown, companies are quick to reorganize their management structures. Diversification projects of companies are closely scrutinized and companies have to react quickly. Toys 'R' Us has largely changed its initially successful sales concepts after having been in Japan for only a relatively short period. Ryohin Keikaku has downsized its internationalization plans and began closing unprofitable stores in continental Europe at the end of the year 2001, only two years after it ventured into these markets (*Nihon keizai shinbun* 22 December 2001).

Looking at these developments, we can conclude that companies are forced now to come up with stable and transparent management systems at a much earlier stage than were their predecessors. The next chapter will show that many of the problems the established large retailers faced at the end of the 1990s can be attributed to problems of corporate governance. However, when looking at innovativeness in

Japanese retailing in general, it can be concluded that the considerable leeway entrepreneurial companies enjoyed in the past was not without advantages. The possibility for Japanese companies to concentrate on long-term developments was once hailed as their major strength but might not be sustainable under the new conditions. While the danger of sudden bankruptcies like those described in the next chapter might be reduced, so might also be the possibility for companies to improve their concepts and strategies and come up with original solutions. The case of the Japanese convenience store is one such case where it has been shown in earlier chapters how Ito Yokado, its efforts having met with a lot of skepticism, reached its current level of success only through years of meticulous trial-and-error processes.

8

Failure and Reorganization of the Mass Merchandising Sector

By the beginning of the 1990s, the group of leading companies of the general merchandising sector had remained basically unchanged for nearly two decades with the same companies occupying the upper spots continuously. Nonetheless, as has been outlined in the previous chapters, these companies had undergone tremendous change during these two decades, developing from operators of general superstores to core companies of conglomerates with diversified portfolios of interests in retail and leisure-related industries. While suspicions concerning the financial strength and soundness of investments had surfaced from time to time, the public and especially the media had still regarded these companies with awe and had generally expected them to profit most from pending measures to free the distribution industry from regulation regarding the opening of new stores and manufacturer-dominated trade practices.

However, a decade later, at the turn of the millennium, the landscape of Japanese retailing appeared dramatically changed. As a result of major financial difficulties Mycal, Daiei and the Saison Group had lost much or even all of their strength (Table 8.1). Looking at the future, only two company groupings, Ito Yokado and Aeon, seemed to be of sufficient strength to truly carry on the tradition of general merchandising in Japan. Within the crisis that hit many Japanese retail companies during the 1990s, the first major firm to go down was Nagasakiya, a pioneer in mass merchandising; this was followed by the department store operator Sogo and finally Mycal and Kotobukiya. Others like the Saison Group, with its major members Seibu Department Stores, Seiyu and Family Mart, avoided bankruptcy; yet Saisom was still forced to sell off major assets, the affiliation of group members was weakened or totally desolved and the superstore business of Seiyu was reduced to its core operations. Daiei,

Table 8.1   Major general retailers, 2000

Company	Consolidated revenues 2000 (bn yen)	Core company revenues 2000 (bn yen)	Number of stores – core company 1999	Number of stores – core company 2001
Ito Yokado	3 104	1 491	176	181**
Daiei	2 914	1 981	308	288
Aeon	2 738	1 548	347	372
Mycal	1 722	1 081*	123	128
Seiyu	1 071	832	191	204
Uny	1 173	781	144	160

*1999. **2002.
Sources: Author's compilation based on NRS 2001, company homepages.

the long-time symbol of Japanese mass-merchandising also appeared to be near bankruptcy at the turn of the millennium. At the beginning of the year 2003 its future still looked uncertain. Up to then, only its size and the consequences of a possible breakdown on suppliers and employees saved it from bankruptcy, and if it can avoid failure in the future the necessary sale of assets and closure of a large number of stores will leave the company just a shadow of its former gigantic self.

This chapter analyzes the above-described developments in two steps. The first part deals with the background of corporate failures in Japanese retailing, looking at issues of corporate control and corporate financing.[1] The second part tries to piece together the emerging patterns of leadership in Japanese retailing with regard to ownership and organization.

Crumbling empires

The previous chapters have described the 1990s as a complex environment for Japanese retailers, providing a mix of distinct threats and opportunities. It has been shown how the position of many existing retailers was threatened increasingly by changes in consumer behaviour and the success of upcoming domestic and foreign retailers with innovative retail concepts. Still, taking up only these factors alone cannot explain the reasons why the shakeout of the retail scene happened so suddenly and rapidly around the turn of the millennium. The following

---

[1]This part has been published in more detail in *International Review of Retail, Distribution and Consumer Research*, vol. 12, no. 1, January 2002, pp. 13–28.

narratives of struggling retailers will therefore show that issues of corporate ownership, governance and finance need to be looked at to explain these developments.

Narratives of struggling retailers

The cases of struggling retailers during the 1990s were widely covered in the Japanese media and throughout these reports a set of common elements emerges. Among these, the most important was the loss of support from banks and the government; other elements were failed management strategies, problems with founder families, a lack of transparency and even suspicion of criminal behaviour.

In the following, the case of one retailer, Nagasakiya, is described in more detail. While not the largest among the failures at the turn of the millennium, it still involved a company that had continuously occupied a prominent position in Japanese retailing. Its smaller size reduces the complexity to a degree that makes it possible to show the interplay of different elements that contributed to the failures of prominent retailers in Japan at the end of the 1990s.

Nagasakiya had to apply for court protection from its creditors in February 2000. By then the company and its affiliates had an accumulated debt of 380 billion yen and were no longer able to fulfill their obligations. At that time Nagasakiya was ranked nineteenth in the retail industry with sales of over 314 billion yen in the fiscal year 1998. With its history Nagasakiya represents the development of mass merchandising in Japan. During the 1960s and up into the 1970s competitors had regarded the chain as a model to follow. Under the leadership of a strong founder personality the outward appearance of the company in many ways resembled the image of the rapidly expanding companies of the 1990s as outlined in the previous chapter. Like these companies Nagasakiya was described as possessing advanced knowledge in product procurement and mass merchandising. In 1963 it had even been the first mass merchandiser to be introduced to the Tokyo Stock Exchange. In the 1970s, the ability of Nagasakiya to profitably sustain stores in the neighborhood of railway stations, based on its strength in store development and supplier relationships, even after other companies had been forced to relocate stores to outer suburbs, was interpreted as proof of the company's superior management capabilities.

However, these strengths gradually deteriorated. The influential role the founder had played became apparent after his retirement from management. Supplier relationships were managed less efficiently, resulting in a weakened supplier base. Uncertainty about the future development of the company was further raised through inconsistencies in personnel policies at the top management level of the company. Not being able to respond proactively to the changes in consumer behaviour during the 1990s, the stores of the company became 'processing zones for dead stock of Nagasakiya's vendors' (Atsumi 2000:21). Consequently, sales in existing outlets decreased on a yearly basis at a rate of 5 to 10 per cent continuously.

However, the company faced additional problems. In the second half of the 1980s a new management led by the son of the founder had decided on a strategy of ambitious diversification with the aim of catching up with other companies in this regard. In 1988, at the height of the bubble economy, the company ventured into leisure, real estate, video rental and consumer finance. One venture alone, a leisure dome in Hokkaido, required an investment of around 11 billion yen. The company also tried to make up for its backwardness in store development in the suburbs by adding another 20 stores to its existing network of 100 stores. Compared with those of other companies, the diversification activities of Nagasakiya proved to be especially unfortunate. The debt of the company spiraled, which eventually resulted in the withdrawal of the founder family from management. In 1993 a former representative of a major bank was brought in as president. By that time, the company was in a state of continuous crisis. Unprofitable affiliates were liquidated, its convenience store chain was sold off and headquarters and various store buildings were sold and leased back. With consumer demand not recovering for a prolonged period of time, this led the company into a vicious cycle. Operating costs increased but could no longer be covered by returns. Nonetheless, the management's confidence in the ongoing support by its lenders remained strong. When lenders finally reached the decision to withdraw their support this came as a shock that extended to the management of other Japanese companies that had up to then believed themselves protected from corporate failure by having established close relationships with financial institutions.

After applying for bankruptcy protection Nagasakiya entered into reorganization under the guidance of a foreign mergers-and-acquisitions fund. However, it took until late March 2002 for the company finally to present a rehabilitation plan after the foreign fund experienced problems in finding local partners to continue its work. An electronics manufacturer with some stakes in the discount store business eventually took the lead and lenders agreed to forgo 85 per cent of the debt of the company (*Nihon keizai shinbun* 27 March 2000, *Gekiryu Magazine* April 2000, Atsumi 2000, Maruta and Toyoda 2000,

Nagano 2000, Takayama 2000, Tanaka 2000, *Nihon keizai shinbun* 25 March 2002). Succeeding events proved that the case of Nagasakiya was no exception. After the collapse of the major department store company Sogo, the former chairman, with a banking background, was convicted of 'executive imprudence' and ordered by the court to pay about six billion yen in damages (*Nihon keizai shinbun* 8 December 2000). Mycal filed for protection under the civil rehabilitation law in September with an amount of debt of around 1.38 trillion yen (*Nihon keizai shinbun* 17 September 2001). Seiyu, a member of the former Saison Group, needed to raise 220 billion yen to liquidate an ailing finance company and even had to give up control over its profitable ventures FamilyMart and Ryohin Keikaku in the process (*Nihon keizai shinbun* 31 January 2000). Seiji Tsutsumi, the founder of the Saison Group, lost all of his posts at group companies and offered to contribute 10 billion yen of his own funds toward the liquidation of real-estate developer Seiyo. Effectively these developments ended his dream of creating an empire for the provision of life-oriented services (*Nikkei Weekly* 24 July 2000) and marked the end to a long period of leadership described as charismatic and colorful. Consequently, two popular books (Downer 1994, Havens 1994) have ensured that the business endeavours of Seiji Tsutsumi and the rivalry with his brother, Yoshiaki Tsutsumi, who controlled the Seibu railway and real estate business, have also become known to a wider audience outside Japan.

Seiji Tsutsumi's long-time rival in the retail sector, Isao Nakauchi, the founder of Daiei, did not fare much better. He was forced to hand over management of his company to a new management team that was cited as denying Nakauchi a retirement allowance until Daiei was back on track to profitability. Nakauchi himself saw the primary reasons for Daiei's downfall to be its failure to sustain the mercantile spirit within a growing organization, and his main slogan 'for the customers' not being understood and practised throughout the company. At the beginning of the year 2002 the company nearly defaulted on its debts. The agreement by its creditors to forgive debt was not without political intervention, with Prime Minister Koizumi voicing his opinion that the failure of a company with more than 2 trillion in debt, 100 000 employees and 3000 suppliers would have more than a limited impact on the Japanese economy (*Nihon keizai shinbun* 24 November 2000, 18 December 2000, 19 January 2002).

At the beginning of the year 2002 the shakeout in the superstore industry was still going on. In December 2001, Kotobukiya, Kyushu's largest supermarket chain with 134 stores, folded under obligations of nearly 300 billion yen. In April 2002, another regional company from Kyushu, Niko Niko Do, followed with group liabilities of about 130 billion yen. Though of smaller size the company had still expanded and diversified ambitiously during the bubble period of the late 1980s by not only opening large-sized stores but also entering into joint ventures for hotel, apparel, department and discount store operations in China (*Nihon keizai shinbun* 20 December 2001, 9 April 2002a).

As pointed out previously, concerns about the state of corporate finance and governance of Japanese leading retail companies had been voiced early on, for example as early as 1971 by Yoshino. In the light of the events described above though, it appears that the general change of business orientation as demanded by Yoshino and others did not take place. After introduction to the stock exchange, founders, in spite of formerly only owning minority stakes, often continued to dominate companies and entered into ambitious diversification during the 1980s. The failure of many of these programs brought companies to the brink of bankruptcy. Nonetheless, companies still managed to enter into decisive store expansion programs during the 1990s, and therefore the question has to be asked how they were able to do so, and also why the situation changed so suddenly for a number of them at the turn of the millennium. The answers lie mainly in developments in the financial sector. Investigating the institutional relationship between financial institutions and retail companies in more detail will thereby add another piece to the jigsaw puzzle of entrepreneurship and developments of retail companies in Japan.

Retailers and financial institutions

The relationship between financial institutions and retailers is documented regularly in the publication *Kigyô Keiretsu Sôran* (General Survey of Company Relationships) published by Toyo Keizai. The publication provides relatively detailed information on the borrowing of funds from certain financial institutions, plus rankings and share ownership of the main shareholders. Information is also given on the previous positions of board members outside their current company, thereby providing hints at possible relationships with other companies, banks or the civil service.

The data for 1999 show one general characteristic of the Japanese industrial organization still firmly in place for the Japanese retail sector, namely the main bank system. Under the main bank system a certain company has a strong relationship with a certain bank that not only acts as its largest institutional shareholder but also as its largest lender. The main bank is entitled to provide the largest share of fee-based services to its client and is also expected to support the client in times of crisis. While these aspects of the system are largely undisputed, others are debatable, and this dispute touches on the core issues of this chapter. Some authors have argued that main banks fulfill a major role in monitoring their clients, doing so not only for themselves but also for other shareholders and lenders (Aoki *et al.* 1994). Others, however, point out that banks are interested mainly in the provision of loans and fee-based services and that banks themselves neither accept special responsibility beyond their own interests nor are able to monitor companies effectively (Scher 1997).

Out of a total of 138 retail companies, traded in 2000 on at least one of the Japanese stock exchanges in Tokyo, Osaka, Nagoya, Fukuoka or Sapporo, 80 companies had one bank as both the largest lender and largest institutional shareholder. To these, 20 corporations can be added where the largest lender was from the banking sector but was surpassed in shareholdings by another financial institution (a life insurance company or a trust bank) that did not directly compete with the main bank. Twelve companies had split the main bank role between several companies. Usually these financial institutions accounted for exactly identical amounts of loans and identical amounts of shares. For the 18 corporations that did not have outstanding loans from financial institutions it was difficult to speak of a clear main bank relationship. Banks were, however, prominent shareholders of many of these companies, or else former bank managers were members of their boards. Finally, only 8 cases could not be classified. The presence of former bank managers on the board in 74 companies gives additional proof for the close relationship between the retail industry and the financial sector.

The directory also shows that even among retail companies listed on the stock exchange founder families still dominated the majority. This was the case for 83 companies. 37 companies were controlled by other companies, often other retailers. A further 18 companies did not fall into either of these two categories. Some of these seem to be dominated by banks, though, which can be concluded from strong links through loans, shareholdings and previous affiliations of members of their management.

Tables 8.2 and 8.3 give more detailed examples of the workings of the main bank system. For Sogo Denki, a retailer of electric appliances, the main bank was the largest lender and the second largest shareholder. Overall, the largest twenty shareholders controlled around 44 per cent

Table 8.2   Example of distribution of ownership and loans – Sogo Denki, 1999

Lender ranking	Amount (m. yen)	Shareholder ranking	%	Shareholder ranking (cont.)	%
1. Hokuyo Bank	10 466	1. Association of Franchisees	3.39	11. Nippon Life Insurance	2.16
2. Bank of Tokyo-Mitsubishi	2 120	2. Hokuyo Bank	3.37	12. Sharp	2.10
3. Hokkaido Bank	700	3. Nagata (Co.) (Founder Family)	3.13	13. Tasei Kaijo Insurance	2.09
4. Asahi Bank	545	4. Sanyo Electric	2.73	14. Dai Ichi Life Insurance	1.88
5. Nippon Credit Bank	230	5. Employee Association	2.60	15. Pioneer	1.68
6. 77 Bank	200	6. Bank of Tokyo-Mitsubishi	2.57	16. Orix Alpha	1.54
7. Fuji Bank	150	7. Matsushita Electric	2.45	17. Hitachi	1.44
8. Daiwa Bank	109	8. Sumitomo Life Insurance	2.37	18. Hokkaido Bank	1.41
		9. Toshiba	2.32	19. Mitsubishi	1.35
		10. Sony Finance International	2.28	20. Kenwood	1.26

Source: Author's compilation based on Toyo Keizai (2000:521).

of the capital. These shareholders could be considered stable shareholders and most of them seemed to own their shares not just for capital gains or dividend earnings. For banks, the ranking of shareholders followed the sourcing of loans. This ranking is usually also reflected in the allocation of fee-based services between the banks. Manufacturers of electric appliances aimed to stabilize their dealings with the company, and even life insurance companies expected to sell insurance contracts to the company and its employees in accordance with their role as stable shareholders (Meyer-Ohle 1993b).

The case of Daiei is different, as it distributed its lending and shareholding accurately among a number of financial institutions. Overall, the founder family controlled the company by a net of cross-shareholdings with affiliated companies. Interestingly, Daiei also owned shares in banks. In 1995 the company reported shareholdings in at least 23

Table 8.3 Example of distribution of ownership and loans – Daiei, 1999

Lender ranking	Amount (m. yen)	Shareholder ranking	%
Sumitomo Bank	33 744	Daiei Holding Corp.	6.53
Fuji Bank	33 744	Fukuoka Dome	5.95
Sanwa Bank	33 744	Marunaka Kosan	4.46
Tokai Bank	33 744	Nakauchi International	4.20
Development Bank of Japan*	31 500	Maruetsu	2.98
Norin Chukin Bank**	24 211	Dai Ichi Life Insurance	2.46
Yokohama Bank	16 507	Tokai Bank	2.46
Bank of Tokyo-Mitsubishi	14 655	Sanwa Bank	2.46
Mitsui Trust Bank	14 288	Sumitomo Bank	2.46
Sumitomo Trust Bank	11 913	Fuji Bank	2.46

*Government related institution. **Central financial institutions for Japan's fishery, agricultural and forestry cooperatives.
Source: Author's compilation based on Toyo Keizai (2000:538).

banks, with values for single companies ranging between 110 million and 7.2 billion yen (Ôkurashô Insatsukyoku 1995:64–5).

Land prices and financing of retailers

Banks did not regard the financing of retailers as a major risk since most companies only needed financing to acquire land. The preference for acquiring land instead of leasing it as well as the low risk associated with this activity by banks can be explained by a look at the development of land prices. Prices for land increased continuously until the early 1990s (Figure 8.1), and as already pointed out in earlier chapters general merchandising companies had profited greatly from rising land prices of land acquired earlier. Since landlords usually asked companies to provide substantial deposits and other advances, leasing was not a cheap alternative and was therefore preferred by only a minority of companies.

Having established close relationships with retailers and given most of their funds for the acquisition of land, banks appeared to have only shown a low level of interest into the actual details of single investment projects (Maruta and Toyoda 2000). A contributing factor here was that the loan market during the 1980s was largely a buyers' market. Manufacturers, as the traditional clients of Japanese banks, had gained international recognition which had given them access to alternative means of financing. In addition, the Japanese government embarked on

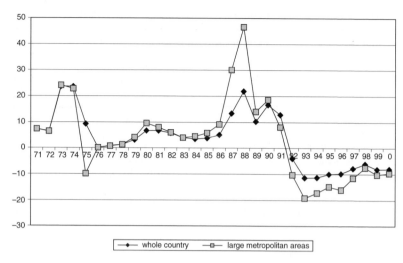

Figure 8.1 Development of prices of land for commercial use, 1971–2000 (change over previous year in per cent).
Source: Author's figure based on Kokudochô (pertinent years).

initiatives to deregulate the banking sector, increasing competition between banks and other financial institutions (Ozawa 1999, Taniguchi 1999). Banks were looking for new clients and discovered the retail and real estate sector (Shimizu 1999). In an overall fierce competition for clients, banks did not go to great lengths to understand the structure of the increasingly complex corporate networks that had been built up by their clients. In a situation, where firms were not forced to provide consolidated reports, some affiliated companies were utilized only to prevent losses from appearing in parent companies' balance sheets. Under these circumstances, standards in risk assessment slipped and money became available for purely speculative investments. Land became accepted as collateral at full market value from a previous standard of 60 per cent of market value. Conveniently these developments set in just at the time when retail companies were looking for means to pursue their ambitious diversification programs (Takayama 2000). For these projects in leisure and real estate development companies usually needed to acquire land and they did so during a period of heavily rising land prices. Companies became vulnerable to fluctuations in land prices and the sliding land prices of the 1990s quickly destabilized companies. The quick decline into bankruptcy of these companies was prevented, however, by sustained stable banking relationships, with the main bank system still largely intact.

New relationships between retailers and banks

The relationships between banks and retailers were challenged, however, by a number of developments towards the end of the 1990s. These led to the eventual withdrawal of support from the banking sector for a number of retail companies:

- Within a larger reorganization of the Japanese financial sector, banks merged into larger entities and were eager to clear their balance sheets before these mergers.
- The Japanese government and international institutions forced banks to dispose of problematic loans.
- Banks had to sell off stable shareholdings to compensate for losses and to prepare for new accounting rules that made it less attractive for them to hold shares in large amounts.
- Some banks with large exposure in the retail sector changed ownerships under a government-led bail-out plan that compensated the new owners for losses in case of the corporate failure of their clients.

These factors were eventually responsible for the nearly simultaneous failure of a number of retail companies. Banks finally renounced the close relationship with their clients from the retail sector. Returning to the example of Nagasakiya, some observers stated that Nagasakiya was chosen early to purposely send a signal to the industry (*Gekiryu Magazine* April 2000, Maruta and Toyoda 2000). The especially strong relationship of Nagasakiya with its main bank was well known in the industry, and described as a 'fat pipe for the provision of loans' (Maruta and Toyoda 2000). Throughout the 1990s the bank was closely involved in the management of the company, with former bank employees acting in leading management positions. In this respect, allegations even surfaced that a company closely affiliated with the main bank had profited from the restructuring by purchasing buildings and land from Nagasakiya at a low value and being able to lease them back to Nagasakiya at too high a rate. In a time of falling real estate prices, real estate costs for the company increased to 45 per cent of overall costs compared with an industry average of 33.9 per cent and a targeted ratio of 25 per cent (Atsumi 2000; Nagano 2000).

These facts question the basics of entrepreneurship in Japan. In mainstream thinking, the rise of Japanese corporations in the 1970s and 1980s has been attributed mainly to increases in productivity and innovativeness. However, it is argued increasingly that while these factors had indeed been the main driving force for growth during the 1960s, growth in later periods was driven mainly by high and continuous levels of capital input that did not lead to comparable returns in productivity and growth rates (Katz 1998). The same argument can also be applied to the retail industry. Takayama (2000) argues that continuous shareholder pressure on American retailers resulted in advances in productivity and profitability through the development of human resources, advanced systems and rationalization. At the same time Japanese retailers could strive for sales growth and diversification, neglecting the aspects of the productivity and profitability of investments. The stabilized relationship with banks and other institutional shareholders certainly contributed to this development. This allowed founder families to stay in control and also to enter into ambitious and prestigious diversification projects. During the 1990s, the relationships also prolonged the necessary restructuring of the mass merchandising sector. As shown in the previous chapter, during the 1990s new companies grew in a different corporate environment.

Reorganization of mass merchandising

Corporations that have vitality, foresight and quickness will survive. It is important to make the first step, since Japanese move quickly once they start changing. This year will also be a year of confusion, but I hope it's positive confusion, which will give rise to new things. (President Motoya Okada of Aeon Co., interviewed in *Nihon keizai shinbun* 16 January 2002)

As outlined above, failed investments from the bubble period, overexpansion during the 1990s, misinterpretations of consumption trends and belated and inconsequent moves to restructure have increased the number of failures in Japanese retailing dramatically. With financial institutions pulling out, founder families losing control and once-dominant conglomerates being dissolved, the question about the consequences for the future organization of the Japanese retail sector has to be raised. However, developments are ongoing and, while speculations in the Japanese and foreign press run high, outcomes are uncertain. For example, coverage on the involvement of foreign companies in Japanese retailing went full circle in just over a year, and changed from 'Foreign retailers shake up retail sector' to 'Foreign retailers finding local market hard to crack' to 'Retail shakeup likely as Wal-Mart weighs in' (*Nihon keizai shinbun* 13 November 2000, *Nikkei Weekly* 17 December 2001, *Nikkei Weekly* 18 March 2002).

Nonetheless, while we must try not to speculate too much about future developments certain patterns of development can be identified. These are found in trends in reorganization through consolidation and mergers and acquisitions, and more specifically on the role of domestic retailers, foreign retailers and general trading companies in this process. Among these developments the most pronounced and maybe the most remarkable is the rising involvement of general trading companies in the retail sector. This trend has been going on for some time and it is possible to analyze it from a number of perspectives, such as differences in strategic approaches and objectives, and the coordination with existing activities of general trading companies in wholesaling and information technology. In contrast, the involvement of foreign companies has progressed to a far lesser extent. Foreign companies have developed some strongholds in the specialty store sector, as has already been outlined in the example of Toys 'R' Us. In comparison, foreign involvement in general mass merchandising is just at the beginning and therefore only a very preliminary assessment can be attempted. The same is true for the realignment among domestic companies. While differences between companies can be outlined, especially between the remaining companies, Daiei, Ito Yokado, Seiyu and Aeon, at present no real verdict on the outcome of developments seems to be possible. In the following, foreign involvement and domestic realignment are discussed first, followed by a more detailed analysis of the involvement of general trading companies.

Mergers of companies and acquisitions of store networks

Compared with the retail sectors in other countries, concentration in the Japanese retail sector is relatively low. This is of course to a certain extent due to the large number of existing small stores, but is also true for larger companies. As has been demonstrated, competition was muted by the Large Store Law and the dominance of manufacturers and the wholesale sector. In addition, companies themselves had managed to stay independent by stabilizing their ownership and funding through long-term relationships with financial institutions and other stable investors. Overall, the number of takeovers and mergers had remained low.

This changed during the 1990s, with a number of companies not being able to survive on their own and others seeking fast expansion.

The most active company in the reorganization of the Japanese retail industry so far has been the Aeon Group, assisting other companies in their activities to rebuild or simply taking over stores of failed companies. Having applied for protection from creditors, Mycal was believed to have received offers to assist in rebuilding its operations from several domestic and foreign retailers, among them Ito Yokado, Aeon and Wal-Mart. In the end Aeon was chosen. Out of 140 mostly large stores Aeon is expected to take over about 80. Aeon also assisted Yaohan, a company that filed for court protection as early as 1997. In spring 2002 the company changed its name and with its 36 stores became a member of the Aeon Group. Aeon has also acquired 50 stores from Kotobukiya in Kyushu, an operator of supermarkets that failed in December 2001. Finally, in May 2002 the company announced that it would become the largest shareholder in Inageya, a company with about 120 outlets in the greater Tokyo area. The company was thereby able to expand its store network nationwide quickly (*Nihon keizai shinbun* 27 February 2002, *Nihon keizai shinbun* 4 March 2002, *Nihon keizai shinbun* 22 May 2002). Aeon has been described by Larke (1994:215) as being at the beginning of the 1990s a little smaller than some other retailers, yet possessing a firm business base with the ability to spot success in international ventures (especially specialty stores), concentrating on the retail sector and avoiding the temptation to diversify widely. Indeed, the wide base of the Aeon Group in the retail sector, established firmly not only in general superstores but also in the field of food supermarkets, specialty stores and to a lesser degree convenience stores, became the foundation for the company's ability to become actively involved in the restructuring of Japanese retailing.

At the beginning of 2002, Ito Yokado had shown less initiative in this process. Like Aeon, it kept its focus on the retail markets during the bubble period, developing its Seven-Eleven convenience store chain, food supermarket operator York Benimaru and family restaurant chain Denny's Japan. In addition, the company engaged in areas that complemented its core business and in this quest set up its own banking operations. Having always emphasized profitability over growth, the company did not become saddled with the urgent need to dispose of unprofitable investments. This focus explains to a certain extent the reluctant stance of the company towards mergers and acquisitions, in order not to tarnish its image with investors and the public. Nonetheless, the company considered taking over stores from the Mycal group, and owing to its financial strength seems to be in a strong position to play a more active part in the future reorganization of Japanese retailing (*Nikkei kinyû shinbun* 2 April 2002).

As already pointed out, the two other remaining companies among the traditional large Japanese general merchandisers, Seiyu and Daiei, have lost much of their clout, and throughout the 1990s had basically to focus on the restructuring of their operations. Having to service a high load of debt, they had to sell off many of their stakes in affiliated companies and were thereby reduced to their core operations. Being forced to participate in the elimination of debt incurred by the Saison Group in real estate development and financing, Seiyu had to sell off its convenience store chain FamilyMart and also most of its shares in Ryohin Keikaku. It rebuilt its retail operations around food retailing and in this process even took over a supermarket chain with 75 stores in Kyushu from the struggling department store operator Iwataya. As will be discussed later, it was supported in this process by Sumitomo Corporation and will receive additional support from a tie-up with Wal-Mart in the future.

For Daiei the situation appeared quite different. Like Seiyu, it was forced to sell off or liquidate many of the ventures it diversified into during the 1980s. Among these were its convenience store business and its food supermarket chain Maruetsu. In contrast to Seiyu, though, Daiei started later to restructure its core business; and while Seiyu managed to recover its operations by increasing engagement in the relatively stable food business, Daiei still had to rely largely on its general merchandising business. With the company on the brink of bankruptcy in January 2002, the company's three main creditor banks agreed on a plan to bail out Daiei through the injection of new funds in an equity-for-debt swap, a credit waiver and a capital reduction of 50 per cent. The company agreed to reduce its store network further through the closure of around 60 additional unprofitable outlets and to cut down the number of subsidiaries from 150 to 100 with major assets being sold off (*Nikkei Weekly* 21 January 2002).

The closure of stores is one of the major outcomes of the current reorganization in Japanese retailing. Requiring severance payments for employees, settlements with tenants and landlords, reevaluation of assets and the liquidation of subsidiaries, closing stores proved very costly and many companies did not have sufficient funding to do so. Keeping loss-making stores open, however, further worsened their situation. As in the case of Daiei, the rebuilding measures for companies include funding to break this vicious cycle. The overall move to close stores was expected to reduce considerably the pressure on existing stores. A survey for the year 2002 among the 18 largest superstore operators showed that these expected the closure of 100 stores and the opening of 80 new stores. This was more than the 50 new stores opened during the year 2001 when openings were hindered through the transition to the new Retail Store Location Law of July 2000, but considerably fewer than the 180 stores opened during the fiscal year 2000. In addition, many of the new stores opened were smaller, with a focus on foods (*Nihon keizai shinbun* 16 April 2002).

After the failure and restructuring of general merchandisers the overall focus shifted to food supermarkets. Here, a high number of largely independent chains existed that had often concentrated their operations within a certain area. In the greater metropolitan area around Tokyo (Tokyo, Kanagawa, Saitama and Chiba prefectures) for example, the list of superstore operators that handle food included nine other companies besides Daiei, Ito Yokado, Jusco and Seiyu. Most of these companies expanded during the 1990s and it appeared questionable whether all of them could survive independently in a much more challenging environment (*Gekiryû Magazine* March 2001).

Role of foreign companies

As already mentioned, the future role of foreign companies in the reorganization of the Japanese retail sector is a topic much speculated about. In the Japanese retail sector at the turn of the millennium, the overall share of foreign companies was still very low. Decisive foreign entry into Japan's retail sector started only in the 1990s and focused mainly on specialty retailing with the most important companies being Toys 'R' Us, followed by other major players such as Tower Records and Gap. The success of foreign companies has been mixed. Foreign companies achieved success in areas where local competition was not very strong, such as toys and records but have been less successful in sectors like cosmetics where strong domestic players existed. For example, a joint venture between the British company Boots and general trading company Mitsubishi was dissolved after only two years in the face of strong competition from established companies such as Matsumotokiyoshi (*Nikkei Weekly* 16 July 2001).

In general and food merchandising the situation looked different. As already outlined, the early initiative by Safeway to enter Japan during the 1960s had initially received considerable attention but did not succeed in the end. The failed attempt by DFI in food discount merchandising in the middle of the 1990s has also been outlined in Chapter 6. Nonetheless, Carrefour and Costco entered Japan around the turn of the millennium and opened large stores. The example of Carrefour offers some clues on the challenges that foreign companies face.

Carrefour opened its first store in early December 2000 in a highly competitive retail area in Makuhari in Chiba prefecture (Figure 8.2). Citing the opportunity of lower land prices as its main reason for entry, the company did not compromise in size and opened a store of 17 000 square meters within a shopping complex of a total of roughly 30 000 square meters. It had to compromise in other areas, however. Its initial demands for manufacturers to deal directly with it instead of having to go through conventional wholesale channels largely failed. Subsequently, it started negotiations with wholesalers but again faced resistance when it asked to replace the fixed margins of wholesalers with a cost-based approach. While some wholesalers complained that prices demanded by Carrefour were below purchasing costs, other observers stated that the refusal to deal with Carrefour might have been due to pressure from established domestic clients. Though Carrefour managed eventually to conclude agreements with supply sources, the controversy with some suppliers led to some weaknesses in the assortments of its stores. Subsequently the company opened two more stores in Machida and Izumi. Here it varied its store formats according to differences in consumer composition. After initial success, all three stores were, however, reported as not having reached their sales targets. The underlying reason was seen to be the inability of Carrefour to realize its initial strategy to earn customer support through lower prices. Customers complained about the unattractiveness of stores and assortments and also expressed disappointment that they were not being offered the French flavor they had initially expected. The company has taken measures to improve the situation by bringing in more French products and increasing the amount of private brands. Nonetheless, the difficult situation led the company to revise its expansion plans. Citing additional problems with developers, the company was aiming to develop its store network to only 7 instead of 13 stores by the end of 2003 (*Nikkei Weekly* 25 September 2000, 18 December 2000, 17 December 2001).

When the various problems of Carrefour and the withdrawal of prominent foreign retailers such as Boots and Sephora had just reassured Japanese companies about their position in the Japanese market, Wal-Mart announced in March 2002 that it would take a stake in Seiyu with the option to take over the majority of the company at a later stage. The reason Wal-Mart chose this way to enter the Japanese market was related to the experiences of Carrefour. The company had realized the importance and difficulties of food retailing in Japan and wanted

Figure 8.2   Carrefour store in Makuhari.

a partner that could provide this knowledge. The tie-up between Wal-Mart and Seiyu was mediated by Sumitomo Corporation, one of the large Japanese general trading companies that, together with other general trading companies, developed a high interest in retailing.

Increasing role of general trading companies

General trading companies have become a major force in Japanese retailing within a very short period. Within three years they took control of two of the three major convenience store networks, acquired stakes in two out of five of the large general merchandising companies, and also took control of the largest food supermarket operator. In detail the chronology of events reads as follows. In February 1998, Itochu became the largest shareholder of FamilyMart by acquiring a 30 per cent equity stake in the company from the Saison Group. In spring 2000, Mitsubishi Shoji acquired a 20 per cent stake in Lawson from Daiei, thereby openly confronting Marubeni, which, while being considered the first choice owing to its previous relationship with Daiei, had to content itself with 5 per cent. Mitsubishi became the largest shareholder of Lawson in spring 2001 after Daiei agreed to sell Mitsubishi another 8 per cent stake. In July 2002 Mitsubishi announced plans to become a shareholder in another smaller convenience store company called am/pm, a move that would nearly bring the combined store network of Lawson and am/pm on a par with that of the industry leader, Seven-Eleven. For the general trading companies the investments in the convenience store companies were major decisions. The 170 billion yen paid for Lawson had been the largest single investment by Mitsubishi up to then; Itochu had to raise 135 billion for its stake in FamilyMart. Marubeni, being left behind in the race for influence over the retail sector, finally acquired a 10 per cent equity stake in the leading food supermarket company Maruetsu from Daiei in autumn 2000. It replaced Daiei as the leading shareholder, with Daiei selling another 15 per cent during the year 2001. In addition, Marubeni itself became a shareholder of Daiei by taking over a stake of around 5 per cent. Sumitomo concentrated its interest on member companies of the Saison Group. After acquiring a drugstore chain from the Saison Group in April 2000, the company became the largest shareholder of the operator of food supermarket and general superstores Seiyu by purchasing a nearly 12 per cent equity stake in the company. By combining the stores of Seiyu, its subsidiary Summit, and a smaller regional chain it had acquired a 20 per cent stake in earlier, the company boosted its supermarket network to an impressive 300 outlets within a short time. Mitsui in the meantime teamed up with Seven-Eleven and a number of other companies by setting up a joint e-commerce subsidiary. It has also bought a rather small share of only 1.2 per cent in a leading but financially troubled regional food supermarket chain. In November 2001, the company made a bolder move by taking over 8.6 per cent of Mycal Hokkaido, an affiliate of the troubled Mycal Group. General trading companies have stretched their interest beyond the convenience store and superstore sector. In September 2000, Itochu entered a comprehensive collaboration agreement with Seibu Department Stores and acquired a 4.72 per cent stake in the company from Saison Network (*Gekiryrû Magazine* August 2000, *Nihon keizai shinbun* 17 November 2001, *Nikkei Weekly* 15 July 2002).

The activities described above were not the first ventures of general trading companies in the retail sector. As outlined in earlier chapters, during the 1960s general trading companies together with a number of other firms had tried their hand at the development of supermarkets. However, most companies had failed and the only outcome of substance was the mid-size supermarket chain Summit. This chain had been set up as a joint venture between Safeway and Sumitomo and, as outlined in Chapter 2, had at that time caused fears within the Japanese retail industry similar to those occasioned by the entry of Wal-Mart more than thirty years later. During the early 1970s relationships between retailers and general merchandising companies became closer when general trading companies supported general merchandising companies in the development of shopping centres, helped in their moves to internationalize and also offered to act as procurement agents.

Other factors that promoted the collaboration between general trading companies and general merchandisers was the need to set up comprehensive logistics support when general merchandisers entered into the convenience store business and also when general trading companies became more and more involved in the production of processed food in Japan and overseas (Shôsha Kinô Kenkyûkai 1981:236, Suzuki [Tsuneo] 1990:163, Itôchû Shôji Chôsabu 1997:137).

However, it took until the 1990s for major collaborations between general trading companies and general merchandisers to develop. This happened in two stages. In the first stage, retailers and general trading companies entered into same-level collaborations in the form of strategic alliances. Daiei concluded a comprehensive collaboration agreement with Marubeni. Mitsui intensified ties with the Mycal group and both companies collaborated in logistics. Mitsubishi and Jusco cooperated in the development of shopping centres and supply of products. Ito-Yokado entered into a relationship with Itochu focusing on logistics, product procurement and the opening of stores in China (Meyer-Ohle 2000). However, this phase of equal relationship building did not last very long. When retail empires started to disintegrate, general trading companies jumped at the opportunities and took over equity stakes in retailers, and in doing so did not necessarily stick to the alliances created earlier.

Discourses on the development of distribution systems explicitly or implicitly assume a development path for such systems that include a reduction of layers of middlemen, a concentration of involved companies, and a power shift from the manufacturing to the retail sector. While some of the developments described above point in this direction, the increasing involvement of general trading companies seems to contradict this trend. Initiatives of general trading companies to combine existing strengths in wholesaling and other areas with retail interests have potentially far-reaching consequences for the direction of change in Japanese distribution, and overall seem to add another layer of complexity to the Japanese distribution system. Even though developments are ongoing it thereby seems to be worthwhile to discuss underlying motives and consequences of general trading companies' moves into

Table 8.4   Sales of large five general trading companies, 1999–2001

Company	Consolidated sales (billion yen)		
	2001	2000	1999
Mitsubishi	13 245	14 016	13 109
Mitsui	12 654	13 048	13 200
Itochu	11 400	12 135	12 144
Sumitomo	9 665	10 100	10 672
Marubeni	8 972	9 436	10 222

Sales in business year ending in March 2002/2001/2000.
Source: Author's compilation based on annual reports of each company.

retailing. Far-reaching as these consequences are, there is some overlap with the following chapters on the development of relationships between the retail sector and the wholesale and manufacturing sector as well as with the discussion of development of e-commerce in Japan.

As in the situation of general merchandising companies, the 1990s have been a period of restructuring for general trading companies. As already pointed out, retail activities are only one area of a wide portfolio of activities of general trading companies (for an overview see Asuka 1998:1–14). Table 8.4 shows dramatic decreases in revenues that reflect changes in demand but also the initiatives of general trading companies to divest certain areas of their business. The decline in their core business, the large-volume trade of raw materials, was due to several factors such as traditional clients from the manufacturing sector downsizing or relocating, and a general shift from resource-intensive to knowledge-intensive production. In their search for new growth areas most general trading companies rediscovered consumer markets. In their annual reports, strategies and objectives for consumer markets and the retail sector occupy prominent positions and, as has been shown above, companies are following through on these plans.

Looking closer at the underlying reasons for the entry of general trading companies into the retail sector, five can be identified. The first was the protection and increase of product supply to the retail sector, and it was based on the traditional wholesale activities of general trading companies. As will be outlined in more detail in the following chapter, general trading companies, especially Itochu and Mitsubishi, have built up powerful subsidiaries in the wholesale sector and have made substantial investments during the 1990s to develop their wholesalers into companies with broad assortments and nationwide scope.

The second objective, the exploitation of opportunities within the reorganization of the retail sector, is linked to the financial and organizational capabilities of general trading companies. This strategy was pursued mainly by Sumitomo. Based on its long experience with its subsidiary Summit, the company claimed not to involve itself with the daily affairs of its affiliated retailers and especially not to influence purchasing decisions (*Gekiryu Magazine* June 2000b). At the beginning of the year 2002, the company played a major role in negotiating the tie-up between Wal-Mart and Seiyu (*Nihon keizai shinbun* 9 April 2002b). The third objective was the acquisition of knowledge of consumer behaviour. General trading companies aimed to play a larger role in the development of products for consumer markets, but had a general lack of knowledge in this area. Acquiring stakes in retail companies brought companies closer to this information and also opened up possibilities for the development of new products in collaboration with retailers.

The fourth motive was the integration of retailers in e-commerce strategies. It will be shown in Chapter 10 how convenience store companies have been trying to maneuver themselves into a central position in Japan's emerging e-commerce structure. In this regard, general trading companies have expressed interest not only in providing products but also in developing and maintaining the necessary information technology and infrastructure. General trading companies have set up a number of subsidiaries in the areas of infrastructure, financing, information technology and content creation. They have also become heavily involved in digital data transmission, television channels, satellite operation, international telecommunications, cable television, television shopping and the provision of web-related services. For example, Itochu became the operator of the Excite web search engine in Japan, and through its satellite communication business became involved in Japan's leading digital television provider, SKY-Perfect TV. It also became engaged in the production and provision of content with companies such as Japan Entertainment Network, Star Channel, and Space Shower Network.

The last objective related to the financial accounting of general trading companies. Compared with final consumer demand, demand from industrial customers is highly volatile and also subject to exchange rate fluctuations if products are shipped internationally. With their focus on industrial clients, the revenue flow of general trading companies was thereby highly unstable. The inclusion of retail companies into the consolidated accounts of general trading companies thereby can contribute to the stabilization of revenues.

By taking leading equity stakes in retail companies, trading companies have, however, entered into a complex net of new relationships, and the success of their strategies will depend mainly on their capabilities to balance internal and external interests. While interests within the company might press for a tight integration of retail operations, products and services provided from within the general trading company or subsidiaries and affiliates might not always be the best solutions on the market. This situation is complicated further by the fact that convenience store operations are operated largely as franchise systems, with companies having to compete not only for customers but also for sustained support by franchisees (*Gekiryu Magazine* August 2000). The increased importance of retailing has thereby led to organizational changes within general trading companies. While general trading companies are described generally as being heavily divided along product lines (Uchida 1986:105–43), they have been setting up departments specializing in the handling of retail operations to be able to serve partners in the retail sector in a more comprehensive manner.

Finally, returning to the overall restructuring of Japanese mass retailing, the activities of different players have been discussed; however, owing to the ongoing nature of developments no distinct outcomes can be shown. What may be concluded, however, is that ownership, governance and organizational patterns will be much more diverse than in the past. With retail competition moving away from the simple competition between different store formats towards competition between integrated systems along the whole supply chain, diverse patterns of ownership and organization will further drive innovation and change in the industry.

9
Building Supply Chains

Besides changes in the legal environment, consumer demand and entre-preneurial climate, the years of the 1990s and since have also seen major developments in the procurement markets. As in most other areas, change has been reciprocal with retailers both being influenced by changes and making them. In the preceding chapters of this book the situation on the supply side has already been discussed in some detail. The characteristics of Japanese procurement markets were described as having developed in response to the needs of the high number of small retailers, and as having shown a high resilience against initiatives for change from the retail side. On the whole, the development and expansion of new retail formats did not lead to a drastic overhaul of the distribution system as experienced in other highly industrialized countries.

During the 1990s, however, initiatives to change the configuration of the product flow between manufacturer and consumer gained importance. These initiatives led to major changes in the composition of actors, and required a reallocation of functions and a mobilization of resources. This chapter takes up these developments. While focusing on developments of the 1990s and since, this needs to be done within a discussion of the overall development of Japanese distribution channels in the past.

Patterns of stability and change in Japanese distribution channels

While change usually receives most of the attention it is often stability that really characterizes economic relationships. This argument was forcefully brought forward by the network approach. Commenting on change and stability in distribution channels from the viewpoint of the network approach, Gadde (1993:62–3) reached three major conclusions:

- While most researchers tend to focus their interest only on periods and events of explicit change, the basic characteristic of distribution channels is stability.
- Development may happen by *mobilization*, describing clearly visible changes in the structure of actors and resources. However, change can also be achieved through *coordination*, meaning the constant adaptation of the way tasks are shifted between actors and the way resources are used by actors in an otherwise stable network structure. Though less visible, these efforts may be the more important ones.
- Apparent stability in the actor structure therefore does not necessarily mean low performance, since coordination efforts require and reinforce some form of basic stability.

As already pointed out, the Japanese distribution system seems to be a prime example for stable relationships. At least, this is the case in quantitative terms. While the retail sector has shown some change, the wholesale sector has demonstrated an astonishing pattern of structural constancy that persisted even throughout the 1990s (Table 9.1).

The underlying reasons for this stability are to be found mainly in the attitudes shown by manufacturers, wholesalers and retailers toward their position and role in the distribution channel. On the one hand, manufacturers and, to a smaller extent, wholesalers tried to gain control over other members within distribution channels. On the other hand, as shown in previous chapters, big retail companies concentrated efforts not on their purchasing activities but on the development of sales concepts. In all, actors in Japanese distribution focused on smaller changes and did not aim for drastic reorganization; in the language of the network approach, coordination rather than mobilization was the dominant feature of change in Japanese distribution.

Manufacturers strove to achieve a dominant position in distribution channels by building up distribution networks that were used exclusively for or at least gave priority to distributing their own goods. They took stakes in wholesale companies' capital and gradually increased their influence. Wholesalers that had once been independent were thereby gradually transformed into quasi-sales companies of certain manufacturers. However, manufacturers went to different lengths regarding their organizational and regional integration. Pursuing control

Table 9.1   Development of Japanese wholesaling and retailing, 1960–99*

Size of establishment (no. of employees)	1960	1966	1974	1982	1991	1994	1999
Wholesaling	**Percentage of total wholesale sales**						
1–4	5.6	4.3	5.1	5.3	5.8	5.1	5.1
5–9	12.2	9.2	9.2	10.7	11.2	10.5	10.5
10–19	17.0	12.3	12.1	12.9	14.3	14.0	14.3
20–49	21.6	17.8	17.7	17.7	18.9	19.5	19.7
50 or more	43.6	56.4	57.0	53.4	49.9	51.2	50.4
Retailing	**Percentage of total retail sales**						
1–4	47.0	40.8	34.2	32.9	27.2	23.3	18.3
5–9	22.6	20.6	21.1	22.0	20.5	20.2	18.3
10–19	10.6	11.7	12.4	12.5	15.2	16.6	18.8
20–49	6.7	9.1	11.3	12.5	15.0	16.7	17.9
50 or more	13.1	17.8	21.2	20.1	22.0	23.2	26.7

* The Census of Commerce for the year 1999 lists a total of 425 850 wholesale and 1 406 884 retail establishments. The number of retail establishments reached its peak with 1 732 500 in 1982 and has been declining since; the number of wholesale establishments reached its peak in 1991 with 461 623. The high share of total sales for establishments with more than 50 employees in the wholesale sector partially results from the inclusion of the large general trading companies, which execute a large portion of Japan's international trade with raw materials.
Source: TSC (b) (pertinent years).

as far as the retail level, some manufacturers or dependent wholesalers organized small-scale retailers into a chain structure, in which retailers, having formerly been independent, were now dealing mainly in products of one manufacturer. Widely known as *ryûtsû keiretsu*, the largest network was built up by Matsushita and at the beginning of the 1990s consisted of 28 wholesale companies and 27 000 retail stores. These strategies were not pursued to the same extent in all industries, but they were prevalent in leading and fast-growing fields of the Japanese economy, such as electric appliances, automobiles and cosmetics. Pursuing these strategies enabled manufacturers to reach three inter-related goals (Mishima 1993:211–18):

- Expanding and protecting their market share by making exclusive use of a network of wholesalers and retailers.
- Controlling prices on the retail and wholesale level.
- Developing into full-line manufacturers by denying competitors – especially smaller, narrow-line manufacturers – access to the retail level.

Manufacturers controlled their distribution channels by a carefully designed set of trade practices. First of all, they established a pricing scheme that carefully assigned margins to each level in the distribution system down to the retail level, where recommended prices for products existed. Despite being in violation of official antitrust policy these prices were often strictly enforced and controlled by manufacturers. Within this system rebates were given; however, more important than rebates based on the overall amount of merchandise ordered at one time, or actual functions performed by a retailer in the distribution process, were rebates based on the fulfillment of individually agreed sales targets over a longer period, the amount of articles kept in storage, or the share of a particular manufacturer's products of overall sales by a retailer. Other incentives for retailers and wholesalers to become closely integrated with manufacturers were the delegation of personnel from manufacturers to wholesalers or from wholesalers to retailers, the possibility of returning unsold merchandise, the exclusive right to represent the manufacturer in a certain area and the provision of exclusive information and support (Itô *et al.* 1991:135).

In food distribution the systematization of distribution channels was due to the initiative of wholesalers. Primary food wholesalers took control over secondary regional wholesalers, while at the same time there were mergers between wholesalers. As already mentioned in Chapter 8, general trading companies brought relatively influential wholesale groups under their control, so that competition in food wholesaling became a competition between major groups (Miyashita 1993:183–7). While becoming powerful players in term of size, these companies nonetheless could not overcome limitations in terms of the breadth of assortments and also regional scope of operations. As has been pointed out in the analysis of the development of convenience stores, wholesalers usually carried only a limited range of product groups, thus requiring retailers to deal with a large number of wholesalers if they wanted to provide assortments beyond the narrow lines of a certain product group.

This product specialization was also reinforced by governmental policies. When pursuing policies to modernize the Japanese distribution system, Japanese government agencies did not question the existing high degree of product specialization on the wholesale level and supported efforts to rationalize the flow of products and information between specialized actors on a product-by-product basis. Wholesale companies were thus encouraged to make heavy product-specific investments in warehousing, logistics and information technology and it thereby became difficult for them to widen their area of expertise at a later stage (Bartlett 2000).

The position of large retail companies has been outlined in detail previously and need therefore only be summarized now. Overall, a reliance on the services of the wholesale sector and manufacturers enabled retailers to focus on their growth strategies and expansion of market share. Wholesalers not only assisted retailers in financing by stocking their stores and reducing the need to keep inventories, but also reduced the risk of introducing new product lines. The spectacular conflicts between large manufacturers of consumer goods and superstore operators about the right to set prices which dominated the late 1960s gradually faded away in the 1970s. Superstore operators became more compliant to manufacturers' wishes to control the pricing of merchandise. Manufacturers and wholesalers eased the expansion of superstore chains by gradually taking over more activities and risks (Atsumi 1993:30, Yahagi 1993a:137–9, Yahagi 1994:27).

Several factors have already been discussed that supported the decision of Japanese superstore operators to concentrate on expansion and sales growth. In the 1960s these were growing consumer markets and the chance for retailers to develop new locations in rapidly growing suburban areas without much retail competition. In the 1970s and 1980s existing stores were protected by the Large Store Law. Consumers had a limited choice of stores offering one-stop shopping and therefore they started to accept superstores more for their wide assortments and services than for low prices.

Relationships between the different actors in the distribution channel were further stabilized by the importance of personnel relationships that formed over time. Gerlach (1992) characterized the Japanese economic system as alliance capitalism, deriving this assessment from the state of company relationships. Companies maintained relationships that went beyond normal commercial transactions, were heavily dependent on personal relationships and even built up reciprocal obligations over time. For the retail sector some of the relationships formed over time were so strong that it literally took an earthquake to drive change: in January 1995, an earthquake devastated most of Kobe and with it large parts of its retail infrastructure. After department store operators had rebuilt their premises they voiced some surprising comments. On the one hand, companies complained about lost revenues and the cost of rebuilding store operations. On the other hand, operators pointed to positive aspects that resulted from the interruption of business caused by the catastrophic event. Store operators not only were given the opportunity to redesign sales floors but also were able to end long-standing business relationships. Contracts with tenants who did not contribute sufficiently to overall store attractiveness could be cancelled and accounts with weak suppliers could be closed (*Nikkei ryûtsû shinbun* 18 January 1996:1).

In summary, interest in the development of short, easy-to-comprehend distribution channels had not been very high and at the same time general characteristics of Japanese company interrelationships reinforced the status quo. Most small operators were satisfied with a small but guaranteed income and large companies strove less for profitability than for sales growth and a high market share. In fact, while there was continuous criticism in regard to the efficiency of marketing channels, the Japanese distribution system was at the same time praised for its high level of product availability and consumer choice (see for example Goldman 1992).

The delegation of functions and risks to the wholesale and manufacturing sector is reflected in low retail margins and the high turnover of merchandise. This is most obvious in the case of the department store. While in other countries the department store is a retail format with high margins and low inventory turnover, in Japan department stores purchase a large share of their merchandise on commission, do not keep high stocks, or else hold the right to return unsold merchandise, and thus show high turnover rates and comparatively low margins (Maruyama 1995:202) (Table 9.2).

The discussion and comparison of distribution margins and productivity is a complex topic and is not pursued here. Research at the beginning of the 1990s (for an overview see Nishimura 1993 or Ito and Maruyama 1995) has shown that despite the many tiers of the distribution system, gross margins of the distribution sector (combination of wholesalers and retailers) of Japan compared with those of the United States were not necessarily higher and in some cases proved to be even lower.

What are of interest here, though, are opportunities for actors within the system to innovate and drive change. In this sense the use of wholesalers can be interpreted in the following way. By making use of the possibility or giving in to the necessity to delegate functions to the wholesale sector, retailers deprived themselves or were deprived of the opportunity to control a part of their strategic portfolio and thereby to differentiate themselves from competitors. Seen as a whole, actors in the Japanese distribution network were highly interlocked. The system offered room for small adjustments, but, within a set of given players,

Table 9.2   Margins and inventory turnover in Japanese and US retailing, 1992

Japan			United States	
Store format	Gross margin (%)	Inventory turnover p.a.	Store format	Gross margin (%)
Department store	24.4	16.2	Department store	30.3
General superstore	22.4	21.8	Discount department store	24.0
Food superstore	21.9	32.7	Grocery store	24.4
Home centre	17.9	14.0	Furniture and home furnishing stores	42.0
General discount store	14.2	12.3	Warehouse clubs and superstores	15.0
Electric appliances store	17.8	7.0	Electronics and appliances stores	29.0
Men's clothing discount store	32.7	5.4		

Source: Author's compilation based on Ryûtsû Mondai Kenkyûkai 1995:53–6 and US Census Bureau 2001.

did not encourage major changes in the activity structure. This does not mean that change did not take place at all. In the sense of the network approach, however, change took place by coordination rather than by mobilization.

The most prominent and successful example of change in distribution channels was change brought about after the introduction of convenience store. As has been outlined in previous chapters of this book, a new type of retail institution with highly specific needs was introduced that could not be accommodated within the existing patterns of the distribution system. While the need for a different pattern of distribution was clearly visible, convenience store operators had, nonetheless, to be content to drive change slowly.

For convenience stores it was small sales floors, limited storage space, broad assortments and long business hours that posed special requirements to suppliers in the form of small delivery lots and a high frequency of deliveries. These could however not be fulfilled by wholesalers who were closely linked to certain manufacturers and whose merchandise were limited to a certain product line. The efforts of convenience store companies to overcome this situation have already been described in some detail (Chapter 4). Up until the 1990s companies organized the joint distribution of goods, set up joined distribution centres, introduced quality control for their suppliers, became pioneers in the coding of merchandise, overcame price differentials between suppliers, negotiated a reduction of packages and lot sizes, and introduced advanced information systems. The establishment of distribution centres resulted in a gradual shift of functions from wholesalers to retailers and manufacturers. Retailers negotiated with manufacturers recommended wholesale prices for their franchise members and, where the physical distribution of goods was concerned, manufacturers often delivered directly into distribution centres (SIJ 1992:114–20, 185–96, Ryûtsû Mondai Kenkyûkai 1995:86).

With convenience store companies having proceeded so far already in the organization of their supply chains, Seven-Eleven finally went even one step further. In November 1997 it got 25 wholesalers to establish a separate new company with the exclusive purpose of supplying the company's convenience stores with daily miscellaneous goods and sundries. The establishment of this company can be seen as its final move to transform a manufacturer-oriented distribution structure into a retail-orientated one. Commercial transactions and the physical distribution of merchandise were united again and in addition the new company operated on a national level (*Gekiryû Magazine* October 1997) (Figure 9.1).

Looking at the underlying patterns of change in the case of convenience stores shows that, change was not undertaken in a radical manner but implemented step by step, always taking into account the existing actors and their current position. Only after convenience store companies had established themselves as major players in Japanese retailing did they attempt to directly influence manufacturers' marketing strategies, and even after doing so they continued to pursue their strategies within the given set of actors.

Recognizing the need to change

The Japanese distribution system of the 1990s has been described as undergoing revolutionary change. Change was related to a number of factors, most importantly deregulation, stricter application of fair trade regulations, changes in consumer behaviour, entry of foreign retailers and increasing imports through the appreciation of the yen. The outcome of these trends was a decline in consumer prices that proved challenging not only for retail companies but for all companies engaged

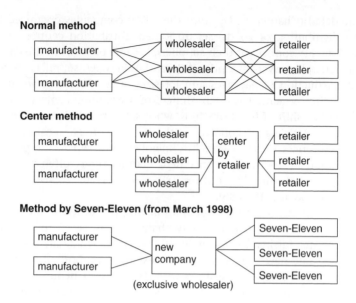

Figure 9.1   Distribution channels in the household goods industry.
Source: *The Nikkei Marketing Journal*, 2 September 1997:2, translated by Hendrik Meyer-Ohle.

in the production and distribution of consumer goods. Faced with drastic decreases in sales and profits (Figure 9.2), manufacturers and retailers tried to rationalize their operations. These attempts revealed major shortcomings in the companies' earlier strategies.

Retailers had delegated key functions to wholesalers and manufacturers and thereby limited their strategic choices to adapt to the changed market conditions. Companies found themselves lacking capabilities in the area of logistics but shortcomings were also reported in the area of sales promotion and development of assortments. Having lost control over assortments and having neglected the development of independent skills in merchandising and logistics, established companies found it difficult to fulfill the complex patterns of consumer demand of the 1990s in regard to price, quality and originality, especially in competition with the successful companies of the 1990s described earlier (Fujita 1995:5, Ryûtsû Mondai Kenkyûkai 1995:108–10, Teranaka 1995:20).

Manufacturers for a long time sustained distribution channels that helped them in their quest for market share and control. However, smaller members of these channels became heavily dependent on capital and personnel support by manufacturers. Set up in a situation of growing

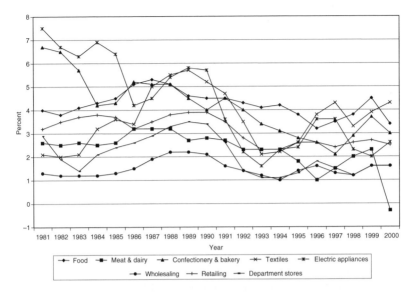

Figure 9.2   Development of ratio of ordinary income to sales over major industries, 1981–2000 (average in per cent). The number of companies included changed over the years.
Source: Author's figure based on Nihon Seisaku Tôshi Ginkô (1991, 1996, 1997, 2002).

markets and less knowledgeable consumers, manufacturers found it hard to adapt distribution channels to saturated markets and the needs of sophisticated consumers. In consumer electronics, the main features of the traditional channel were closeness to consumers' homes and advice in the selection of products and after-service. However, consumers became more mobile and knowledgeable themselves, and interest in low prices increased. For cosmetics, change was driven by the Japanese Fair Trade Commission. It forced manufacturers to relax control over retailers and also encouraged large-scale retailers to not follow manufacturers' recommended prices. In processed foods, manufacturer-recommended retail prices quickly lost their impact after increased competition in the retail sector led to many products being continuously sold at so-called bargain prices. With manufacturers guaranteeing wholesale margins, wholesalers were usually reimbursed by manufacturers for rebates granted to retailers. However, rebates granted to retailers and subsequent demands by wholesalers for reimbursements reached such a scale during the 1990s that manufacturers were unable to pay them, so that large manufacturers were led eventually to switch to an open price system. The control over prices thereby partly shifted away from the manufacturer to the retail level (Nihon Keizai Shinbunsha 1995:176–8, Ryûtsû Mondai Kenkyûkai 1995:99–112).

Manufacturers had also to rethink their objectives in product development. The rapid development of new products had become a major element in the drive for manufacturers' market share expansion. However, the over-reliance on this strategy with ever-increasing variations of articles with shorter and shorter life cycles brought even the Japanese distribution system to its limits. The system became vulnerable to fluctuations in demand that quickly led to the piling up of large quantities of stock, forcing companies to think about new methods of synchronizing production and sales (Takaya 1994:16–24).

Finally, every actor in the Japanese distribution sector was confronted increasingly with alternative models of organizing relationships between retailers and manufacturers. Previous calls for change had mostly envisioned a radical change from a manufacturer-dominated to a retailer-dominated distribution structure and had thereby always been quickly dismissed as unrealistic and unsuitable for the Japanese situation. In contrast, models of collaborative merchandising and supply chain management developed by leading convenience store chains proved the existence of a middle ground and thereby received serious attention from retailers and manufacturers alike. Other examples that did not go unnoticed were emerging alliances between leading manufacturers and retailers overseas, such as those involving Wal-Mart. In both cases relationships went beyond aspects of merchandising and included also issues like the effective use of information technology and a redesign of logistics. In summary, the existing stable structure of the Japanese distribution system was seriously challenged from different angles during the 1990s, with actors under heavy pressure to come up with new solutions; instead of the usual coordination between existing actors, a general mobilization of resources in a new structure was called for.

Changing strategies by manufacturers and wholesalers

Change during the 1990s and since has been occurring on many levels and in many areas. As in the case of previous developments, the eventual outcome can only be speculated about. What can be outlined and discussed, however, are the processes leading to change. Here certain patterns can be identified, which will be shown below. As outlined above, not only retailers but also manufacturers and wholesalers were

facing with increasing pressure for change during the 1990s. Companies were faced with the need not only to raise efficiency within their
operations to regain profitability but also to come up with larger solutions to ensure their future position in the distribution system. To do so
retailers, manufacturers and wholesalers alike changed their strategies
significantly, with changes covering arrangements for the physical distribution of goods, trade practices, assortments, spatial reach and
internal organization (Table 9.3).

Concerning change in the manufacturing sector, Watanabe (1997:144)
proposed the following model of successive change:

1. review of business philosophy and objectives;
2. change to an organization that can cater to the needs of large retailers;
3. review of channel strategy;
4. review of product strategies in regard to product proliferation;
5. review of production and stock-keeping systems;
6. strengthening of logistics and information systems.

Indeed, change could be seen in all these areas, though it was often
more of an incremental than a systematic nature.

In formulating their marketing strategies, manufacturers were and are
still faced with the original problem of how to cater to the different
interests of small and large retailers, with the number of small ones continuing to be high. While the relationship between large retailers and
manufacturers was of a somewhat ambiguous nature, varying between
conflict and collaboration, the relationship with the small retail sector
was quite clear. Here manufacturers clearly dominated, controlled
the activities of retailers with a sophisticated set of trade practices. As
such, the sales arms of manufacturers targeted and were designed for
the support of wholesalers and small retailers. While manufacturers in
principle followed a vision of a systematization of sales channels, the
setup of their marketing organization in practice was made up of a large
number of affiliates organized more or less along regional, functional
and product lines. As already pointed out, these patterns of organization resulted from the gradual intensifying of relationships with once-
independent companies on the wholesale level.

While taking up a certain commitment to these companies by taking
over capital stakes, many manufacturers had not fully integrated these
firms in order to not disrupt existing leadership patterns or not lose
the possibility to differentiate employment conditions between core
companies and affiliates. This argument runs parallel to that used for

Table 9.3 Areas of change in supply chains

	Manufacturing	Wholesaling	Retailing
Logistics	Reorganization of logistics, shortening of lead times and reduction of inventories, industry-wide collaboration, separation of logistics operations	Strengthening of logistics, providing comprehensive logistics services	Strengthening of logistics (exclusive distribution centres)
Trade practices	Reform of rebate systems, gradual abolition of recommended prices	Caught in between retailers and manufacturers' strategies – change to market-based prices	Everyday-low-price independent from manufacturers, increase of share of products handled on own risk
Organizational change (M&A)	Merger of sales companies, setting up of own store network (textile), building own capabilities of retail support	M&A of wholesalers, acquisition of retailers and setting up of retail departments (general trading companies)	Mergers and acquisitions to increase buying power
Products/assortments	Concentration/reduction of number of products, rethinking of traditional full-line strategies, development of retail format or retail customer-specific products	Widening of assortments	Strengthening of private brands, development of new sources, development of exclusive brands with manufacturers
Spatial reach	Streamlining of national networks	Increasing coverage	Striving for national coverage

Source: Author's compilation.

the relationship of manufacturers and their suppliers, especially in the Japanese automobile industry. Here, large companies have been careful to keep the number of core employees low, being faced with the responsibility of securing long-term employment, advancement opportunities, high wages and a number of other benefits for their employees.

From the 1990s on, manufacturers have initiated or intensified measures to streamline their organizations. Within a general trend to concentrate on core competencies with the aim to raise profitability, and also in the light of stricter rules for the consolidation of affiliates with regard to financial reporting, companies are reviewing the position of their affiliates. Other factors leading to a review of organizational patterns were the rising importance of large retailers with nationwide store networks as well as the necessity to introduce new information technology, both factors that challenged regionally and functionally fragmented organizations on the supplier level.

Reacting to these changes, a number of manufacturers began to refocus their sales organizations and to reorganize logistics. Matsushita, for example, in March 2001 announced plans to merge 22 of its 28 regional sales firms into one entity. Nichimen, a leading textile producer, absorbed a number of distributors to concentrate its resources. Suntory sold its 55 per cent stake in a wholesaler of liquor and foods to Ryoshoku, arguing that it wanted to concentrate on its liquor business (*Nihon keizai shinbun* 5 October 2001, 14 February 2002). At the same time companies started to review their logistics operations. Matsushita, for example, merged two logistics service providers. Other manufacturers increased the independence of their logistics affiliates, enabling them to offer their services to other companies. While activities of Kao in this regard will be outlined later in more detail, other example are the outsourcing of physical distribution by electronics retailer Best Denki to electric appliance manufacturer Sanyo's logistics company or retailer Eiden's collaboration with Toshiba in the area of logistics (*Nihon keizai shinbun* 6 September 2001).

Manufacturers supported their strategies to reorganize logistics with changes in their trade practices, again with the aim of refocusing these on cost and resource efficiency (Ryûtsû Mondai Kenkyûkai 1995:103). A good example here was the case of Shiseido. The company traditionally gave rebates to retailers on the amount of goods stocked by them and not the amount sold. This strategy guaranteed the availability of products for customers and also made it more difficult for other manufacturers to get access to retailers' shelf and storage space. However, retailers felt motivated to increase stocks beyond needs and either disposed of them by selling them to discount stores or wholesalers, thereby undermining the goal of the company of sustaining its brand image, or else had excess stock returned to Shiseido. After writing off 43 billion yen in distributed inventories – this being partly due also to a change in regulations concerning the labeling of products – the company in addition changed its rebate system to a system based on actual sales but which also had components to motivate retailers to actively retail products and keep returns of merchandise to the manufacturer at a low level (*Nikkei kinyû shinbun* 18 October 2001).

Manufacturers also made significant changes in product policies. A number of manufacturers began reducing the number of products offered. This has been especially significant in the area of household products and cosmetics. After a thorough analysis of sales and margins in August 2001, Kao announced plans to slash the number of household products it offered by half from 2000 to 1000. The rationale behind this move was summarized by the president of the company: 'I think we'll receive complaints from regular users of some products. But we're not in an age where one company can dominate and we need to improve profitability, even if that means decreased revenues' (Takuya Goto, president of Kao, cited in *Nihon keizai shinbun* 30 August 2001). Kao's main rival, Lion, entered into a similar strategy and announced a cut in its core brands from currently 57 to only 21, with the marketing director of the company stating 'Our conventional full-line strategy is taking its toll and our profit margins are going down' (Yasuhisa Kinugasa cited in *Nikkei Weekly* 5 February 2001). Similarly, cosmetics manufacturer Shiseido announced plans to drastically reduce the number of its brands from around 100 to between 30 and 35.

Companies support these strategies of focusing on core areas by increasing their support to retailers, a function that was usually performed by the wholesale sector but has increasingly become unstable because of changes in the wholesale sector. Manufacturers also began increasingly to work together with certain retailers to jointly develop and offer exclusive brands, thereby trying to overcome initiatives by retailers to develop private brands on their own.

Overall, manufacturers thereby changed their marketing approach considerably from one that pursued market share growth through control over distribution channels, provision of full line assortments, and control of prices to one that focuses on growth and profitability through a focus of resources on core capabilities. As will be discussed later, these changes had considerable consequences for activities in the retail sector.

Wholesalers were caught in the squeeze between retailers and manufacturers. As already pointed out, the decline of wholesaling in Japan had repeatedly been predicted but for various reasons the wholesale sector had largely been able to sustain its crucial role in Japanese consumer goods distribution. However, initiatives of manufacturers to review distribution channels and of retailers to improve their supply chain management in the 1990s have become a serious threat to the position of wholesalers. Wholesalers were no longer assured of guaranteed incomes through long-standing and exclusive relationships with manufacturers, nor could they rely on growth-obsessed retailers to delegate major functions to them without properly assessing costs and additional advantages and disadvantages.

Players in the wholesale sector had to react to this situation and it was the large companies that took the initiative. Basically, all larger companies subscribed to the same objective of becoming general wholesalers that could serve large retailers with comprehensive and unified assortments and services on a nationwide basis.

Looking at these activities in more detail, the first step leading wholesalers took in this direction was the unification of the handling of the three major product groups (liquors/beverages, processed foods, confectionary) that up to then had been handled largely by specialized companies. The strategy for many companies to reach this goal was to take over smaller wholesalers or, where affiliations with other specialized companies already existed, to intensify these. In doing so, companies took care to increase the spatial coverage of their operations and therefore had to buy into a number of regional wholesalers. While this consolidation of the wholesale industry has not come to an end yet, companies have already entered into the next stage of reorganization. In this stage they have begun to focus on the strengthening of functions in the area of logistics, retail support, product development, information systems and capabilities for the handling of more demanding products such as chilled and frozen merchandise. Again, companies have been doing so by mergers and acquisitions but have also entered into on-par collaborative activities with companies from within and without the wholesale industry.

As has already been pointed out in Chapter 8, a major role in the reorganization of the wholesale sector is played by wholesalers affiliated with general trading companies (Table 9.4). General trading companies originally built up their interests in food wholesaling during the late 1960s and throughout the 1970s but they intensified activities during the 1990s considerably, especially by unifying their operations and

Table 9.4 Major grocery wholesale companies, 2000

Company	Sales (bn Yen)	Affiliation	Main products handled
Kokubu	1021	Independent	Processed foods, liquor
Yukijirushi Access	661	Formerly Snow Brand, now Itochu and other general trading companies	Dairy products, chilled and frozen foods, processed foods
Ryoshoku	634	Mitsubishi Corporation	Processed foods
Itochu Shokuhin	484	Itochu	Processed foods
Meidiya	481	Independent	Liquor, processed foods
Kato Sangyô	387	Mitsui	Processed foods
Nihon Shurui Hanbai	386	Independent	Liquor
Asahi Foods	315	Mitsubishi Corporation	Processed foods
Yamae Hisano	223	Independent	Processed foods, liquor

Source: Author's compilation based on Nikkei MJ (Ryûtsû Shinbun) 2001, web pages of companies.

supporting affiliated wholesalers in their takeover activities. The previous chapter has also described the move of general trading companies into the retail sector. While it was initially discussed how and to what degree this engagement would affect the procurement decisions of retailers, this development has started to show significance in the realignment of wholesalers. In particular, medium-sized wholesalers that were strongly dependent on sales to these convenience stores were and are being drawn under the umbrella of the respective wholesale groups (*Gekiryû Magazine* February 2002).

With large wholesalers quickly upgrading their capabilities, the gaps within the wholesale sector widened and many smaller companies have lost their accounts with large retailers. The initiatives of retailers and manufacturers in reviewing logistics and information systems have required that wholesalers who wanted to sustain relationships with large as well as small retailers should build up distinctively different sales systems in regard to sales organization, logistics and information networks, and many smaller wholesalers have not been able to do this. In contrast, large wholesalers have been intensifying initiatives to transform themselves from sales agents for manufacturers into procurement agents for the retail sector.

Strategies by the retail sector

As shown already, the change in distribution channels from the 1990s on has been driven from different directions, often with competing solutions. The most visible area of change during the 1990s was logistics. Companies not only recognized the existing inefficiencies in this area, but also identified it as a key area to secure their future position in distribution channels. Hence, wholesalers, manufacturers and retailers alike are competing for leadership in this area as the three following examples demonstrate. Changes in logistics, however, go hand in hand with changes in other areas which will be discussed afterwards.

In 1993, the major food wholesaler Ryoshoku took over the logistics for Sotetsu Rozen, a food supermarket operator with 75 food outlets in Kanagawa prefecture. Instead of delivering directly to the stores, wholesalers were advised to deliver to a distribution centre operated by Ryoshoku from where merchandise was to be jointly distributed to the retailer's outlets. Changes did not stop with the physical distribution of goods, but extended to commercial transactions. Sotetsu Rozen reduced the numbers of suppliers for processed food from 23 to only 5, assigning a share of 75 per cent to Ryoshoku. The new organizational setting was described as an instant success, with reductions in the number of store deliveries, the time for unloading of trucks and, especially, the rate of undelivered articles. Ryoshoku also extended retail support to the company. With only four buyers, Sotetsu had in the past not properly utilized the information collected through its point of sale systems. After taking over logistics Ryoshoku assigned a staff of ten to Sotetsu Rozen and began to systematically analyze the company's sales data and develop proposals for changes of sales floors and assortments (*Nikkei ryûtsû shinbun* 29 September 1994, 8 December 1994).

Kao, the leading company in the Japanese toiletries and household goods industries, realized the importance of logistics early on. Freeing itself from the need to go through wholesalers, it systematically developed its own sales and logistics operations, introducing sophisticated technologies. When Ito Yokado wanted to reorganize its logistics for daily necessities and sundries in 1996, and asked manufacturers to deliver goods into a distribution centre, Kao refused, pointing to the

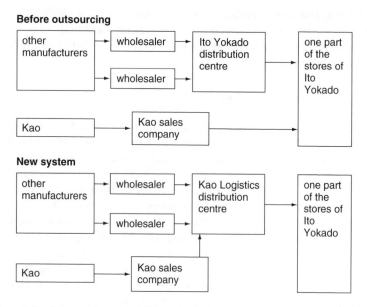

Figure 9.3   Changes in store delivery for household goods for one part of the stores of Ito Yokado.
Source: *The Nikkei Marketing Journal*, 24 June 1997:2, translated by Hendrik Meyer-Ohle.

existence of its already existing efficient infrastructure for store deliveries. The compromise the companies eventually reached together stunned competitors of Kao: Kao logistics was put in charge of running the distribution centre and logistics for Ito Yokado, thereby forcing other companies to deliver goods through a competitor's logistics agent (Figure 9.3) (*Nikkei ryûtsû shinbun* 24 June 1997).

Concerning retailer-led change in the organization of logistics, the activities of Seven-Eleven in reorganizing its supply channels by eventually taking over a leadership role, though still in a collaborative setting, have already been outlined. Another example of a retailer-dominated approach is that pursued by the Aeon Group. In 2001 Aeon announced an ambitious reorganization of its supply chain management. After completion of the project in 2004 the company is set to be the first large retailer in Japan controlling a comprehensive nationwide logistics network. The network is to be comprised of one national distribution centre for the handling of seasonal and slow-moving goods, three cross-docking centres to control the flow of goods, ten regional distribution centres and a number of cross-docking centres for collection of goods for store delivery from the other centres. In addition, 19 planned processing centres will handle fresh merchandise and raw materials used for merchandise produced within the stores. The system will not be owned and operated by Aeon itself but by a group of six specialized logistics providers. Aeon wants to leverage on its logistics network to create new relationships with suppliers. It has called on 25 leading manufacturers of processed foods, confectionary and daily necessities for direct delivery into its logistics network and all but two have agreed to do so. Out of these, four have also agreed to change to direct commercial transactions. The company gradually hopes to raise the share of direct dealings with manufacturers to 50 per cent of overall dealings, hoping to reach 70 per cent in the long run (HKH 2001).

The three examples show the reorganization of logistics and transactions under different leadership. The objectives of the activities by the Aeon group are the most far-reaching. With the new system the company is setting the stage for direct dealings with manufacturers on a large scale. Starting out with only a small number of manufacturers, the company wants to gain experience gradually in this regard, especially since among the first four manufacturers that agreed to direct dealings were the Japanese subsidiaries of Procter & Gamble and Unilever. Further, in organizing its system Aeon has been careful not to include any of the leading general food wholesalers. The company argued that the volume of its dealings reached that of some of the large wholesalers, and it would actually rank seventh in processed food, sixth in confectionary and second in household goods, this enabling it to cut out this distribution stage (*Gekiryû Magazine* March 2002). Instead of utilizing the wholesale sector the company has decided to collaborate with specialized logistic providers that have each accumulated knowledge in a certain area, for example retail logistics, fresh fish distribution, or frozen foods. Aeon even included one company because of its existing distribution network and port operations in Southeast Asia and China, thereby preparing itself for an increase in imported products from Asia. Aeon plans to shoulder the costs for the operation of the logistics network and thereby aims to create a new relationship with manufacturers. Instead of the current black box approach, Aeon strives for an open book and cost-based approach in negotiating prices with manufacturers (Hayashi 2001).

Looking at the approach taken by Aeon, it resembles in many ways practices adopted by leading retailers outside Japan. It also questions the validity of many of the statements made when Carrefour entered the Japanese market. Carrefour's original demands in many ways resembled those of Aeon. However, it was turned down by most suppliers and this was interpreted at that time as a demonstration of the strength of the Japanese wholesaling system as well as established and traditional Japanese business customs (*Nikkei Weekly* 25 September 2000, 18 December 2000). However, in the Japanese market size and buying power increasingly matter. Carrefour had not even opened one store when making its demands, and had at the same time already revealed that its business presence in Japan would not develop very quickly. Quite to the contrary, the Aeon group only announced its plans for a new logistics network by the time it had clearly established itself as the new leading company in Japanese mass retailing.

Looking at other Japanese companies, not too many in the mass retailing of foods and household goods have built up the same capability, and put themselves in a position, to drive change by themselves. This is especially true because many of the other companies have already committed themselves to wholesaler-led systems. Through the activities of general trading companies exchange relationships have also been backed up increasingly by ownership patterns. These patterns have been quite common in other areas of the Japanese economy but, as has been described in Chapter 8, may have contributed to problems in corporate governance, distorted incentive structures and inefficiencies. General trading companies have to come up with solutions to resolve conflicts of ownership and commercial dealings or commit to the alternative, which would see a reorganization of Japanese food retailing around groups led by certain general trading companies. These groups would consist of a number of collaborating or merged supermarket companies that all rely on the services from wholesalers and other service providers from the same group. In whatever direction these relationships are set to develop, the drive for companies to come up with efficient solutions will be spurred on by the existence of competing models and this might be the main difference from the past where patterns across companies and industries largely resembled each other.

Change in the relationships with suppliers that serve the need of the larger retailers did not take place only in the distribution of foods and household necessities. In consumer electronics it had been mainly the rapid product proliferation of manufacturers and the existence of recommended retail prices that had led to harmonious relationships between large retailers and manufacturers. The rapid introduction of new products by manufacturers required retailers to collaborate closely with manufacturers because of the danger of overstocking certain articles and missing necessary changes in recommended retail prices to prepare for product changes. Collaboration was further promoted through the high number of seasonal products in Japanese electric appliances. Manufacturers used their power over retailers largely to force them into the use of their existing sales network. While general conditions were negotiated directly between retail chains and head-quarters of manufacturers, the distribution of goods, stocking of stores, warehousing, payments and so on were taken care of by regional sales organization or manufacturer-affiliated wholesalers (Hitaka 1999). During the 1990s change was driven from both directions. Manufacturers amended many of their trade practices and marketing strategies by reducing assortments, slowing down the speed of product alterations, and partly doing away with recommended retail prices. On the other hand, as has been shown by the examples in Chapter 7, some electric appliance retailers reached a size where their demands for changed conditions could no longer be ignored. Through the introduction of distribution centres, retailers have begun to reduce the number of daily deliveries to their stores, under the old system reportedly being up to 50 and occupying up to a third of the work force, to one or two. Comply-ing with these demands required manufacturers to set up separate sales and logistics systems for large and small stores (*Nihon Keizai Shinbun* 6 September, 2001).

In apparel, manufacturers and retailers alike were faced with new competitors that vertically integrate manufacturing and retailing. Their business models as described in Chapter 7 heavily challenged existing systems such as the concession sales system that separated ownership and decision-making. To solve this situation some manufacturers have moved to systems that let them take over all responsibilities in leased sales floors or totally independent store formats (Che 1999, *Nihon Keizai Shinbun* 5 December 2001).

Overall, the years of the 1990s and since have seen major changes in the supply chain management of Japanese retailers. Faced by the need to rationalize, and being aware of foreign and homegrown examples of change, companies have finally recognized procurement as an area where major competitive advantages can be gained. As has been out-lined, these changes have not been completed yet and results are still uncertain. One certain result is a simplification of trade practices and supply channels. The system seems to be changing finally to one that caters to the needs of large retail companies and this fact may well disadvantage small retailers further in their quest for survival. In the sense of the network approach, the 1990s and early 2000s have seen a major mobilization of resources and a breakup of existing relationships. Companies have been entering into new relationships and have made substantial efforts to enter into these relationships in a position of strength. Commitment to new relationships, however, usually requires high specific investments and therefore Japanese retailing might well be heading for a new phase of stability where supply chain management is concerned. This should be interpreted not necessarily as a state of stagnancy with no development, but in the sense of the network approach, being perceived potentially as a situation in which in a given set of actors coordinating efforts prevail, centring on the activity structure.

10
Convenience Stores and the Organization of E-Commerce

While transactions on the internet are virtual the exchange of goods and payments still require a real space. Until now, the convenience store was limited to a size of 100 square meters with an assortment of 3000 items. But, in the future, through the use of e-commerce techniques, it will become possible to handle several 10 000 items on the same 100 square meters. Also, with transactions conducted on the net it will be possible to raise sales without effect on the operation cost of stores since stores do not need to keep stocks, there is no problem of missing articles or responsibility for product loss and it does not incur additional costs for personnel. (Homepage of FamilyMart at www.family.co.jp/inf/ec/cvs.html)

Previous chapters of this book have dealt with the interaction between the availability of new technologies and knowledge and the emergence of new retail formats in Japan. For the period of the 1990s and since, the largest development in this regard has been the internet and its possibility of offering new means of interaction between consumers and businesses. While this new technology was seen initially as a grand possibility for outsiders to enter the retail scene – and a few companies actually managed to do so – or as a dramatically new way of doing business with fast and tremendous growth prospects, many of these assumptions have since had to be reconsidered. Change has been less dramatic and established retailers have often taken a leading role in the development of the new technology. The question concerning e-commerce has thereby shifted from the replacement of bricks-and-mortar operations to possible combinations of e-commerce and existing retail operations. In Japan, it has been especially convenience store operators that have embraced the new technologies. Companies and observers alike pointed to a number of characteristics of the current business models of convenience stores that would put them in a central position in overcoming many of the problems associated with the expansion of e-commerce in Japan. This chapter will deal with the engagement of convenience stores in e-commerce under the following perspectives. First, e-commerce activities of convenience stores will be outlined. These will then be discussed within the overall development of e-commerce in Japan and in regard to the consequences of the introduction of e-commerce into business models of convenience store operators.

Examples of e-commerce initiatives by convenience stores

All major convenience store companies have engaged in the area of e-commerce (Table 10.1). Web ventures of companies have developed at different speeds with the three largest ones setting the pace. In the

Table 10.1   Leading convenience store companies, 2001

Company (affiliation)	Sales (bn yen)	Change from previous year (%)	Number of stores	Internet venture
Seven-Eleven Japan (Ito Yokado)	1 963	6.3	8 153	www.7dream.com
Lawson (Daiei–Mitsubishi)	1 221	5.5	7 378	www.at-lawson.com
FamilyMart (Seiyu–Itochu)	783	3.3	5 546	www.famima.com
Sunkus & Associates	342	10.3	2 593	http://www.toki-meki.com/
Circle K (managed jointly under C&S Holding from 1 July 2001)(Uny)	447	14.1	2 588	
Daily Yamazaki (Yamazaki Baking)	361	–5.3	2 571	www.daily365.net
MiniStop (Jusco)	192	11.2	1 375	https://www.e-ministop.com/
am/pm Japan (Japan Energy–Mitsubishi)	167	n.a.	1 182	http://www.ampm.co.jp http://delice.ampm.co.jp

Source: Author's compilation based on NRS (2000:192, 350).

following, the web-based ventures of the three largest convenience store companies will be introduced in more detail and will be contrasted briefly with the distinctly different approach by the company am/pm. The following overview of strategies is based on information provided by the three companies on their homepages, from an observation of the web pages as such and the newsletters distributed to their members. Additional information was taken from *Chain Store Age* 15 January 2000, *Shûkan Daiyamondo* 4 March 2000, *Chain Store Age* 15 March 2000, and Katô (2000).

7dream.com

Seven-Eleven Japan launched its website 7dream.com in June 2000. The site was developed and is managed by a separate venture, 7dream.com, a joint venture with Seven-Eleven as majority shareholder and NEC, NRI, Sony, Mitsui, JTB and Kinotrope as minority shareholders. The company was set up with the purpose to provide an e-commerce infrastructure focusing on convenience stores, to offer key services and products, and to develop payment services for other companies.

Seven-Eleven offers access to its online services in two ways. One is through the internet, the other through multimedia terminals in its stores. In addition to on-screen functions, these terminals are equipped with printing facilities for stickers and pictures and the ability to download digital content on minidisks and other storage devices. On its site 7dream.com offers a wide array of products that differ from the merchandise found at convenience stores. The most distinct difference is that food products are not included. The selection of products and categories available on the website seems to be focused in two ways. One is a customer group focus, with a clear focus on the main user group of convenience stores, young working single people. The other is a focus on certain product groups and here the company mainly offers products that have proved to be highly sellable over the internet by not requiring extensive customer advice. Following these principles the company offers books, CDs, software and computer-related articles, fashion accessories, character goods and automobile accessories. Content and services include travel, car rental, insurance and even health consulting. Customers are given the option to pay for purchases in the stores of Seven-Eleven. Smaller purchases can also be picked up in the stores or products can be delivered to customers' homes requiring customers to pay a delivery fee. Larger products are only delivered directly to customers' homes.

The main aim of the venture is therefore clearly not to increase the sales of the Seven-Eleven store network. Products and services are offered by companies Seven-Eleven is involved in, by partners in the 7dream.com venture and by other companies. The involvement of Seven-Eleven is symbolized mainly by titles like 7dream Rent-A-Car or Seven-Dream Insurance Shop. Nonetheless, the main suppliers of services and products are stated clearly. For car rentals, for example, the company basically offers links to several competing operators. The affiliation to the mother company of Seven-Eleven, Ito Yokado, can be seen only in a mail order business for larger items and a site for the promotion of computer games. Most of the offers available on the website are not exclusive to Seven-Eleven and can be accessed from other sites, too. This is even true for some of the services offered by companies in which Seven-Eleven owns an equity stake.

To increase loyalty by its customers, 7dream.com has also launched a membership club. It distributes a weekly newsletter which introduces special offers for members and also introduces new features of the online site. In probably its most innovative initiative the company also utilizes its site to interact with its users to develop new products. Users are asked to suggest new products for development. If the site's operators deem suggestions viable, then they create an online forum to discuss realization. Already, Seven-Eleven has succeeded in developing two new products based on suggestions by site users.

at-lawson.com

Lawson collaborates with the general trading company Mitsubishi in the development of e-commerce. The objectives are largely the same as those of Seven-Eleven. Areas of cooperation are the creation of e-commerce portals accessible by mobile phones, the organization of payment and delivery services through the store network, and the installation of ATMs and multimedia terminals in convenience stores. The website www.at-lawson.com as visited at the end of May 2002 offers a mix of products and services as well as information on the activities of Lawson. Under the title of Lawson Shopping Online the entrance page prominently leads to seven sections: character goods, CDs, Videos/DVDs, cosmetics, perfume, pet accessories and a hotel booking service. The selection is much narrower than that offered by Seven-Eleven and even more than at 7dream.com clearly shows targeted customers to be single women and men in their twenties and early thirties. Different payment and delivery options are offered, ranging from payment and next-day delivery at the store to credit card payment and home delivery. Apart from information on its products, Lawson offers information on the activities of Lawson itself in a section called Lawson Research Institute and also information on entertainment events with the aim of selling tickets for them. A special section targeting users with broadband access offers streamed videos with content produced by Lawson and informing about the activities of Lawson. The focus on informing about the activities of Lawson distinguishes the website from that of 7dream.com. Lawson obviously attempts a higher degree of integration of its web-based activities with those of its store networks. Trying to distinguish Lawson from other convenience store operators, the page supports Lawson's activities of developing products for exclusive sale in its stores. The company also uses its web page to motivate more shoppers to use the multimedia terminals it has installed in its stores. Lawson was the first company to introduce multimedia terminals on a large scale. Customers can use these machines to access the services offered by Lawson on its webpage. Based in stores, the company attempts, however, to use these terminals to provide additional information with a regional focus. This applies to special groceries that are not offered on the main webpage of Lawson at all, and also for local information on travel and entertainment events.

On the lower right-hand corner of its webpage, in a rather inconspicuous position, Lawson links to shopping pages offered by other companies. These stores all have in common offering their customers the possibility to pay for and sometimes even collect their merchandise in the Lawson stores. This service is made available to these companies by a separate venture, ECONTEXT. This company wants to provide online sellers with a comprehensive infrastructure. Business clients are able to choose from a number of service packages which start with the mere handling of payment transactions and gradually extend to product delivery, home page design, electronic data exchange with the provider, automated system updates and, finally, systems for the handling of all aspects of credit card payment. In using a prepaid card, the company aims to collect extensive information on customers by asking them to enter their age group and gender before entering their prepaid card information. At the end of May 2002 about 70 companies were making use of the services of Lawson in one way or another, among them prominent companies like HMV, Amway and operators of leading online shopping malls like Rakuten and Shopping@Nifty. While all of these companies made use of the payment option, only a small number of companies allowed customers to pick up merchandise at Lawson's stores. Many of the companies are, however, not using Lawson as their sole agent for collecting payments, but offer customers a choice among stores belonging to different convenience store chains.

famima.com (FamilyMart)

FamilyMart operates its e-commerce platform famima.com in collaboration with Itochu, NTT Data, Toyota, Dai Nippon Printing, JTB and PIA Corporation. The most interesting aspect of the collaboration is its approach to link the new platform closely to individual stores of the FamilyMart Network. Described as a unique e-franchise system, the franchisees of FamilyMart are provided with a virtual presence on the famima.com platform. When signing up for first orders or the membership club, customers are asked to designate a particular store in their neighborhood for delivery of goods. After signing in to the website a link to the website of the designated store appears. On their website, store owners can provide customers with individualized content. While initially being announced as a major innovation in e-commerce not much progress seems to have been made to realize the concept on a large scale. As of May 2002 only a very small number of stores participated and information on the individual pages of participants was limited to a few words of greeting by the store manager and a recommendation of certain products.

famima.com offers its product and services in seven different groups: food and beverages, DVD & CD & Games, books, fashion, toys, entertainment and services. As with other convenience stores, most of these products thereby fall into the categories that have had most success on the internet by being easy to handle and not requiring much explanation. Services are supplied mainly by collaborating companies. When visited, the selection in many of the sub-categories was overall not very deep, with a number of products cross-listed in several categories. Some of the categories offered did not have any content at all. Like Seven-Eleven and Lawson, FamilyMart is offering other companies the use of its store network for the payment of merchandise.

am/pm

The concept of am/pm Japan is quite different from that of other convenience stores. The company has not opted to extend its assortments through the introduction of e-commerce. On its very basic web page it offers information on services and products handled by its stores, together with some limited information on events for which it handles the ticket sales. Nonetheless, the company utilizes the new possibilities of the internet. It has come up with an online ordering system, Cyber Delice Delivery, for all products handled by its stores, with the promise to deliver these products within 60 minutes. Only offering this service in a limited area of Tokyo, the company has equipped its stores with additional personnel and a fleet of scooters for delivery.

The e-commerce involvement of convenience stores can be analyzed under a number of aspects. Questions have to be asked about the reasons underlying the companies' entry into e-commerce, patterns in regard to services and products offered, organizational principles underlying their engagement, and finally the successfulness of activities. While these issues will be addressed, it has to be pointed out that looking at developments at such an early stage is not without problems. Nonetheless, it is felt that, while some of the features described above might still be subject to change, Japanese companies have come up with interesting models of e-commerce that overall contribute to the discussion on the combination of e-commerce with existing retail businesses.

Too good to resist: factors behind the drive into e-commerce

While often being described as falling behind in international comparison, especially when compared with developments in the US, the development of e-commerce in Japan was still impressive, at least where developments on the supply side were concerned (Table 10.2). Between July 1995 and May 2000 the expansion of the internet in Japan was monitored in a databank by the Centre of Cyber Communities Initiative (CCCI), a joint venture between Keio University and Nomura Research Institute. Based on this databank, the first internet shopping site was opened by the operator of a Japanese noodle restaurant in 1994. As of May 2000, the databank was unfortunately discontinued afterwards, 25 621 sellers offered products and services on the internet, showing a development from only 66 stores in May 1995 to 1507 in 1996, 4750 in 1997, 10 211 in 1998 and 15 942 in 1999 (CCCI 2000:243). Among the stores entered in the database, the largest share of companies was active in foods and beverages (27.4 per cent), followed by culture and hobby-related sites (21.1 per cent), fashion (15.8 per cent), services (8.4 per cent) and computers and software (5.2 per cent). Approximately half of these sites were operated by companies classified as retail and wholesale businesses (47.5 per cent), followed by food producers with 11.2 per cent and providers of various services (8.3 per cent). Individual operators accounted for 5.6 per cent of all sites (CCCI 2000:244). With 83.9 per cent, the majority of shopping site operators ran their web-based ventures as a side business in addition to existing bricks-and-mortar businesses.

Compared with the development described above, the entry of most existing large retailers and convenience stores into e-commerce can be

Table 10.2   Leading e-commerce companies

Company name	Sales e-commerce (m. yen)		Goods	Start of operation
	FY 1999	FY 2000		
Sofmap Co.	3 000	10 000	PCs, peripherals	Dec 1995
Kokuyo Co.	2 000	–	Office supplies, stationery	Oct 1997
Askul Co.	1 680	–	General consumer goods	Mar 1997
Kinokuniya Co.	1 660	3 500	Books	Oct 1996
Senshukai Co.	1 494	5 000	General consumer goods	Jun 1997
Laox Co.	1 000	–	PCs, peripherals	Dec 1997
Nikkei Business Publication, Inc.	875	1 500	Books	Jun 1996
Book Service Co.	870	2 000	Books	May 1996
Sega Enterprises Ltd	710	1 300	Game software, toys	Apr 1999
Kojima Co.	600	800	PCs, peripherals	Mar 1996

Source: Based on *Nikkei Marketing Journal* 10 July 2000 (available on Nikkei Interactive: www.nikkei.co.jp).

described as quite late. Their eventual move into e-commerce can be attributed to various factors, among them the recognition of possible advantages of convenience stores in e-commerce, developments in their core businesses and finally interests of shareholders.

The development of e-commerce in Japan faced a number of obstacles that pointed to the involvement of convenience stores as a possible means to overcome these. Among the problems faced by early innovators in e-commerce in Japan were the following:

• Insufficient usage of credit cards in Japan, high charges by banks and credit card companies, and a general preference for cash transactions.
• Long working and commuting hours, narrowing time slots for home delivery.
• Comparatively late introduction of information technology into workplaces.
• Lack of facilities at workplaces to use company computers for private purposes.

Table 10.3 Concerns of Japanese consumers towards e-commerce

Concern voiced	%
Possibility of private data being given to third parties	73.4
Product delivered different from product advertised	
(taste, colour, quality)	72.7
Product is not delivered	52.8
Insufficient trust in internet store	47.8
Difficulty to correct mistakes after ordering	44.0
Unordered merchandise delivered and charged	43.8
Different product delivered	37.4
Possibility of higher prices	28.0
Time lag till delivery of product too long	27.4
Difficult to find product on the net	18.8

* More than one answer possible.
Source: Based on internet user survey (conducted 11/12/1999), Yûseishô (2000).

Table 10.4 Payment options offered by Japanese internet retailers

Payment options	No. of stores offering option	%
Registered cash mail	3 563	13.9
Postal transfer	8 932	34.9
Bank transfer	12 639	49.3
Cash on delivery	13 571	53.0
Credit card	2 397	9.4
Prepaid payment	71	0.3
Electronic payment	908	3.5
Others	1 311	5.1
n.a.	2 765	–

Source: Based on CCCI (2000:245).

Asked about their attitudes towards internet shopping, consumers voiced concerns about privacy, product quality and mistakes in the delivery and ordering process (Table 10.3).

In particular, the payment for products ordered on the internet proved to be a major obstacle for the expansion of e-commerce in Japan. Many consumers did not have credit cards and for retailers the processing of credit card payments was often complicated and time-consuming. This was also reflected in the databank of CCCI, where only a minority of retailers offered the possibility to pay by credit card (Table 10.4).

For many of the problems outlined above, the utilization of convenience store networks and their existing infrastructure in logistics and information technology as outposts and backbones for e-commerce seemed to present compelling solutions:

- Convenience stores directly located in the neighborhood of consumers' homes and workplaces could act as pickup and payment points for merchandise.
- Stores were already equipped with the technology to accept payments by customers and were using this technology to collect a wide range of utility charges.
- Japanese consumers associated convenience stores with convenience, speed, reliability, and efficiency, factors that are important in gaining consumers' trust and providing them with the necessary reassurance when trying out new ways of shopping.
- The customer base of convenience stores consisted of young but relatively affluent customers, many working single people, besides students and pupils. In addition, these groups were seen as being responsive to new ways of shopping and were also the first to adopt new technologies. Based on these qualities convenience stores have established a solid track record as a reliable testing ground for new products.
- Convenience store operators built up an advanced business-to-business infrastructure combining logistics and information technology that could also be utilized to support e-commerce.

While these points were already persuasive reasons for convenience store operators to try their hands at e-commerce, the overall situation of convenience stores at the end of the 1990s provided additional motivation. As already pointed out, the situation of convenience stores and operating companies at the end of the 1990s became more difficult. In many areas, saturation led to a stagnation of sales for existing stores, and this also began to reflect in balance sheets and share prices of the network operators. Companies were thereby looking for ways to increase traffic in existing stores as well as new opportunities to raise their revenues and thereby their share prices (*Chain Store Age* 15 January 2000).

Finally, the engagement of convenience stores into e-commerce was also driven by changes in ownership. As already mentioned, general trading companies took control over two of the three largest convenience store chains. General trading companies bought the stakes not only to strengthen the position of their affiliated wholesale operations but also to complement their already substantial interests in telecommunication and information services, and have since been putting these resources to work to develop the presence of convenience stores in e-commerce.

Different patterns and objectives of e-commerce initiatives

The examples given above have already pointed out differences in the strategies of convenience store operators. Three main underlying objectives and related strategies can be identified:

1. e-commerce and provision of information to support the existing store network;
2. e-commerce as a separate extension of the current program; and
3. the internet as an opportunity to provide services to other businesses in the form of an e-commerce infrastructure.

The first strategy regards activities on the web as supporting the existing store network. Activities are used to increase store traffic, raise store loyalty, create new sources of revenue for franchisees or attract new customer groups. Consequently, operators of the website closely link their e-commerce strategies with existing stores, promote new products on their websites and point to the possibility of home delivery from their stores for the existing product range as well as store pick-up and payments for items that are not handled in the stores themselves. The e-franchise concept of FamilyMart that aims at providing information to customers linked to stores in their neighbourhood clearly pursues these objectives. The home meal delivery system of Seven-Eleven also points in this direction. Elderly people can use the convenience stores for ordering and paying for meals and this service might thereby contribute to overcome the dependence of convenience stores on younger customers (*Chain Store Age* 15 January 2000). The introduction of multimedia terminals can also be seen in this way. It allows access to online services for customers that do not have access otherwise. Based on this strategy, convenience stores could eventually become customized interfaces between local communities and the virtual world.

The second strategy is the expansion of revenue sources for the core company beyond existing revenues from the operation of convenience stores. E-commerce is regarded as a separate venture by offering a wide range of services and products that are not available in the stores.

To realize these strategies companies leverage their experience in marketing and market research, their strong brand name and also their existing databases of customers. This strategy seems to be pursued mainly by Seven-Eleven with its separate venture 7dream.com. This business model might still contribute to convenience stores by increasing customer traffic through the option to pay and collect merchandise at stores. However, the e-business side appears to be largely independent and might become increasingly so with home delivery systems already advanced in Japan and safe online payment options quickly developing.

The third strategy aims at the creation of an infrastructure for other companies to sell products online. Other companies are given access to the advanced infrastructure of convenience stores. In its most advanced stage, sellers could source the operation of their whole e-commerce infrastructure to convenience store operators and might thereby be able to have a sophisticated e-commerce infrastructure at comparatively low initial costs. For convenience stores, opening their infrastructure to other companies not only increases revenues through fees charged from sellers and buyers; it also creates scale economies for their own services and the infrastructure serving their store networks. In offering these services companies build on their existing logistics, store and information networks. In addition, they can also point to their relatively unbiased position in the current distribution structure of Japan. Owing to their small size, they handle only a comparatively small assortment of basic products and services, allowing for the addition of a wide range of web-based services by other companies.

As has been described for a number of other innovations, the concepts advanced by Japanese convenience store companies have initially met with a lot of skepticism. Critics have asked how big a change the e-commerce ventures of convenience stores would bring to the so far mostly successful model of the Japanese convenience stores and have come up with a number of arguments, some of these focusing on the difficulties of integrating e-commerce and brick-and-mortar strategies in a franchise setting. The following issues were brought up:

1. A lack of space in convenience stores. Space for the storage of products for pickup, multimedia and banking terminals has to be created and franchisees might be reluctant to sacrifice space that could otherwise be used for the presentation of products (*Gekiryû Magazine* June 2000a).
2. Problems in the distribution of tasks and responsibilities. Despite constant reminders on the web pages that stores act only as agents handling delivery and payment, customers may still hold stores

responsible if problems arise. In a fierce competition for customers, store owners might find it hard to reject customers who demand refunds or to return merchandise.

3. The increasing complexity of store operations. As already pointed out, convenience stores have developed their systems to a point where they can be basically operated by part-timers and fringe employees without constant supervision. This has been described as one of the major achievements of this store format (Ribault 1999). E-commerce might thereby on the one hand increase the customer flow; on the other hand it might result in the need to intensify the attention given to each customer and store owners might have to invest more in additional personnel and their training.

4. Distribution of profits and costs between franchisees and network operators (Katô 2000, *Nikkei Business* 28 February 2000). Store operators will have to perform some tasks that they will not be reimbursed for. In addition, some stores might profit more from online activities than others. So far, network operators have gone to great lengths to avoid inequality between franchisees.

While often seen as a relatively simple addition to the convenience store, the introduction of e-commerce can thereby result in a profound alteration in the business model of convenience stores, with changes ranging from store layout to franchiser–franchisee relationships and qualification of employees. Compared with other uses of internet sites, the organization of e-commerce in a franchise setting therefore complicates the situation and forces network organizers to come up with solutions quickly and prove that their models will have positive effects for not only investors but also for franchisees.

Convenience store companies are not pursuing their e-commerce strategies on their own (Table 10.5). The list of companies involved in their e-commerce ventures is impressive. This is especially the case for Seven-Eleven, which in organizing its e-commerce activities again demonstrated its preferences and capabilities for collaboration (*Chain Store Age* 15 March 2000). The companies in Seven-Eleven's venture bring together knowledge of hardware development, systems design, consumer goods and service marketing, project management and web page design. In the distribution of books and automobile-related services the activities also include Softbank, active not only in e-commerce but also the operator of the Yahoo platform and finance venture companies and thereby one of the most active players in Japan's internet economy.

Table 10.5   Organization of e-commerce

Ventures (projects)	Partners (ownership share in ventures, %)	Business area
Seven-Eleven		
7dream.com	Seven-Eleven (51), NEC (13), NRI (13), Sony (6.5), Sony Marketing (6.5), Mitsui (6), JTB (2), Kinotrope (2)	E-commerce infrastructure centring on CVS, provision of key services and products, provision of payment services for other companies
E-Shopping Books	Softbank E-Commerce (50), Seven Eleven (30), Tohan (10), Yahoo Japan (10)	Online bookstore
CarPoint	Softbank Commerce (45), Microsoft (37), Seven Eleven (10), Yahoo Japan (8)	Provision of automobile related products and services
PlayStation.com (Japan)	Sony Computer Entertainment, Bandai, Enix, Culture Convenience Club, NTTDocomo, Capcom, Koei, Konami, Square, DigiCube, Namco, Happinet, Seven Eleven	E-commerce related to PlayStation
Seven Meal Service	Seven Eleven (60), Nichii Gakkan (30), Mitsui (5), NEC (5)	Home and store delivery of precooked meals
Lawson		
Lawson E-Planning	Mitsubishi Corp (49) Lawson (51)	Incubator for e-business, collaboration with partners from other industries and collaboration with venture companies
EContext (www.econ.ne.jp)	Lawson (46), Digital Garage (34), Toyo Information Systems (10), Mitsubishi Corp. (10)	Open platform for provision of payment and delivery services (provider for other convenience store chains, total 20 000 outlets)
I-Convenience, Inc.	Lawson (51) Matsushita (18), NTTDocomo (13), Mitsubishi Corp (18)	E-kiosk – Provision of services for mobile internet users
FamilyMart		
www.famima.com	FamilyMart (50.5) Itochu (14.5), NTT Data (10), Toyota	Operation of e-commerce franchise system,

Table 10.5 (Continued)

Ventures (projects)	Partners (ownership share in ventures, %)	Business area
	(10), Dai Nippon Printing (5), JTB (5), Pia Corporation (5)	introduction of multi-media terminal in stores
E-Plat	FamilyMart (35), Circle K Japan (25), Sunkus & Associates (10), Three F (10), Ministop (10), Toyota (5), NTT (5)	Platform for e-commerce and contents provision

Source: Author's compilation based on web pages of companies and press releases.

The approach of Lawson and FamilyMart is based heavily on their relationships with general trading companies, though they have still attracted some prominent partners such as Matsushita, Dai Nippon Printing, NTTDocomo and Toyota. Trading companies have been investing very actively in IT and multi-media infrastructure with the aim of developing this area as a major new pillar besides their traditional trading activities (Nakatani 2001). The engagement of general trading companies in this area is, however, not without problems. Operators will have to balance carefully the desire of general trading companies to utilize and develop their capabilities with the need to source the best capabilities to compete with the network put together by other competitors, especially Seven-Eleven.

While the internet has often been hailed as place where new companies can easily challenge established players, the activities of convenience stores appear to reinforce the position of incumbent companies. With the exclusion of car parts and books, a field where Seven-Eleven collaborates with Softbank and challenges existing retailers, in other areas such as travel, services for the elderly, digital content provision or insurance the situation is different. Established companies collaborate with convenience stores to firmly establish themselves in e-commerce. While the internationalization of the Japanese economy and industries has been much discussed over the last decade, it is interesting to notice that foreign companies do not seem to be involved in a significant way.

The difficult road to success

E-commerce is a very new area in Japanese distribution and it is therefore still too early to evaluate the success of the strategies of convenience stores. So far, the area where convenience store operators are most successful is the collection of payments for transactions done on the internet. A large number of companies have subscribed to these services, among them the operator of the largest virtual shopping mall in Japan, Rakuten, with more than 5000 store tenants. At the same time, however, these shopping malls are seriously competing with convenience stores, often offering a wider range of products and having a higher frequency of visitors. Yahoo Shopping is linked to the Yahoo search engine and email services, and Yahoo also operates the leading auction site in Japan, offering an impressive 3.5 million articles as of April 2002. Rakuten has taken over the infoseek search engine.

In contrast, e-commerce sales of convenience stores are described as sluggish. Companies had to revise their objectives. 7dream.com only managed sales of 3 billion yen in the fiscal year 2000 instead of the 7 billion yen originally expected; sales of other companies are described as equally disappointing. This result has led some convenience store companies to reconsider their strategies. Seven-Eleven and FamilyMart have changed their plans to set up multimedia terminals in all of their stores and have instead focused on the upgrading of their merchandise. In addition, 7dream.com has listed some of the store concepts it has originally developed for its website also with other shopping malls. The site of Lawson has undergone a major revamp. The company now seems to pursue a more integrated approach to its web activities with the website focusing equally on the unique products and services offered by the brick-and-mortar operations of Lawson as well as products sold over the internet. In the medium run, however, the e-commerce ventures of convenience stores might yet become successful. Alternative sophisticated payment and, especially, home delivery systems have yet to prove their cost advantages over the store delivery and collection method. Home delivery of small quantities can be extremely costly, and while many companies of the e-commerce sector are currently shouldering costs and accepting losses on home deliveries to build up their customer base, this policy seems to be hardly sustainable in the long run. Including the customer in the value chain by letting him pick up merchandise at stores or other distribution centres, and sharing the existing infrastructure of convenience stores, might therefore prove to be a viable and sustainable alternative under cost considerations.

Part IV
Conclusions

11
Half a Century of Dynamics in Japanese Retailing

This book has looked at innovations and dynamics in Japanese retailing over a period of fifty years. During this period Japanese retail companies have continuously shown their innovative strength. What started with the introduction of new techniques has developed into a wide portfolio of retail formats. During the 1990s these formats are increasingly being supplemented with sophisticated support systems that strengthen the position of retailers in the value chain between manufacturers and consumers. In the following, the process underlying these developments will be taken up again and summarized as follows. First, developments in Japanese retailing will be contrasted with the theoretical work on dynamics in retail and distribution systems. Then patterns of innovative behaviour in Japanese distribution will be identified and an evaluation made of factors influencing developments.

It was shown in the introductory chapter that the discussion of cyclical phenomena for a long time dominated the study of developments in retailing. Later, this discussion changed to a discussion of the general underlying factors driving dynamics in retailing; nonetheless, it has been pointed out that – though not universally applicable and being only of little prognostic value – cyclical developments have been observed for a number of major retail formats in the US and Europe (Goldman 1975:54, Brown 1990:144). An overview on developments in Japanese retailing over a period of roughly 50 years thereby recommends at least a short look at developments in Japan from the perspective of cyclical theories.

The retail format, as well as its operators, that has been given the most attention in this book is the general superstore, and its development seems to closely resemble the pattern pointed out in McNair's Wheel of Retailing theory. The main underlying factors for its initial success during the late 1950s were comparatively low prices based on a reduction of operating costs through the introduction of self-service, volume sales of fast-moving articles and the lack of services and amenities. Near the end of the 1960s companies moved to the second stage. Stores were enlarged, amenities added and assortments upgraded through the inclusion of new categories and more items. Soon stores were characterized as having lost some of their original price aggressiveness and their operators criticized for not being able to curb and control costs. A major reorganization of corporate structures was demanded. During the third stage, from the early 1980s on, operators of general merchandising stores focused mainly on the addition of services and amenities. During the second half of the 1980s, some companies even developed their concepts in the direction of department stores. The massive emergence of discounters from the end of the 1980s then led into the fourth stage, where other companies and other formats began to fill the position vacated by the general superstores by entering the market with formats based on price aggressiveness.

The development of the general superstore can also be described in terms of the life cycle model, proposed for retailing mainly by Davidson *et al.* (1976). The introductory period of this store format was during the late 1950s. The general superstore differentiated itself from the dominating narrow-line oriented retailers mainly through price aggressiveness but also through wide assortments. Strong sales growth was characteristic of the growth period until the early 1970s. Profitability and sales growth reached a maximum during this period. However, the concept of the general superstore was increasingly copied by other operators. At the same time, companies from the traditional retail sector reacted by lowering prices and increasing their competitiveness through the organization of voluntary chains. In addition, the cost structure of operators of general superstores changed. The declining sales many operators experienced in their stores at the end of the 1970s can be interpreted as overcapacity due to a saturation of the market in many locations. Further, new companies emerged with new retail formats such as home centres, discount stores and food supermarkets and quickly gained in strength. From the 1980s on, companies therefore sought to relaunch their original format by developing new concepts that deviated from the original ones and targeted a younger customer base. These strategies prevented companies and formats from slipping into the next stage characterized by total loss of competitiveness. During the 1990s, however, the cycle continued with general superstores showing a rapid loss of sales and profitability and some major operators even being forced into bankruptcy.

While the application of cyclical theory to the Japanese general superstore as above has some merit, and we can find developments resembling cases that have been described for other countries, this approach nonetheless has severe limitations. Being of a highly affirmative nature, it simplifies developments and neglects the importance of environmental conditions and entrepreneurial initiative. This can be shown by looking at some environmental factors as well as developments of other retail formats.

The environmental factor that has received the most attention for Japan has been the regulation of retailing through distribution policy. In fact, most developments could be described in relation to this factor: regulations for department store operators hindered their expansion from the second half of the 1950s on, but at the same time protected stores in existing locations, encouraging operators to move away from aggressive pricing strategies. This policy promoted unintentionally the introduction and expansion of new retail formats and techniques by creating a supply–demand gap for discounting stores and stores with wide assortments. This demand was recognized by superstore operators, who quickly developed their stores in the direction of general superstores. From the 1970s on, this led to countermeasures by the authorities fearing for the well-being of smaller retailers. As had been the case for department stores, superstore operators condemned the new governmental policies, but at the same time enjoyed protection of their existing stores from the threat of new discounters. During the 1980s distribution policy favoured the coexistence of large and small retail store, which allowed large store operators to build stores that abandoned price aggressiveness for sheer size, amenities and services. At the same time, policies unintentionally favored medium-scale specialty discounters that did not need to fear competition from large stores. In addition, the regulative environment favored the emergence and rapid development of convenience stores by channeling the resources of general merchandisers into the development of this format and hindering operators of food superstores from adjusting their opening hours. Not being able to grow in their core area, general merchandising companies also diversified into non-retail related areas. During the 1990s, retail policy was relaxed. Unsure about the length of this window of opportunity, companies entered into ambitious expansion plans that not only led to a drastic intensification of retail competition but also resulted in the eventual downfall of a number of once-leading companies. In this sense, retail policy also seems to be able to explain the major developments in Japanese retailing; however, similar explanations highlighting singular factors could be drawn up for consumer conduct or the situation of procurement markets.

For other Japanese retail formats and companies, cyclical retail theory seems to be less applicable and this is not only due to their shorter span of development. In the following, developments will be summarized, but in such a way as to go beyond the reference to cyclical theory by highlighting general patterns that seem to be noteworthy to developments in Japan.

The first development that has to be raised here is the position of food superstores in Japanese retailing. These could establish themselves in the market as independent retail formats only after their operators had overcome the preference of consumers for fresh food and the subsequent problems of procurement, the handling of merchandise and the organization of human resources. These problems have caused the overall development of superstore retailing in Japan to be driven by operators of general superstores rather than by those of food superstores as has been the case in other countries. The establishment of food superstores as a competitive retail format in its own right happened only during the 1970s and was based not on aggressive pricing policies but on the quality of products and assortments offered. With the number of food superstores increasing rapidly during the 1990s in a deregulated environment, price has become more important. However, the activation of pricing policies required major changes in the organization of supply chain management.

Other formats developed following examples from overseas and often they were introduced among skepticism about their appropriateness to the Japanese market. Among these formats were the convenience store and the home centre. The original idea for home centres was taken from the American retail market. However, the concept was developed pragmatically from a DIY orientation to a focus on general household goods with a wide and often shallow assortment, sometimes even paired with a discount orientation. Only later, when consumer needs had developed further, did some home centre operators develop concepts with a closer resemblance to original models.

The convenience store was a format that was not established on the basis of an active pricing policy. At first sight, convenience stores went through a process of trading up, with the number of services introduced increasing steadily. However, most of these services were charged directly to consumers and thereby contributed to profitability and revenues in their own right. At the same time, convenience stores even managed to lower prices of some of their products. These achievements are due mainly to the continuous innovativeness of convenience store operators, in contrast to cyclical theories that often assume a spread of inertia and inactiveness in growing organizations. This continuous innovativeness can be attributed largely to the entrepreneurial strength of one company, Seven-Eleven, but has also to be related to the organizational characteristics of convenience store chains, these not only having to satisfy customers and owners but operators also competing to keep and attract franchisees. Nonetheless, the convenience store at the turn of the millennium found itself in an increasingly threatened position with the market having reached a certain degree of saturation and facing increasing competition from other retail formats. The drive into e-commerce activities brought a new wave of innovation into the sector and might eventually result in significant alteration of the business model of convenience stores in Japan. While innovative activities in many regards were focusing mainly on format design, this was not the case for convenience stores. Here, success could be accomplished only through constant innovations along the whole value chain between producer and consumer. As such, operators of convenience stores became the early forerunners in the development of comprehensive systems, supplying other retailers with indigenous models of supply chain management and the use of information technology, apart from the widely studied but sometimes not applicable cases of retail development outside Japan.

The development of retail concepts comprising comprehensive support systems intensified during the late 1980s and 1990s, with a number of companies in different sectors not only coming up with innovative sales concepts but also supporting these with innovations in product development, category management, information technology and logistics. Many of the stores opened during this period can be characterized as category killers, though some of them built their concepts around certain themes such as one-price shopping, simple and ecologically conscious design, or unisex casual clothing. With their concepts they challenged existing retailers, especially large superstores that were challenged to catch up with these stores in the above-mentioned capabilities.

The introduction of new formats or techniques into Japanese retailing, therefore, usually followed a pattern of development that can be divided into different phases. The first of these was the introduction of a new retail format, often based on American models. The introduction is often described as untimely or precipitate, a characterization often justified later to a certain extent by the need to adjust the format or technique to the Japanese market. This phase of adaptation was of varying length, and took longer for home centres or food superstores than for the convenience store. During this period, significant changes were made to the original concepts, reaching a degree where the final result might be difficult to trace back to the original role model. Only after this phase could retail formats enter into a phase of growth, with the development thereafter being subject to the individual capabilities of the company to sustain competitiveness in an ever-changing environment.

New techniques were transferred to Japan consciously and by different mechanisms. The place to look for new inspiration has mostly been the United States. During the early stages it was the interests of an American manufacturer of cash registers as well as the activities of publishers of Japanese industry journals and consultancy companies that informed the market about the state of retailing in the United States. Japanese retailers were educated on certain techniques in seminars and study trips to the United States, and they introduced enthusiastically what they had seen into their own stores. From there on, they often became role models of change for other Japanese retailers in their own right. In a situation of general growth of retail markets, and also in striving for general recognition of their contributions within the growth of the Japanese economy, innovative retailers collaborated in the introduction of new technologies by sharing their knowledge with other companies. The introduction of convenience stores during the 1970s introduced a different mechanism. Here, knowledge was acquired through the conclusion of franchise agreements with American partners, though this did not hinder Japanese companies from coming up with their own solutions and refinements.

The straight transmission of new techniques through foreign direct investment became important only during the 1990s. While some of these activities by foreign retailers recorded substantial and fast success, frequently built on the flexibility of retailers to deviate from their original intentions, others, often those that stuck closely to their original models did not do so well or failed altogether. Even those cases (for example, Safeway, Boots, Wellsave, Carrefour) left their mark on Japanese retailing, though. The announcement of their intention to enter the Japanese market or, often enough, just their showing subtle signs of interest in it, usually led to an intensive discussion of their concepts in Japan, with domestic players preparing for the arrival of the new competitors by adapting those features of competitors that they deemed appropriate for their domestic market.

Overall, innovation in Japanese retailing saw a pattern that moved from the introduction of certain techniques to a focus on retail formats and consumer-orientated strategies and finally to the creation of comprehensive systems. Within this change, the long-lasting preoccupation with retail formats is especially noteworthy. Markin and Duncan (1981:65), introducing the evolutionary approach to retail theory, noted that in regard to the development of retailing, change and not preservation of the status quo should be regarded as normal: 'What is, is wrong.' Japanese companies certainly prescribed to this position. As outlined, Japanese companies showed a relatively low inclination to standardize concepts nationwide and to sustain a certain format design over a longer period of time. With the exception of convenience stores, newly opened stores usually showed a number of new features, and old stores were left in their original state, leading to a high degree of diversity of stores operated by the same company. Indeed, observers with a knowledge of the US retail markets have continuously criticized inconsistencies in the format development strategies of Japanese retail companies – not only regarding the processes surrounding the introduction of convenience stores into Japan but also in the ongoing discussion about discount stores there (see for example Uchiro 1983, Miya 1987, Ishihara 1990, Goldman 2000).

The underlying reason for this pragmatic handling of format development can be seen mainly in the sales and revenue orientation of companies. Most companies concentrated on sales growth and in that sense the preference for closely adapting store concepts to locations and perceived changes in consumer preferences was only rational. Strategies thereby resembled the intensive product proliferation strategy of Japanese consumer goods manufacturers that also strove for sales growth and market domination. In this way, Japanese retailers have also come under criticism during the 1990s for neglecting aspects of efficiency and profitability. The overall characterization of the innovative activities of Japanese retailers as pragmatic also corresponds to general results in the adaptation of new techniques into Japan. Moritz (1992:168–75) states that in this process actors were always goal-oriented and less inclined to follow certain set principles or theories. Certain useful features, rules or aspects were adapted without too much concern for consistency with the original theoretical concept. The pragmatic stance of retailers can, however, also be attributed to the uncertain state of their environment that required them to sustain a high level of flexibility. Retail policies were not only prone to constant change, but also regulated stores on an individual basis. The replacement of outdated stores with new stores in the same or an alternative location was made nearly impossible.

In this sense, entrepreneurial initiative and conduct did not happen in a vacuum, and in the following the main underlying environmental factors will be summarized once more. Factors driving change in Japanese retailing have been analyzed on different levels. The most direct influence was exerted by the goals and decisions of entrepreneurs and companies to introduce into the market, or further develop, certain techniques or whole retail formats and systems. In doing so, they enjoyed different levels of freedom that were determined by the behaviour of transaction partners and competitors in sales or procurement markets and also the situation in the external environment.

The introduction of new techniques and formats in the US and Europe has often been associated with the initiative of certain entrepreneurs or companies. These innovators have often managed to build up impressive companies with a large number of sales branches within a short time. It has been shown that in Japan the situation was no different. Japanese retailing has continuously produced innovative entrepreneurs. The objectives of these entrepreneurs often went beyond pure aspects of sales growth or profitability and extended to a general propagation of merchandising and corporate philosophies. The importance of entrepreneurs has to be valued especially highly since many of their innovative activities were not greeted by the markets with open arms. This is certainly not a fact special to Japan; however, it has been pointed out that a number of formats were introduced into Japan based on foreign models but under drastically different and often less favourable environmental conditions. While some of these concepts have been described as inconsistent by domestic and foreign critics, most were nonetheless the result of painstaking processes of trial and error before becoming finally accepted by the market.

Among factors that influenced innovative behaviour, the discussion in this book has to a certain degree highlighted Japanese distribution policy. Other factors, however, have also been described in detail and here innovators enjoyed more freedom. This is especially true for the situation of the consumer markets in regard to the existence of competitors and consumer behaviour. Taking a dialectic perspective on retail development in Japan leads to the conclusion that innovative retailers had mainly to differentiate themselves from the mass of small, family-led stores. The difference from other large-store concepts was a lesser concern. In contrast to a large number of small, narrow-line retailers a lack of stores existed that offered multiple lines. General superstores introduced this concept in suburban locations and thereby competed with smaller traditional retailers rather than with department stores. Another innovative format, the convenience store, had developed in the US as an antithesis to large superstores, but in Japan developed rather as an antithesis to small traditionally run shops.

Innovative initiatives were also promoted by the general situation of consumer markets. Especially during the 1960s, Japanese retailers faced a growing market. New suburban areas developed and presented themselves as locations for new large-scale superstores. New families showed demand patterns that could largely be met by general superstores, promoting the development of this format. Later, needs became more specific and contributed to the growth of home centres and other category-oriented stores. Other store formats profited from the increased segmentation of consumer markets, such as the convenience store that catered to the specific needs of students and single people. Overall, consumers responded positively to new shopping opportunities; ties to traditional retail stores seemed to be not as tight as often they were said to be. Another question, however, increasingly asked during and since the 1990s, is how successfully operators managed to adapt their existing formats to changing consumer needs. While some newcomers came up with innovative new concepts that proved their worth in a time of prolonged economic stagnation, established retailers are struggling to change concepts from traditional mass merchandising to ones that fulfill the needs of increasingly diversified, selective and sophisticated consumers.

Another factor discussed in detail throughout this book has been the situation in procurement markets. The predictions of the early 1960s that the emergence of new retail formats would necessarily change the power relationships in distribution channels did not come true. On the contrary, in the light of changes in the retail sector manufacturers became even more inclined to increase their control over downstream distribution channels. Companies in large-scale retailing that had gradually changed their focus from price aggressiveness to the expansion and upgrading of assortments began to value stable supplier relationships, including the various supportive measures offered by wholesalers and manufacturers in regard to financing and merchandising, more than continuous battles to lower purchasing prices. While new retail concepts were regularly introduced into the market with a discount policy based on alternative routes of procurements, the limitations of these channels soon became obvious after companies entered into chain development and operators had to switch to regular channels. The existing distribution structure reached its limit, however, when it was faced with the needs of a small-scale retail format, the convenience store. Convenience store operators recognized the strategic importance of this area from the beginning and gradually drove change in their procurement markets. During the 1990s, wholesalers, manufacturers and retailers alike came under pressure to change the established situation in procurement markets. Advancements in information and logistics technology as well as crumbling profits and revenues called for a new distribution of functions along the value chain. New relationships emerged that led to various solutions to the reorganization of distribution and procurement channels. The variety of competing solutions had come to characterize Japanese distribution at the end of the 1990s.

Since the regulative environment has already been mentioned repeatedly in this conclusion it will only be mentioned briefly again. While the high importance of distribution policy for Japanese retail development has often been denied, the drastic developments in the Japanese retail landscape after the liberalization of regulations should bring an end to this dispute. Regulation has obviously hindered the development of large store retailing in Japan. It has, however, been shown that the consequences of regulation were far more complex than a mere suppression of the opening of large stores. In the light of regulation, some Japanese retailers demonstrated their innovative capabilities by channeling resources to the development of smaller formats and using to their own advantage the protection that the law granted not only to small retailers but also to established stores. The many problems established stores and retailers have faced since the 1990s can in this sense also be described as an over-reliance on and over-adaptation to the stipulations of previous regulations.

Finally, the developments in Japanese retailing can be seen within the overall development of the Japanese economy, management and industrial organizations. So far, the study of Japanese distribution and retailing has been largely an isolated area, discussing issues closely related to retailing such as format development or supplier relationships but mostly neglecting to establish linkages and parallels with and to studies on other areas of Japanese economy and business. While this book has also to a large extent focused on issues of retail management and development, nevertheless, continuous strong charismatic leadership by founders, quick growth and a growth focus, the urge to diversify and close inter-company relationships and bank-centred corporate governance and financing are characteristics of the general Japanese business setup. Owing to developments during the 1990s, many of the once-established findings on Japanese management and economic development are currently undergoing a process of reevaluation. Many of these can also be applied to retailing. For example, it has been asked whether growth in the manufacturing sector has really been based on productivity increases or whether it has been, rather, due to capital input because of the close relationship between banks and their clients. The same can be asked for the retail sector, where decisive and ambitious growth was not always based on clear developments in customer needs. Another point increasingly questioned, and also applicable to the retail sector, is the still frequently assumed dichotomy between large enterprises and small enterprises, or the so-called traditional and modern sectors. Large enterprises were often seen as forward looking and modern, and small ones characterized as traditional and remaining in a state of overall dependency. During the 1990s and since, however, it has been many of the larger companies that, owing to traditional features in management and organization, have been slow to change while many smaller companies have been quick to adjust to changes in the environment.

Around the turn of the millennium, entrepreneurs in Japanese retailing thereby face an environment significantly different from that faced by their predecessors. With regard to distribution policy, procurement markets, consumer conduct and also aspects of corporate financing and governance, a convergence with the situation in other highly developed countries can certainly be seen. Nonetheless, a degree of difference remains, as the many foreign retailers that are currently trying their hand in the Japanese market will readily certify. Through the increased flow of retail techniques not only to Japan but also increasingly from it, this difference will continue to be a source of innovation in its own right.

References

Abe, Yoshifumi (1993) 'Hyakkaten, kakushin ni idomu' [Department stores, striving for reform], in Nikkei Ryûtsû Shinbun (ed.), *Ryûtsû gendaishi* [Modern history of distribution], Tokyo: Nihon Keizai Shinbunsha, pp. 40–56.

Abe, Yukio (1993) '1992 nendo CVS saishin chôsa deetashû' [Latest data collection on convenience stores, 1992], *Shokuhin shôgyô* (special issue), October: Konbiniensu sutoa no subete [Everything about convenience stores], pp. 25–42.

Abe, Yukio (1994) 'Kyôteki no buki wa manabitori jakuten wa kô semeyo' [Studying the weapons of the opponent and attacking the weaknesses], *Shôgyôkai*, no. 3, pp. 39–42.

Achrol, Ravi Singh and Philip Kotler (1999) 'Marketing in the new economy', *Journal of Marketing*, vol. 63 (special issue 1999), pp. 146–163.

Agergård, E., P.A. Olson and J. Allpass, (1970) 'The interaction between retailing and the urban centre structure: a theory of spiral movement,' *Environment and Planning*, vol. 2, pp. 55–71.

Anonymous (1987) 'Tokubetsu kikaku – Nikkei kouri chôsa 10 nenkan bunseki – ôgata kourigyô, seichô kara seijuku e no kiseki' [Special project – analysis of the last 10 years of Nikkei's retail survey – large retail companies: on track from growth to maturity], *Kikan shôhi to ryûtsû*, no. 39, pp. 12–90.

Aoki, Masahiko, Hugh Patrick and Paul Sheard (1994) 'The Japanese main bank system: an overview', in Masahiko Aoki and Hugh Patrick (eds), *The Japanese Main Bank System: Its Relevance for Developing and Transforming Economies*, Oxford University Press, pp. 3–50.

Arakawa, Yûkichi (1992) 'Konbiniensu sutoa' [Convenience store], in Yûkichi Arakawa (ed.), *Ryûtsû kôzô, shôgyô keiei oyobi ryûtsû seisaku* [Distribution structure, retail management and distribution policy], Tokyo: Chikura Shobô, pp. 91–118 (article originally published in *Shôgyô ronshû*, vol. 19 (1974), no. 3/4).

Araya, Masaru (1973) 'Konbiniensu sutoa wa hatashite dokuritsu suupaa no "kyû-seishu" tari eru ka' [Can the convenience store, as expected, be the saviour of independent supermarket companies?], *Hanbai kakushin* (special issue), pp. 260–263.

Arita, Hideaki (1994) 'Wan furoa 1300 tsubo no fuudo & doraggu ni chôsen' [Striving towards the 1300 tsubo sized food and drug store], *Hanbai kakushin*, March, pp. 63–65.

Asahi shinbun, 7 April 1998, 'Ôte kusen, jimoto no chûken kentô – suupaa gyôkai' [Supermarket industry – fierce battle with leading companies, local medium-sized companies put up a good fight].

Asuka, Shunichi (1998) *Sôgô shôsharon* [Theory of the general trading company], Tokyo: Chuô Keizaisha.

Atsumi, Shunichi (1971) 'Chotto matte konbiniensu sutoa' [Just a minute, convenience store], *Hanbai kakushin*, no. 10 (October), pp. 111–115.

Atsumi, Shunichi (1976) *Kourigyô seichô no himitsu* [The secret of growth of the retail industry], Tokyo: Kawade Shobô.

Atsumi, Shunichi (1993) 'Nihongata suupaa sutoa wa katoki no foomatto da' [The Japanese superstore in a period of change], *Hanbai kakushin*, September, pp. 26–33.

Atsumi, Shunichi (2000) 'Hikari kagayaku sai sentan cheen no hensetsu to zasetsu' [The betrayal and collapse of the shiniest spearhead chain], *Hanbai kakushin*, April, pp. 18–23.

Azuma, Toru (1993) 'Nihon ni okeru daikibo kouri tenpo kisei no genryû' [The origin of regulations for large stores], *Kitami Daigaku ronshû*, vol. 29, pp. 49–88.

Bartlett, Brent L. (2000) 'Product specialization among Japanese wholesalers: the role of policy and consequences for market access,' in Michael R. Czinkota and Masaaki Kotabe (eds), *Japanese Distribution Strategy*, London: Business Press/Thomson Learning, pp. 164–178.

Beem, Eugene R. and A.R. Oxenfeldt (1966) 'A diversity theory for market processes in food retailing', *Journal of Farm Economics*, vol. 48, no. 3, pp. 53–95.

Brown, Stephen (1987) 'Institutional change in retailing: a review and synthesis', *European Journal of Marketing*, vol. 21, no. 6, pp. 5–36.

Brown, Stephen (1988) 'The wheel of the Wheel of Retailing', *International Journal of Retailing*, vol. 3, no. 1, pp. 16–37.

Brown, Stephen (1990) 'The Wheel of Retailing: past and future', *Journal of Retailing*, vol. 66, no. 2, pp. 143–149.

CCCI (Centre for Cyber Communities Initiative) (2000) *CCCI katsudô hôkokusho* [Report on activities by CCCI], Centre for Cyber Communities Initiative.

Chain Store Age, 15 January 2000, 'E no nami ni noru' [Riding the e-commerce wave], pp. 24–37.

Chain Store Age, 15 March 2000, 'Konbiniensu sutoa no EC senryaku' [E-commerce strategies of convenience stores], pp. 82–88.

Che, Yon Fun (1999) Onwaado Kashiyama ni okeru itaku torihiki hôshiki to tsuika seisan hôshiki no senryakuteki hokansei [Strategic complementarities between the method of consignment sales and the method of supplementary manufacturing as for Onward Kashiyama], in Fumio Kondô and Yasunaga Wakabayashi (eds), *Nihon kigyô no maaketingushi* [Marketing history of Japanese businesses], Tokyo: Dôbunkan Shuppan, pp. 130–152.

Czinkota, Michael R. and Masaaki Kotabe (eds) (2000) *Japanese Distribution Strategy*, London: Thomson Learning.

Daiee (Kabushiki Kaisha Daiee Shashi Hensanshitsu) (1992) *For the CUSTOMERS – Daiee guruupu 35nen no kiroku* [For the customers – The chronicle of 35 years of the Daiei Group], Osaka.

Davidson, William R., Albert D. Bates and Stephen J. Bass (1976) 'The retail life cycle', *Harvard Business Review*, vol. 42 (Nov./Dec.), pp. 89–96.

Davies, Ross L. (ed.) (1995) *Retail Planning Policies in Western Europe*, London: Routledge.

Dawson, John (1979) *The Marketing Environment*, London: Croom Helm.

DMC (Dodwell Marketing Consultants) (1988) *Retail Distribution in Japan*, Tokyo: Dodwell Marketing Consultants.

Doi, Masashi (1982) 'Ôte 6 sha no takakuka senryaku kaku susumu' [The advancing diversification strategies of the six major companies], *Hanbai kakushin*, September, pp. 28–36.

Downer, Lesley (1994) *The Brothers: The Saga of the Richest Family in Japan*, London: Chatto & Windus.

Dreesmann, A.C.R. (1968) 'Patterns of evolution in retailing', *Journal of Retailing*, vol. 44, no. 1, pp. 64–81.

El-Ansary, Adel I. (1984) 'Selective innovative forms in retailing and wholesaling in the United States: an economic analysis', in Angeli Franco (ed.), *The Economics of Distribution*, Milan: no publisher, pp. 469–490.

Etgar, Michael (1984) 'The Retail Ecology Model: A comprehensive model of retail change', *Research in Marketing*, vol. 7, pp. 41–62.

Evans, Kenneth R., John W. Barnes and John Schlacter (1993) 'A general systems approach to retail evolution: an existing institutional perspective', *The International Review of Retail, Distribution and Consumer Research*, vol. 3, no. 1, pp. 79–100.

Fortune, 7 February 1994, 'Retailing Revolution in Japan', p. 31.

Fujita, E. (1995) 'Naze fuenai . . . ? Hyakkaten no chokuyûnyu' [Why are they not increasing. . . ? Direct imports by department stores], *Nikkei ryûtsû shinbun*, 16 May 1995, p. 5.

Gadde, L.-E. (1993) 'Evolution processes in distribution networks', *Advances in International Marketing*, vol. 5, pp. 43–66.

Gekiryû Magazine, October 1997, 'Butsuryû kakaku no shinchôryû' [New trends in the reorganization of logistics], pp. 50–53.

Gekiryû Magazine, April 2000, 'Gyôkai no shukuzu o kaima miseta Nagasakiya tôsan geki' [The Nagasakiya bankruptcy drama that showed a glimpse of the future shrinking of the industry], pp. 96–99.

Gekiryû Magazine, June 2000(a), 'Shôsha 'kawashimo senryaku' no abunai sokumen' [The dangerous side of the downstream strategies of general trading companies], pp. 36–39.

Gekiryû Magazine, June 2000(b), 'Mô tomaranai? Sumitomo Shôji no Seiyû shihai' [Not going to end? The control of Sumitomo Corp. over Seiyu], pp. 14–16

Gekiryû Magazine, August 2000, 'Sôgô shôsha 'riteeru senryaku' no zentô' [Future prospects of the retail strategy of general trading companies], pp. 53–72.

Gekiryû Magazine, March 2001, 'Ryûtsû saihen sôkanzu' [Mapping the interrelationships in the reorganization of distribution], pp. 21–31.

Gekiryû Magazine, February 2002, 'Tonya – shôsha no riteiru shinshutsu de nuri kaerareru keiretsu kankei' [Wholesaler – group affiliations are realigned through the entry of general trading companies into retailing], pp. 60–63.

Gekiryû Magazine, March 2002, 'Ion jitsuryoku dankai ni haitta EDPL senryaku' [Aeon: EDPL strategy enters into level of real strength], pp. 10–26.

Gerlach, Michael (1992) *Alliance Capitalism: The Social Organization of Japanese Business*, Berkeley: University of California Press.

Gist, Ronald R. (1968) *Retailing: Concepts and Decisions*, New York: Wiley.

Glöckner-Holme, Irene (1988) *Betriebsformen Marketing im Einzelhandel* [Retail format marketing], Augsburg: FGM.

Goldman, Arieh (1975) 'The role of trading-up in the development of the retailing system', *Journal of Marketing*, vol. 39, no. 1, pp. 54–62.

Goldman, Arieh (1992) 'Evaluating the performance of the Japanese distribution system', *Journal of Retailing*, vol. 68, no. 1, pp. 11–39.

Goldman, Arieh (2000) 'Discount retailing in Japan', in Michael R. Czinkota and Masaaki Kotabe (eds), *Japanese Distribution Strategy*, London: Business Press/ Thomson Learning, pp. 47–63.

Haley, John F. (1986) 'Administrative guidance versus formal regulation: resolving the paradox of industrial policy', in Gary R. Saxonhouse and Kozo Yamamura (eds), *Law and Trade Issues of the Japanese Economy*, Seattle: University of Washington Press, pp. 107–128.

Hanbai kakushin, August 1971, 'Konbiniensu sutoa buumu no haikei o megutte' [About the background of the convenience store boom], pp. 134–136.

Hanbai kakushin, February 1972, 'Chigasaki Daikuma' [The Daikuma store in Chigasaki], February, pp. 48–53.

Hanbai kakushin, April 1980, 'Daiee no shingyôtai "Toposu"' [Daiei's new format 'Topos'], pp. 94–96.

Hanbai kakushin, April 1981, 'Kochira misoka ni (?) shikashi chakuchaku to Topos 3 go mise oopen!' [Is the secret in here? The third Topos eventually opened], p. 24.

Hanbai kakushin, January 2001, 'Matsumotokiyoshi daihyô Matsumoto Namio' [Interview with Matsumotokiyoshi chief representative Namio Matsumoto], pp. 42–47.

Hasa, Hiroaki (2000) 'Konseputo Japan' ni gyôshuku sareta shinasoroe no hirosa to fukasa [Depth and breath of assortment have been condensed into the 'Concept Japan'], *Hanbai kakushin*, August, pp. 34–37.

Hashizume, Noboru (1982) 'Nihon no HC no jôshiki o yaburu Doito Kawagoe ten no "1000 tsubo" "2 sô tenkai" no daitan na kokoromi' [The bold experiment of the Doit Kawagoe Store with 1000 tsubo and expanding over two stories, that breaks with common sense in regard to the Japanese home-centre], *Hanbai kakushin*, January, pp. 132–136.

Hata, Nokumi (2000) 'Yunikuro ga konnani hitto suru ni wa riyû ga aru' [There are reasons why Uniqlo can produce hit products in such a way], *Hanbai kakushin*, January, pp. 32–35.

Havens, Thomas R.H., (1994) *Architects of Affluence: the Tsutsumi Family and the Seibu-Saison Enterprises in Twentieth-Century Japan*, Cambridge, Mass.: Council on East Asian Studies, Harvard University; distributed by Harvard University Press.

Hayao, Kenji (1993) *The Japanese Prime Minister and Public Policy*, Pittsburgh: University of Pittsburgh Press.

Hayashi, Kaoru (1988) 'Daiee disukaunto jigyô no jittai o ou!!' [Chasing the truth about Daiei's discount business!!], *Hanbai kakushin*, July, pp. 113–117.

Hayashi, Kaoru (2001) 'Choku biki "dokuji nettowaaku" o jiku to suru shinbutsuryû infura no zenbô [The full picture of the new logistics infrastructure to implement 'direct dealings' in 'an exclusive network'], *Hanbai kakushin*, July, pp. 117–119.

Hayashi, Shûji (1962) *Ryûtsû kakumei* [Revolution in distribution], Tokyo: Chuô Kôronsha.

Hayashi, Shûji (1964) *Ryûtsû kakumei II* [Revolution in Distribution II], Tokyo: Chûô Kôronsha.

Hayes, Louis D. (1992) *Introduction to Japanese Politics*, New York: Paragon House.

Hitaka, Kenichi (1999) 'Kaden ryûtsû ni okeru ôgata senmonten to meekaa no torihiki kankei' [Exchange relationships between large stores and manufacturers in the distribution of electric appliances], in Fumio Kondô and Yasunaga Wakabayashi (eds), *Nihon kigyô no maaketingushi* [History of marketing of Japanese businesses], Tokyo: Dôbunkan Shuppan, pp. 107–129.

HKH (Hanbai Kakushin Henshûbu) (1977) 'DIY no teihen o kakudaishi kokyaku zukuri o susumeru Tôkyû Hanzu no "te zukuri kyôshitsu"' [The 'built by hand classes' by Tokyu Hands that are widening the base for DIY and increasing new customers], *Hanbai kakushin*, September, pp. 128–131.

HKH (Hanbai Kakushin Henshûbu) (1980) 'Nihonteki DS to DIY mise, hoomu sentaa no chigai wa doko ni aru no ka' [Where are the differences between home centres and Japanese style discount stores and do-it-yourself-stores?], *Hanbai kakushin*, November, pp. 118–123.

HKH (Hanbai Kakushin Henshûbu) (1981a) 'Seiyû Sutoa no CVS Famirii Maato wa doko made tachinaotta ka?' [How far can Seiyu Stores' Family Mart convenience stores catch up?], *Hanbai kakushin*, September, pp. 191–194.

HKH (Hanbai Kakushin Henshûbu) (1981b) 'Sebun Irebun ni môzen to 'charenji seishin' moyashi hajimeta saishuppatsu kumi no Rooson Japan to Famirii Maato no jishin' [The self-confidence of Lawson Japan and Family Mart that have been caught by the spirit seriously to challenge Seven-Eleven], *Hanbai kakushin*, February, pp. 61–64.

HKH (Hanbai Kakushin Henshûbu) (1982) 'Supesharitei HC 2 sha no kurieiteibu de yuniiku na maachandaijingu jikken sutadii – Doito to Tôkyû Hanzu' [Study of the creative and unique merchandising of the two specialty home centre companies – DOIT and Tokyu Hands], *Hanbai kakushin*, January, pp. 126–131.

HKH (Hanbai Kakushin Henshûbu) (1993c) 'Daiee tenpo senryaku kenkyû' [Research on the store strategy of Daiei], *Hanbai kakushin*, July, pp. 56–60.

HKH (Hanbai Kakushin Henshûbu) (1998) 'Daisô 100 en pawaa no kenkyû' [Daiso – studying the power in the 100 yen sector], *Hanbai kakushin*, May, pp. 158–160.

HKH (Hanbai Kakushin Henshûbu) (1999) 'Shimamura (Saitama-ken)', [Shimamura – Saitama Prefecture], *Hanbai kakushin*, February, pp. 95–99.

HKH (Hanbai Kakushin Henshûbu) (2000a) '100 en shoppu Za Daiso' [100 yen shop The Daiso], *Hanbai kakushin*, May, pp. 154–158.

HKH (Hanbai Kakushin Henshûbu) (2000b) 'Intabyuu Yanai Tadashi' [Interview with Tadashi Yanai], *Hanbai kakushin*, January, pp. 26–31.

HKH (Hanbai Kakushin Henshûbu) (2001) 'Ion sôgô butsuryû shisutemu no settokuryoku to gekishindo' [The persuasiveness and revolutionary qualities of the new general logistics system of Aeon], *Hanbai kakushin*, July, pp. 112–116.

HKH/Takayama (Hanbai Kakushin Henshûbu and Kunisuke Takayama) (1989) *Nihon cheen sutoa monogatari* [History of Japanese chain stores], (*Hanbai kakushin* Special Edition, 30 June 1989), Tokyo: Shôgyôkai.

Hollander, Stanley C. (1966) 'Notes on the retail accordion', *Journal of Retailing*, vol. 42, (Summer), pp. 29–40.

Hollander, Stanley C. (1981) 'Retailing theory: some criticism and some admiration', in Ronald W. Stampfl and Elizabeth C. Hirschman (eds), *Theory in Retailing: Traditional and Nontraditional Sources*, Chicago: American Marketing Association, pp. 84–94.

Igarashi, Takuo (1977) 'Daiee vs Ito Yokado – Hokkaidô haru no jin' [Daiei against Ito Yokado – the fight for Hokkaido in spring], *Hanbai kakushin*, May, pp. 118–124.

Ikeda, Nokumi (2000) 'Yunikuro ga konnani hitto suru ni wa riyû ga aru' [There are reasons why Uniqlo can strike out like this], *Hanbai kakushin*, January, pp. 32–35.

Ishihara, Takemasa (1993) 'Chûshô shôgyô seisaku no kiseki' [The locus of the policy for small- and medium-sized commerce], in Nikkei Ryûtsû Shinbun (ed.), *Ryûtsû gendaishi* [Modern history of distribution], Tokyo: Nihon Keizai Shinbunsha, pp. 237–252.

Ishihara, Yasuhiro (1977) 'Kono moku de tashikameta – ôte suupaa cheen no damesa kagen, disukauntaa no odoroku beki yasusa kagen' [Determined by these points – the insufficiencies of the large supermarket chains, the surprising cheapness of the discounters], *Hanbai kakushin*, March, pp. 42–47.

Ishihara, Yasuhiro (1980) 'Haado guzzu disukauntaa (Daikuma, Rojaasu Bauru, Aiwaarudo) ga Nihon no shôhi shijô ni motarashita mono' [What the hard goods discounters (Daikuma, Rogers Ball, Iworld) have brought into Japan's consumer market], *Hanbai kakushin*, November, pp. 130–132.

Ishihara, Yasuhiro (1985) 'Keeyoo HC no seichô senryaku tettei bunseki' [Thorough analysis of the growth strategy of Keiyo home centre], *Hanbai kakushin*, March, pp. 152–156.

Ishikawa, Tatsuya and Yasuhide Yajima (2001) *The Household Savings Rate Paradox – The Population is Aging, but Workers' Households are Saving More*, NRI research paper no. 153, Tôkyô: NRI Research Institute.

Itô, Motoshige, Shigeru Matsushima and Norishiba Yanagawa (1991) Ribeeto to saiban kakaku iji kôi [Rebates and measures to control resale prices], in Yoshirô Miwa and Kiyohiko Nishimura (eds), *Nihon no ryûtsû* [Japanese distribution], Tokyo: Tokyo Daigaku Shuppankai, pp. 131–157.

Ito, Takatoshi and Masayoshi Maruyama (1995) 'Is the Japanese distribution system really inefficient?', in Paul Krugman (ed.), *Trade with Japan: Has the Door Opened Wider?*, University of Chicago Press, pp. 149–173.

Itôchû Shôji Chôsabu (1997) *Seminaaru Nihon no sôgô shôsha* [Seminar Japan's general trading companies], Tokyo: Tôyô Keizai Shinpôsha.

Iwanaga, Tadayasu (1988) 'Sengo waga kuni no ryûtsû seisaku no hatten' [Development of Japanese distribution policy in the post-war period], in Yutaka Tanaka (ed.), *Nyûmon shôgyô seisaku* [Introduction to commercial policy], Tokyo: Sôseisha, pp. 11–142.

Izraeli, Dov (1973) 'The three wheels of retailing: a theoretical note', *European Journal of Marketing*, vol. 7, no. 1, pp. 70–74.

JCSC (Japan Council of Shopping Centres) (1993) *Japan Council of Shopping Centres*, Tokyo: Nihon Shoppingu Sentaa Kyôkai.

Kane, Kiuchi (1999) 'Matsumotokiyoshi (Chiba-ken)', *Hanbai kakushin*, February, pp. 86–89.

Katayama, Mataichirô (1993) 'Gendaika no dôtei' [The road to modernization], in Nikkei Ryûtsû Shinbun (ed.), *Ryûtsû gendaishi* [Modern history of distribution], Tokyo: Nihon Keizai Shinbunsha, pp. 3–19

Katô, Masahi (1995) *Shôhi suru hito* [People as consumers], Tokyo: Yotsuya Raundo.

Katô, Naomi (2000) 'Cheen e-tantôsha, netto kanren benchaa ni kikimakuru' [Listening intensively to the e-business managers of chain stores and net-related ventures], *Konbini*, June, pp. 16–29.

Katz, Richard (1998) *The System that Soured: The Rise and Fall of the Japanese Economic Miracle*, Armonk, NY: Sharpe.

Kawano, Satoshi (1992) 'Senzenki shôtengai seisaku no tenkai' [Development of shopping districts in the pre-war period], *Keizai to bôeki*, no. 161, pp. 123–141.

Kawasaki, Shinichi (1993) 'Nichi-Bei cheen sutoa gekidô no 30 nenshi' [30 Years of rapid change in the history of Japanese and American chain stores], *Hanbai kakushin*, May, pp. 49–69.

Keizai Sangyôshô (METI) (no date) *Dai kibo kouri tenpo no todoke jôkyô – heisei 12 5 gatsumatsu kakutei ban* [The situation of reports for large scale retail stores – end of May 1990, final settlement edition] (Report downloaded as PDF file from http://www.meti.go.jp/policy/index27 – 2.html).

Koch, Matthias (1998) *Rüstungskonversion in Japan nach dem Zweiten Weltkrieg* [Military industry conversion after the Second World War], Munich: Iudicium.

Kojima, Kensuke (1993) 'Nihongata GMS wa ima no gyômu kôritsu o tettei shite kaizen seyo' [Thoroughly investigating the current efficiency of Japanese-style general merchandising stores and then introducing reforms], *Hanbai kakushin,* December, pp. 66–71.

Kokudochô (different years), *Chika kôji* [Public announcement of land prices], available at http://tochi.mlit.go.jp/chika/index.html#kouji.

Konishi, Yukiko (2001) 'Kojin shôhi teimei no haikei' [Background of sluggish personal consumption], *Ryûtsû jôhô,* 2001.8 (no. 386), pp. 4–10.

Kowata, Yoshiyuki (1993) 'Ryûtsû henkaku to disukaunto sutoa' [Changes in the distribution system and discount stores], *Ryûtsû seisaku,* no. 53, pp. 16–23.

Koyama, Shûzô (1993) 'Kouri gyôtai no shinka' [Evolution of retail formats], in Nikkei Ryûtsû Shinbun (ed.), *Ryûtsû gendaishi* [Modern history of distribution], Tokyo: Nihon Keizai Shinbunsha, pp. 20–39.

Koyama, Shûzô and Yôko Togawa (1992) *Depaato · Suupaa* [Department stores and supermarkets], Tokyo: Nihon Keizai Hyôronsha.

Kruger, David and Ichiko Fuyuno (2001) 'King of the Mall,' *Far Eastern Economic Review,* vol. 164, no. 34, pp. 34–35.

KS (Kansai Suupaamaaketto) (1985) *Kansai suupaa 25 nen no ayumi* [Kansai Supermarket – a walk through 25 years], Itami: Kansai Suupaamaaketto.

Kubomura, Ryûsuke, Yoshiro Tajima and Hiroshi Mori (1982) *Shôgyô seisaku* [Commercial policy], Tokyo: Chuô Keizaisha.

Kuhlmeier, Arno (1980) *Die Betriebstypeninnovation als Bestandteil der Absatzpolitik im Einzelhandel* [The innovation of retail formats as part of retail distribution policy], (Schriften zur Handelsforschung nr. 62), Göttingen: Otto Schwartz.

Kunimasa, Tsunehiro (1985) 'Seikyô shutten kisei no udoki' [Developments concerning regulations for store openings by consumer cooperatives], *Hanbai Kakushin,* July, pp. 22–23.

Kurahashi, Yoshio (ed.) (1993) *Zaidan hôjin Nihon Shoppingu Sentaa Kyôkai 20 nen no ayumi* [Foundation Japan Council of Shopping Centres, a walk through 20 years], Tokyo: Shoppingu Sentaa Kyôkai.

Kusano, Atsushi (1992) *Daitenhô – keizai kisei no kôzô* [Large Store Law – the structure of economic regulations], Tokyo: Nihon Keizai Shinbunsha.

Larke, Roy (1992) 'Japanese retailing: fascinating, but little understood', *International Journal of Retail & Distribution Management,* vol. 20, no. 1, pp. 3–15.

Larke, Roy (1994) *Japanese Retailing,* New York: Routledge.

Maeda, Kazutoshi (1992) 'Ryûtsû kakumei' [Revolution in distribution], in Morikawa Hidemasu (ed.), *Bijinesu man no tame no sengô keieishi nyûmon* [An introduction to the post-war history of management for businessmen], Tokyo: Nihon Keizai Shinbunsha, pp. 167–194.

Makita, Seiichiro (1993) 'Disukaunto sutoa no hensen to seichô yôin' [Main causes of change and development of discount stores], *RIRI Ryûtsû Sangyô,* no. 9, pp. 2–8.

Markin, Rom J. and Calvin P. Duncan (1981) 'The transformation of retailing institutions: beyond the Wheel of Retailing and life cycle theories', *Journal of Macromarketing,* vol. 1, no. 1, pp. 58–66.

Maruta, Takashi and Masahiro Toyoda (2000) 'Nagasakiya tôsan ni nanio manabu ka' [What can we learn from the Nagasakiya bankruptcy?], *Chain Store Age*, 15 April, pp. 65–69.

Maruyama, Masayoshi (1995) 'Kourigyô no kosuto kôzô to keiei kôdô' [Cost structures and management performance in retailing], in Kenichi Miyazawa (ed.), *Kakaku kakumei to ryûtsû kakushin* [Price revolution and reform in retailing], Tokyo: Nihon Keizai Shinbunsha, pp. 197–210.

Masuda, Daizô (2000) *Ryûtsû shisutemu no kôzu – seikatsusha e no paradaimu shifuto* [Stucture of the distribution system – a paradigm shift towards the consumer/people], Tokyo: Chuô Keizaisha.

Matsumotokiyoshi Co. Ltd. (2001) *Annual Report 2001*, Tokyo: Matsumotokiyoshi.

McNair, Malcolm P. (1931) 'Trends in large-scale retailing', *Harvard Business Review*, vol. 10, no. 1, pp. 30–39.

McNair, Malcolm P. (1958) 'Significant trends and developments in the postwar period', in Albert D. Smith (ed.), *Competitive Distribution in a Free High-Level Economy and its Implication for University*, University of Pittsburgh Press, pp. 1–25.

Meyer-Ohle, Hendrik (1993a) 'Wer kauft wo? Zur Einkaufsstättenwahl japanischer Konsumenten' [Who shops where? On the store choice of Japanese consumers], *Japanstudien*, Jahrbuch des Deutschen Instituts für Japanstudien der Philipp-Franz-von-Siebold-Stiftung, vol. 5, pp. 171–207.

Meyer-Ohle, Hendrik (1993b) *Lebensversicherung und Konsument in Japan* [Life insurance and consumers in Japan], Marburg: Förderverein Marburger Japan-Reihe.

Meyer-Ohle, Hendrik (1995) *Dynamik im japanischen Einzelhandel – Einführung, Durchsetzung und Fortentwicklung neuer Betriebstypen 1954–1994* [Dynamism in Japanese retailing, introduction, diffusion and development of new retail types 1954–1994], Wiesbaden: Gabler.

Meyer-Ohle, Hendrik (1996) 'Revolution in der japanischen Distribution? Großunternehmen des Einzelhandels in einer Phase der Neuorientierung' [Revolution in Japanese distribution? – Large retail companies in a period of reorientation], *Handelsforschung, Jahrbuch der Forschungsstelle fur den Handel Berlin (FfH) e.V.*, 1996, pp. 379–397.

Meyer-Ohle, Hendrik (2000) 'Collaboration for change in Japanese consumer goods distribution: strategic alliances, team merchandising and "enemies in the same boat"', in Michael R. Czinkota and Masaaki Kotabe (eds), *Japanese Distribution Strategy*, London: Business Press solidus Thomson Learning, pp. 117–134.

Meyer-Ohle, Hendrik (2001) 'Product supply or e-commerce – old and new paradigms in the role of general trading companies in Japanese retailing', *2001 AJBS Conference Best Paper Proceedings*, Association of Japanese Business Studies, Seinäjoki Polytechnic Seinäjoki Business School, pp. 111–121.

Midori no Machizukurika (2001) *Shikishi chûshin shigaichi kasseika kihon keikakusho* [Basic plan for the revitalization of the central district], Shiki: available at: http://www.shiki-toshiseibi.com.

Mimura, Yumiko (1992) *Gendai Nihon no ryûtsû shisutemu* [The current Japanese distribution system], Tokyo: Yuhikaku.

Mishima, Mari (1993) 'Ryûtsû keiretsuka no ronri' [Theory of the systematization of distribution channels], in Ken Ariga (ed.), *Nihonteki ryûtsû no keizaigaku* [Economics of Japanese distribution], Tokyo: Nihon Keizai Shinbunsha, pp. 207–254.

Miya, Eiji (1985a) *Gendai Nihon kouri keiei senryakushi* [History of business strategies in contemporary Japanese retailing], Tokyo: Yuhikaku.

Miya, Eiji (1985b) 'Amerika to Nihon ni okeru kouri kakushin no sai' [Differences in retail reform of retailing in the US and Japan], *Kyôto Gakuen Daigaku ronshû*, vol. 14, no. 1, pp. 45–79.

Miyaji, Toshio (1996) *Yasuuri ô no 'shôjin tetsugaku' ni manabu* [Learning from the 'merchant philosophy' of the king of discount], Tokyo.

Miyashita, Naofusa (1993), 'Oroshiuri keiei no kakushin' [Revolution in wholesale management], in Nihon Keizai Shinbun (ed.), *Ryûtsû gendaishi* [Modern history of distribution], Tokyo: Nihon Keizai Shinbunsha, pp. 176–187.

Miyazawa, Kenichi (ed.) (1995), *Kakaku kakumei to ryûtsû kakushin* [Revolution in pricing and renewal in distribution], Tokyo: Nihon Keizai Shinbunsha.

Momose, Shigeo (1983) *Konbiniensu sutoa* [Convenience store], Tokyo: Nihon Keizai Shinbunsha.

Morishita, Norihiko (1990) *Itoo Yookadoo – Itô Masatoshi shôbai no tessoku* [Ito Yokado – the hard-and-fast rules of trade of Itô Masatoshi], Tokyo: Baru Shuppan.

Moritz, Eckehard Fozzy (1992) 'Konfuzius – Japan – Technik. Ein alter Hut neu aufgesetzt', [Confucius – Japan – technology, an old hat worn in a new way], *Deutsches Museum – Wissenschaftliches Jahrbuch 1991*, pp. 131–175.

Munekata, Mamoru (1994) 'HC gyôtai no saikôchiku wa genjô hitei kara hashimaru' [Beginning the reconstruction of the home-centre from the negation of its current state], *Hanbai kakushin*, March, pp. 122–126.

Muramatsu, Michio and Ellis S. Krauss (1987) 'The conservative policy line and the development of patterned pluralism', in Kozo Yamamura, and Yasuba Yasukichi (eds), *The Political Economy of Japan – vol. 1: The Domestic Transformation*, Stanford University Press, pp. 516–554.

Murata, Shôji and Yumiko Mimura (1987) 'Suupaa cheen no jiko kakushin' [The self-revolution of the supermarket chains], in Ryusuke Kubomura and Ryûtsû Mondai Kenkyû Kyôkai (eds), *21 Seki no ryûtsû* [Distribution in the 21st century], Tokyo: Nihon Keizai Shinbunsha, pp. 121–133.

Nagano, Minoru (2000) 'Shijô saidai to natta ryûtsû kigyô yaburetan no [butai ura]' [Backstage of the largest downfall of a distribution enterprise in history], *Hanbai kakushin*, April, pp. 24–27.

Naikakufu (2001) *Kôtsû anzen hakusho* [White paper on traffic safety], Tokyo: Zaimushô Insatsukyoku.

Nakamoto, Hirotsugu (1995) *Gendai no shôhi keizai to shôhisha kôdô* [Current economics of consumption and consumer behaviour], Tokyo: Zeimu Keiri Kyôkai.

Nakamura, Takafusa (1981) *The Postwar Japanese Economy*, Tokyo: University of Tokyo Press.

Nakatani, Iwao (2001) *IT kakumei to shôsha no miraizô* [IT revolution and general trading companies' visions of the future], Tokyo: Tôyô Keizai Shinpôsha.

Nihon keizai shinbun, 12 April 1990, 'Daitenhô kondo wa Nichi-Nichi masatsu' [The Large Store Law will create Japanese-Japanese friction].

Nihon keizai shinbun, 16 April 1990, 'Daitenhô to shôtengai' [The Large Store Law and shopping streets].

Nihon keizai shinbun, 31 March 1994 (morning edition), 'Itô Yôkadô, shinshôsha riyô ni hairyô moderu mise o Saitama ni' [Ito Yokado, model store for the use by disabled persons in Saitama].

Nihon keizai shinbun, 31 January 2000, 'Saison cuts deal to unload real-estate debt' (retrieved in English from Nikkei Net Interactive).

Nihon keizai shinbun, 27 March 2000, 'U.S. fund to rehabilitate Nagasakiya' (retrieved in English from Nikkei Net Interactive).

Nihon keizai shinbun, 13 November 2000, 'Foreign retailers shake up retail sector' (retrieved in English from Nikkei Net Interactive).

Nihon keizai shinbun, 24 November 2000, 'Daiei announces revival plan, to cut 4000 jobs' (retrieved in English from Nikkei Net Interactive).

Nihon keizai shinbun, 8 December 2000, 'Tokyo court orders former Sogo chairman to pay 6 bln yen' (retrieved in English from Nikkei Net Interactive).

Nihon keizai shinbun, 18 December 2000, 'Daiei to appoint new management at Jan hldr mtg,' (retrieved in English from Nikkei Net Interactive).

Nihon keizai shinbun, 30 August 2001, 'Kao to halve number of products to 1,000' (retrieved in English from Nikkei Net Interactive).

Nihon keizai shinbun, 6 September 2001, 'Big electronics retailers rationalize distribution systems' (retrieved in English from Nikkei Net Interactive).

Nihon keizai shinbun, 14 September 2001, 'Daiei plans more PAS clothing stores despite Uniqlo protests (retrieved in English from Nikkei Net Interactive).

Nihon keizai shinbun, 14 September 2001, 'Yamada Denki to strengthen business in Osaka area' (retrieved in English from Nikkei Net Interactive).

Nihon keizai shinbun, 17 September 2001, 'Failed Mycal holds creditors' meetings' (retrieved in English from Nikkei Net Interactive).

Nihon keizai shinbun, 5 October 2001, 'Ryoshoku to absorb Suntory wholesale food unit' (retrieved in English from Nikkei Net Interactive).

Nihon keizai shinbun, 17 November 2001, 'Mycal Hokkaido to increase capital via private placement' (retrieved in English from Nikkei Net Interactive).

Nihon keizai shinbun, 5 December 2001, 'Earnings gap in 6 apparel firms to widen in FY01' (retrieved in English from Nikkei Net Interactive).

Nihon keizai shinbun, 20 December 2001, 'Long-established local retailers go under as economy worsens' (retrieved in English from Nikkei Net Interactive).

Nihon keizai shinbun, 22 December 2001, 'Ryohin Keikaku to close European stores amid slow sales' (retrieved in English from Nikkei Net Interactive).

Nihon keizai shinbun, 16 January 2002, 'Executive interview: Aeon boss touts direct ties with makers' (retrieved in English from Nikkei Net Interactive).

Nihon keizai shinbun, 19 January 2002, 'Analysis Daiei revival 1st step toward averting crisis' (retrieved in English from Nikkei Net Interactive).

Nihon keizai shinbun, 14 February 2002, 'Nichimen to make Nichimen Infinity 100% unit via TOB' (retrieved in English from Nikkei Net Interactive).

Nihon keizai shinbun, 27 February 2002, 'Failed retailer Kotobukiya to sell 50 outlets to Aeon' (retrieved in English from Nikkei Net Interactive).

Nihon keizai shinbun, 4 March 2002, 'Retailers' struggle: survivors prosper by buying failed firms' (retrieved in English from Nikkei Net Interactive).

Nihon keizai shinbun, 25 March 2002, 'Failed Nagasakiya to slash debts by 85%' (retrieved in English from Nikkei Net Interactive).

Nihon keizai shinbun, 16 April 2002, 'Major supermarket operators to close 100 outlets in FY02' (retrieved in English from Nikkei Net Interactive).

Nihon keizai shinbun, 9 April 2002 (a), 'Supermarket operator Niko Niko Do files for court-led rehabilitation' (retrieved in English from Nikkei Net Interactive).

Nihon keizai shinbun, 9 April 2002 (b), 'Wal-Mart to launch Japan operations in fall' (retrieved in English from Nikkei Net Interactive).

Nihon keizai shinbun, 22 May 2002, 'Aeon buys major stake in Inageya from Shuwa' (retrieved in English from Nikkei Net Interactive).

Nihon keizai shinbunsha, (1995) *Ryûtsû TODAY* [Distribution today], Tokyo: Nihon Keizai Shinbunsha.

Nihon Seisaku Tôshi Ginkô [Development Bank of Japan] (ed.) (1991, 1996, 1997, 2002) *Sangyô betsu zaimu deeta handobukku* (Handbook of industrial financial data), Tokyo: Nihon Keizai Kenkyûjo.

Nihon shokuryô shinbun, 22 September 2000, 'Yanô Fuudo Sentaa, 'Fuudogaaden Niizaten' oopen' [Yano Food Centre opens Foodgarden Niiza store].

Nihon shokuryô shinbun, 24 February 1997, 'Samitto, 600 tsubo gata SSM 'Asakadai-ten' 3 gatsu itsuka kaiten' [Summit, opening of 600 tsubo sized SSM 'Asakadai store' on March 5].

Nihon shokuryô shinbun, 9 February 1998, 'Seiyu 'weruseebu' zen 14 ten heiryô e' [Towards the closure of all 14 Wellsave stores].

Nikkei Business, 28 February 2000, 'Konbini no mirai' [The future of the convenience store], pp. 26–34.

Nikkei kinyû shinbun, 18 October 2001, 'Shiseido shifts rebates from product stocking to sales' (retrieved in English from Nikkei Net Interactive).

Nikkei kinyû shinbun, 2 April 2002, 'Interview: Ito-Yokado head prioritizes profit increase' (retrieved in English from Nikkei Net Interactive).

Nikkei Marketing Journal, 10 July 2000, 'E-commerce market registers sharp growth in FY99' (retrieved in English from Nikkei Net Interactive).

Nikkei Marketing Journal, 15 January 2002, 'Fast retailing chief aims to defy criticism' (retrieved in English from Nikkei Net Interactive).

Nikkei MJ (Ryûtsû Shinbun) (2001) *Ryûtsû keizai no tebiki 2002* [Handbook of the distribution industry], Tokyo: Nihon Keizai Shinbun.

Nikkei ryûtsû shinbun, 29 September 1994, 'Aranami koeru keiei senryaku (31) – Sôtetsu Roozen' [Management strategies to cross the stormy seas (31) – Sotetsu Rozen].

Nikkei ryûtsû shinbun, 8 December 1994, 'Sôtetsu Rôzen, ikkatsu butsuryû shisutemu, seisen nozoku zenuriba ni dônyû' [Sotetsu Rozen, introduction of a bundled delivery system to all salesfloors with the exception of fresh merchandise].

Nikkei ryûtsû shinbun, 29 August 1996, '17nen buri shutten saikai, Hokushin Shôji 'Rojaasu'' [Resumption of store openings after 17 years – Hokushin Shôji 'Rogers'].

Nikkei ryûtsû shinbun, 16 May 1995, 'Kategoriikiraa vs. kizon suupaa Saitama, Shiki-eki shûhen' [Category killers against existing supermarkets, Saitama area around Shiki station].

Nikkei ryûtsû shinbun, 18 January 1996, 'Kôbe kara hyakkaten ga kawaru' [Since Kobe department stores are changing].

Nikkei ryûtsû shinbun, 15 May 1997, 'Seisen uriba 5 wari ni kakudai' [Increasing the sales floor for fresh merchandise to 50%].

Nikkei ryûtsû shinbun, 20 May 1997, 'Sôgô DS no Rojaasu – seisenhin hanbai kakudai [General discounter Rogers – expanding the sale of fresh merchandise].

Nikkei ryûtsû shinbun, 24 June 1997, 'Yôkadô – hatchû deeta, mainichi shôkyo' [Yokado – order data deleted daily].

Nikkei ryûtsû shinbun, 15 July 1997, 'Shokuhin bunya shutten aitsugu, Saitama-ken Niiza-shi' [Successive opening of new stores in the food sector – Saitama prefecture, Niiza city].

Nikkei ryûtsû shinbun, 2 September 1997, 'Ryôkuwaza senyô oroshiuri no shôgeki – konbini, hanbairyoku buki ni' [The impact of the mighty specialist wholesaler – convenience stores, utilizing sales strength as a weapon].

Nikkei ryûtsû shinbun, 2 June 1998, 'Cheen opereeshon minaoshi' [Review of chain operations].

Nikkei ryûtsû shinbun, 23 July 1998, 'Raifukoopo, kogataten no kaisô suishin' [Life Corporation, drive to remodel small stores].

Nikkei ryûtsû shinbun, 10 September 1998, 'Chûken suupaa M&A jidai he' [Towards the era of M&A between medium-sized supermarkets].

Nikkei ryûtsû shinbun, 6 October 1998, 'Saizen sakana uriba haiken – Raifu Koopo-reeshon Asaka-ten' [Exploring the most advanced fish salesfloor – Life Corporation Asaka-store].

Nikkei ryûtsû shinbun, 7 January 1999, 'Makuake daiten ritchihô jidai' [Beginning of the era of the Large-Scale Retail Stores Location Law].

Nikkei ryûtsû shinbun, 15 October 1998, 'Seiyû, heitensû hangen' [Seiyu, number of stores to be closed halved].

Nikkei ryûtsû shinbun, 19 October 2000, 'Rodjaasu – butsuryû taisei' [Rogers – logistics set-up].

Nikkei Weekly, 24 July 2000, 'Saison group asks for help in cleanup'.

Nikkei Weekly, 25 September 2000, 'Carrefour runs into supply snags'.

Nikkei Weekly, 18 December 2000, 'Carrefour brings new ways of selling'.

Nikkei Weekly, 14 May 2001, 'Discount retailers on shakeout track'.

Nikkei Weekly, 16 July 2001, 'Mitsubishi–Boots venture to end as business flopps'.

Nikkei Weekly, 11 June 2001, 'Rivals' merger unlikely to alter scene'.

Nikkei Weekly, 17 December 2001, 'Foreign retailers finding local market tough to crack'.

Nikkei Weekly, 5 February 2001, 'Battles over turf reshape personal-care industry'.

Nikkei Weekly, 18 June 2001, 'Changes sweep consumer electronics'.

Nikkei Weekly, 20 August 2001, 'Growing Matsumotokiyoshi to face efficiency concerns'.

Nikkei Weekly, 22 October 2001, 'Mujirushi looks for winning formula'.

Nikkei Weekly, 5 November 2001, 'Making waves'.

Nikkei Weekly, 26 November 2001, 'Toys 'R' Us recasts sales approach'.

Nikkei Weekly, 27 November 2000, 'Matsumotokiyoshi rethinks strategy as market saturated'.

Nikkei Weekly, 21 January 2002, 'Daiei saga begins new chapter with bailout'.

Nikkei Weekly, 18 March 2002, 'Retail shakeup likely as Wal-Mart weighs in'.

Nikkei Weekly, 15 July 2002, 'Big trading houses get serious about retail'.

Nikkei Weekly, 4 November 2002, Toys 'R' Us pinning hopes on baby unit, own products'.

Nishikawa, Ryûichi (1997) 'Fuudo purasu Niiza-ten' [Food Plus Niiza store], *Hanbai kakushin*, February, pp. 85–89.

Nishimura, Kiyohiko (1993) 'The distribution system of Japan and the United States: a comparative study from the viewpoint of final-goods buyers', *Japan and the World Economy*, vol. 5, pp. 265–288.

Nishimuta, Katsumi (1981) 'Mada 5 tenpo no honno 'Mini Sutoppu' da ga Jasuko no 1 chô en kôsô no jûyô na kagi nagiru [Though only 5 Mini Stops exist so far they are still an important part within Jusco's one billion dollar plan], *Hanbai kakushin*, September, pp. 194–196.

Nitto, Haruyuki and Junichi Shiozaki (2001) *Changing Consumption Patterns and New Lifestyles in the 21st Century*, NRI Papers, no. 24, Nomura Research Institute.

NKK (Nichi-Bei Kôzô Mondai Kenkyûkai) (1990) *Nichi-Bei kôzô mondai kyôgi saishû hôkoku* [Final report of the consultations on Japanese-US structural problems], Tokyo: Zaikei Shôhôsha.

NKR (Nihon Kikai Kôgyô Rengôkai) (1963) *Suupaa maketto no gendai* [Current situation of supermarkets], Ryûtsû kikô no bunseki chôsa hôkokusho (2), Shôwa 37 nendo kikai kôgyô kisoku chôsa hôkokusho [Analysis of the distribution structure, survey report 2, reports about the regular surveys on the machinery industry, 1962], Tokyo: Nihon Kikai Kôgyô Rengôkai.

NKR Guruupu (2000) 'Za Daisô 100 en kan – Machida-ten' [100 yen shop The Daisô – Machida store], *Hanbai kakushin*, May, pp. 81–86.

NKS (Nihon Keizai Shinbunsha) (ed.) (1963) *Shinten suru ryûtsû kakumei* [Progressive revolution in retailing], Tokyo: Nihon Keizai Shinbunsha.

NKS (Nihon Keizai Shinbunsha) (ed.) (1990) *Daitenhô ga kieru hi* [The day when the Large Store Law disappears], Tokyo: Nihon Keizai Shinbunsha.

NRS (Nikkei Ryûtsû Shinbun) (different years) *Ryûtsû keizai no tebiki* [Handbook of the distribution industry], Tokyo: Nihon Keizai Shinbunsha.

NSK (Nihon Shôhi Keizai Kenkyûjo) (1993) 'Hoomu sentaa no mitsu no seerusu pointo to kokyaku manzoku' [The three selling points of the home centre and customer satisfaction], *Forum*, August, pp. 11–16.

Ogata [no first name] (1972) 'Kakudai kidô ni utsutta K-maato' [K-mart moved onto the track for expansion], *Hanbai kakushin* May, pp. 114–116.

Ogata, Tomoyuki (1986) *Itoo Yookadô no gyômu kakushin* [Ito Yokado's business reform], Tokyo: Offisu 2020.

Okamura, Noriyuki (2001) 'Gun'yû kakkyo no kaden gyôkai sengoku emaki' [Picture scroll of a country being fought over by rivaling warlords from the consumer electronics industry], *Hanbai kakushin*, April, pp. 80–83.

Ôkurashô Insatsukyoku (ed.) (1995) *Yûka shôken hôkokusho sôran – Kabushiki gaisha Daiee* [Periodic securities report – Daiei, Inc.], no. 19–89, Tokyo: ôkurasho Insatsukyoku.

Okuzumi, Masamichi (1983) *Shôgen – sengô shôgyôshi* [Witness reports – post-war history of retailing], Tokyo: Nihon Keizai Shinbunsha.

Orihashi, Seisuke (1993) *Suupaa gyôkai* [Supermarket industry], Tokyo: Kyôikusha.

Ôshita, Eiji (1993) *Nakauchi Isao no Daiee ôkoku* [Nakauchi Isao's Daiei kingdom], Tokyo: Shakai Shisôsha.

Ôsono, Tomokazu (1992) *Ichime de wakaru kikyô keiretsu to gyôkai chizu* [Company groupings and industries at one glance], Tokyo: Nihon Jitsugyô Shuppansha.

Ôta, Minoru, Masateru Fujino, Shigeru Morino and Shunichi Atsumi (1977) 'Disukaunto gerira no keieiteki potensharitei o kaibô suru' [Analyzing the management potential of the discount guerrilla], *Hanbai kakushin*, March, pp. 30–41.

Ozawa, Terutomo (1999) 'The rise and fall of bank-loan capitalism: institutionally driven growth and crisis in Japan', *Journal of Economic Issues* vol. 33, no. 2, pp. 351–358.

Partner, Simon (1999) *Assembled in Japan – Electrical Goods and the Making of the Japanese Consumer*, Berkeley: University of California Press.

Pauer, Erich (1993) *Nachbarschaftsgruppen und Versorgung in den japanischen Städten während des Zweiten Weltkrieges* [Neighbourhood groups and food provision in

Japanese cities during World War II], Marburger Japan-Reihe, vol. 9, Marburg: Förderverein 'Marburger Japan-Reihe'.

Ribault, Thierry (1999) 'Flexible employment in Japanese retailing: toward a just-in-time employment management', in Daniel Dirks, Jean-François Huchet and Thierry Ribault (eds), *Japanese Management in the Low Growth Era*, Berlin, Heidelberg, New York: Springer, pp. 295–312.

Roth, Victor J. and Saul Klein (1993) 'A theory of retail change', *The International Review of Retail Distribution and Consumer Research*, vol. 3, no. 2, pp. 167–183.

Ryohin Keikaku Company (2001a) *Ryohin Keikaku Co., Ltd 2000*, Tokyo: Ryohin Keikaku (retrieved from www.muji.co.jp/en/corporate/2000_e.pdf).

Ryohin Keikaku Company (2001b) *Muji Annual 2001*, Tôkyo: Ryohin Keikaku.

Ryûtsû Mondai Kenkyûkai (1995) 'Kakaku keisei no henyô to ryûtsû kakushin' [Change in pricing and revolution in distribution], in Kenichi Miyazawa (ed.), *Kakaku kakumei to ryûtsû kakushin* [Pricing revolution and renewal in distribution], Tokyo: Nihon Keizai Shinbunsha, pp. 14–150.

Ryûtsû saabisu shinbun, 8 February 2000, 'Marui 'Famirii' gyôtai 2 goten o Saitama-Shiki ni open' [Marui – second store representing the 'Family' format opened in Saitama Shiki].

Satô, Hajime (1974) *Nihon no ryûtsû kikô* [Japan's distribution structure], Tokyo: Yûhikaku.

Savitt, Ronald (1982) 'A historical approach to comparative retailing', *Management Decision*, vol. 20, no. 4, pp. 16–23.

Savitt, Ronald (1989) 'Looking back to see ahead: writing the history of American retailing', *Journal of Retailing*, vol. 65, no. 3, pp. 326–355.

SCC (Shôkô Chûkin Chôsabu) (1993) 'Daitenhô kaisei no chûshô jimoto suupaa no eikyô' [The impact of the change of the Large Store Law on small- and medium-sized local supermarkets], *Shôkô kinyû*, vol. 43, no. 5, pp. 26–46.

Scher, Mark J. (1997) 'The Japanese main bank relationship: governance or competitive strategy', in David Knights and Tony Tinker (eds) *Financial Institutions and Social Transformations: International Studies of a Sector*, New York: St. Martin's Press, pp. 189–214.

Schoppa, Leonard J. (1997) *Bargaining with Japan: What American Pressure Can Do and Cannot Do*, New York: Columbia Press.

Schumpeter, Joseph Alois (1926) *Theorie der wirtschaftlichen Entwicklung*, Munich: Duncker & Humblot.

Schwartz, Frank J. (1998) *Advice and Consent – The Politics of Consultation in Japan*, Cambridge University Press.

Sezon Sôgô Kenkyûjo (2000) *Ôte ryôbaiten no POS deeta o riyô shita bukka shizû ni kakaru kenkyû* [Research based on price indices using the POS data of leading mass merchandising stores], Tokyo: Sezon Sôgô Kenkyûjo (retrieved from http://www.sri-saison.gr.jp/linktoPDF.htm).

SGK (Shôgyôkai) (1989) *1990 nen Nihon suupaa maaketto meikan* [Japanese supermarket directory 1990], Tokyo: Shôgyôkai.

Shimada, Hiyoshi (1973) 'Kaiten sankagetsu ato ni miru Seiyû Mini Sutoa no jikken ten' [Seiyu Mini Store's trial store three months after opening], *Hanbai kakushin*, no. 5, pp. 43–51.

Shimizu, Yoshinori (1999) 'Problems in the Japanese financial system in the early 1990s', in William M. Tsutsui (ed.), *Banking in Japan, Routledge Library of Modern Japan, vol. III*, London and New York: Routledge, pp. 159–80.

Shiraishi, Yoshiaki (1991) 'The public retail market in the changing distribution system of Japan', *Ryûtsû Kagaku Daigaku ronshû*, vol. 4, no. 1, pp. 13–30.

Shôsha Kinô Kenkyûkai (1981) *Shin sôgô shôsharon* [New analysis of general trading companies], Tôkyô: Tôyô Keizai Shinpôsha.

Shûkan Daiyamondo, 4 March 2000, 'Konbini e kakumei' [Convenience store e-revolution], pp. 26–38.

Shûkan Tôyô Keizai (1991, 1992, 2001, 2002) *Chiiki keizai sôran 2002* [Overview of local economies], Tokyo: Tôyô Keizai.

Shûkan Tôyô Keizai (different years) *Zenkoku ôgata kouri tenpo sôran* [Nationwide overview of large retail stores], Tokyo: Tôyô Keizai.

SIJ (Sebun-Irebun Japan) (1992) *Sebun-Irebun Japan – owari naki inobeeshon* [Seven-Eleven Japan – never ending innovation], Tokyo: Sebun-Irebun Japan.

Sômuchô (1995) *Kisei kanwa suishin no genkyô – Kisei kanwa hakusho* [The state of progress in deregulation – White Paper on deregulation], Tokyo: Ôkurasho Insatsukyoku.

Sômuchô Tôkeikyoku (different years) *Bukka tôkei chôsa nenpô* [Yearly report on the census of retail prices], Tokyo: Nihon Tôkei Kyôkai.

Sorifu Kôhôshitsu (1997) *Kouri tenpo nado ni kan suru seron chôsa* [Opinion poll concerning retail stores and other issues], Tokyo: Sorifu.

Sparks, Leigh (1995) 'Reciprocal retail internationalisation: the Southland Corporation – Ito-Yokado and 7-Eleven convenience stores', *Service Industries Journal*, vol. 15, no. 4, pp. 57–96.

Statistics Bureau (different years) Japan Statistical Yearbook, Tokyo: Statistics Bureau, Ministry of Public Management, Home Affairs, Posts and Telecommunications.

STK (Sôrifu Tôkeikyoku) (1969) *Shôwa 42 nen zenkoku bukka tôkei chôsa hôkoku dai 6 kan* (Report on the survey of prices of 1967, vol. 6), Tokyo: Nihon Tôkei Kyôkai.

Sumiya, Hiroshi (1992) 'Chaneru senryaku no nyuu paradaimu' [The new paradigm of channel strategy], in Hiroshi Sumiya (ed.), *Dai-tenkanki no chaneru senryaku* [Channel strategies in a period of great change], Tokyo: Dôbunkan Shuppan, pp. 3–40.

Suzuki, Tsuneo (1990) 'Post-war development of general trading companies', in Shin'ichi Yonekawa (ed.), *General Trading Companies: A Comparative and Historical Study*, Tokyo: United Nations University Press, pp. 111–169.

Suzuki, Yasuaki (1990) 'Kôkyô seisaku toshite no daitenhô – "chûshô kourishô" sonzoku to no kanren' [The Large Store Law as public policy – concerning the continued existence of small and medium retailers], in Nihon Keizai Shinbunsha (ed.), *Daitenhô ga kieru hi* [The day when the Large Store Law disappears], Tokyo: Nihon Keizai Shinbunsha, pp. 199–226.

Suzuki, Yasuaki (1993) 'Daitenhô no hensen' [Change of the Large Store Law], in Nikkei Ryûtsû Shinbun (ed.), *Ryûtsû gendaishi* [Modern history of distribution], Tokyo: Nihon Keizai Shinbunsha, pp. 191–210.

Takaoka, Sueaki (1993) 'Cheen sutoa keiei kara mita hyakkaten no kadai' [Problems of department stores from the perspective of chain store management], *RIRI*, May, pp. 15–22.

Takashi, Eimatsu (1983) 'SM gyôkai 'gendai & shôrai' tenbô' [Supermarket industry, current situation and future prospects], *Hanbai kakushin*, April, pp. 192–195.

Takaya, Kazuo (1994) *Cho kakaku hakai to 'sei hai han' dômei* [Great price destruction and manufacturer, distributor, reseller alliances], Tokyo: Sanno Daigaku Shuppanbu.

Takayama, Kunisuke (1982) '"Tanshitsu hokanteki" takakuka kara sôgô ningen kôfuku sangyô ka e' [Moving from supporting and qualitative diversification towards an industry that supports the general happiness of the people], *Hanbai kakushin*, September, pp. 39–43.

Takayama, Kunisuke (2000) 'Jinchi no shûchû tônyû de tôsan ni itaru fu no isan kara dasshutsu seyo!' [Escape from the bad inheritance leading to bankruptcy by instilling concentrated input of knowledge!], *Hanbai kakushin*, April, pp. 32–35.

Takayama, Kunisuke (2001) 'Ôbei kourigyô no kaigai shinshutsu ga, waga kuni ryûtsûgyô ni ataeru inpakuto to taiô' [The advance of European and US retailers: the impact on and reaction by our distribution industry], *Ryûtsû to shisutemu*, no. 108 (2001.6), pp. 3–11.

Tamura, Masanori (1984) 'Ryûtsû shisutemuron' [Theory of distribution systems], in Masanori Tamura and Takemasa Ishihara (eds.), *Nihon ryûtsû kenkyû no tenbô* [Prospects of Japanese distribution research], Tokyo: Chikura Shobô, pp. 1–49.

Tamura, Yôzô (1995) 'Kûdôka suru daitoshiken de sôgyôki no shôbai o kokoromiru' [Trying methods of the founding period in hollowed-out city centres], *Hanbai kakushin*, November, pp. 178–181.

Tanaka, Hiroyuki (2000) '"Yume" to "genjitsu" no kairi wa uzumaruka – Saisei e no saigo no shinario' [Will the gap between dream and reality be closed? The final scenario towards rebirth], *Chain Store Age*, 15 April, pp. 32–34.

Taniguchi, Tomohiko (1999) 'Japan's banks and the 'bubble economy' of the late 1980s', in William M. Tsutsui (ed.), *Banking in Japan, Routledge Library of Modern Japan, vol. III*, London and New York: Routledge, pp. 181–209.

Tatebayashi, Masahiko (1991a) 'Kouri ryûtsû seisaku no keisei katei (I)' [The formation process of policies for retail distribution (I)], *Hôgaku ronshû*, vol. 130, no. 3, pp. 61–82.

Tatebayashi, Masahiko (1991b) 'Kouri ryûtsû seisaku no keisei katei (II)' [The formation process of policies for retail distribution (II)], *Hôgaku ronshû*, vol. 130, no. 5, pp. 75–101.

Teranaka, Sumiko (1995) 'Hyakkaten, kakaku no tekiseika hitsuyô' [Department stores, need for the adjustment of prices], *Nikkei ryûtsû shinbun*, 6 June 1995, p. 20.

The Economist, 5 February 1994, 'Shop tactics in Tokyo', p. 69.

TKS (Tôyô Keizai Shinpôsha) (1991) *Shôwa kokusei sôran, dai ni ken* [Shôwa statistics, vol. 2], Tokyo: Tôyô Keizai Shinpôsha.

Tôda, Takeshi (1982) 'Jihyô – ryôbaiten fubai undô ga okotte iru?' [Commentary on current events – Do mass merchandising stores experience a boycott?], *Hanbai kakushin*, September, pp. 24–26.

Toyo Keizai (2000) *Kigyô keiretsu sôran 2000* [General survey of company relationships], Tokyo: Toyo Keizai Shinpôsha.

Toyo Keizai (2001) *Ôgata kouri tempo sôran 2002* [Directory of large retail stores], Tokyo: Toyo Keizai Shinpôsha.

Toys 'R' Us Japan Ltd (2002) *Annual Report 2001*.

TS (Tsûshô Sangyôshô) (1980) *Shôkô seisaku shi, dai 7 ken: kokunai shôgyô* [History of policies for commerce and industry, volume 7: domestic commerce], Tokyo: Tsûshô Sangyôshô Kenkyûsha.

TSC (a) (Tsûshô Sangyô Daijin Kanbô Tôkei Chôsabu) (different years) *Shôgyô tôkeihyô dai 3 ken sangyô hen (shi-ku-chô-zon hyô)* [Census of commerce volume 3, industrial classification (cities, city districts, towns and villages)], Tokyo: Tsûsan Tôkei Kyôkai.

TSC (b) (Tsûshô Sangyô Daijin Kanbô Tôkei Chôsabu) (different years) *Shôgyô tôkeihyô sangyô hen* [Census of commerce, industrial classification], Tokyo: Tsûsan Tôkei Kyôkai.

TSC (Tsûshô Sangyô Daijin Kanbô Tôkei Chôsabu) (1976) *Shôwa 49 nen serufu saabisu mise ni kan suru tôkeihyô* [Report on the 1974 survey for self-service stores], Tokyo: Tsûsan Tôkei Kyôkai.

TSC (Tsûshô Sangyô Daijin Kanbô Tôkei Chôsabu) (1983) *Shôwa 57 nen serufu saabisu mise tôkeihyô* [Report on the 1982 survey for self-service stores], Tokyo: Tsûsan Tôkei Kyôkai.

TSC (Tsûshô Sangyô Daijin Kanbô Tôkei Chôsabu) (1985) *Shôwa 57 nen shôgyô tôkeihyô, gyôtai betsu tôkeihen* [Report on the 1982 census of commerce, statistics for retail formats], Tokyo: Tsûsan Tôkei Kyôkai.

TSC (Tsûshô Sangyô Daijin Kanbô Tôkei Chôsabu) (1993)*Heisei 3 nen shôgyô tôkeihyô, gyôtai betsu tôkeihen* [Report on the 1991 census of commerce, statistics for retail formats], Tokyo: Tsûsan Tôkei Kyôkai.

TSC (Tsûshô Sangyô Daijin Kanbô Tôkei Chôsabu) (2000)*Heisei 11 nen shôgyô tôkeihyô, gyôtai betsu tôkeihen* [Report on the 1999 census of commerce, statistics for retail formats], Tokyo: Tsûsan Tôkei Kyôkai.

TSCK (Tsûshô Sangyôshô Sangyô Seisakukyoku/Chûshô Kigyôchô) (1984) *80 nendai no ryûtsû sangyô bijon* [Vision for the distribution industry of the 1980s], Tokyo: Tsûshô Sangyô Chôsakai.

TSK (Tsûshô Sangyôshô Kigyôkyoku) (1968) *Sangyô Kôzô Shingikai Ryûtsû Bukai chûkan hokokushû* [Compilation of the interim reports of the Council for Industrial Structure, Distribution Sub-council], Tokyo.

TSK (Tsûshô Sangyôshô Kigyôkyoku) (1971) *70 nendai ni okeru ryûtsû – Sangyô Kôzô Shingikai dai 9 kai chûkan tôshin* [Distribution in the 1970s, 9th interim report of the Council for Industrial Structure], Tokyo: Ôkurashô Insatsukyoku.

TSS (Tsûshô Sangyôshô Shôseika) (1989) *90 nendai no ryûtsû bijon* [Vision for distribution in the 1990s], Tokyo: Tsûshô Sangyô Chôsakai.

Tsuki, Izumi (2000a) 'Kiseki V-ji kaifuku o jitsugenshita yotsu no kakushin' [The four reforms that led to the miraculous V-shaped recovery], *Hanbai kakushin*, January, pp. 21–25.

Tsuki, Izumi (2000b) 'Aitsugi kuridasu shin senryaku ni shika wa naika?' [Don't the new strategies that are rolled out successively have blind spots?], *Hanbai kakushin*, September, pp. 36–43.

US Census Bureau, (2001) *Reports, Series BR/00-A, Annual Benchmark Report for Retail Trade and Food Services: January 1992 to December 2000*, Washington, DC.

Uchida, Hiroshi (1986) *Struggle for Control: Corporate Strategy and Investment Decisions of the Sogo Shosha*, Diss. Harvard University, Ann Arbor: UMI Dissertation Information Service.

Uchino, Tatsurô (1983) *Japan's Postwar Economy*, Tokyo Kôdansha International Ltd.

Uchiro, Tamiyo (1984) 'Kore kara no seichô kabu hoomu sentaa' [Growth stocks of the future – home centre], *Hanbai kakushin*, April, pp. 68–70.

Uchiro, Tamiyo (1989) 'Juntendoo no senryaku to shisutemu' [Strategy and system of Juntendô], *Hanbai kakushin*, September, pp. 146–149.

Watanabe, Tatsurô (1997) *Ryûtsû chaneru kankei no dôtai bunseki – seihan no kyôdô kankei ni kansuru riron to jisshô* [Dynamic analysis of the relationship in distribution channels – theory and actual proof in regard to the cooperative relationships between industry and commerce], Tokyo: Chikura Shobô.

WSK (Waseda Daigaku Shijô Chôsa Kenkyûkai) (1965a) *Super Market* [Supermarket], Tokyo.

WSK (Waseda Daigaku Shijô Chôsa Kenkyûkai) (1965b) *Suupaa maaketto to shôhisha* [Supermarkets and consumers], Tokyo.

Yahagi, Toshiyuki (1992) 'Konbiniensu sutoa shistemu ron (ue)' [Theory of the convenience store system, part I], *Keiei shirin*, vol. 29, no. 2, pp. 121–136.

Yahagi, Toshiyuki (1993a) 'Ryûtsû chaneru no hendô' [Changes in distribution channels], in Nikkei Ryûtsû Shinbun (ed.), *Ryûtsû gendaishi* [Modern history of distribution], pp. 119–149, Tokyo: Nihon Keizai Shinbunsha.

Yahagi, Toshiyuki (1993b) 'Konbiniensu sutoa shistemu ron (shita)' [Theory of the convenience store system, part II], *Keiei shirin*, vol. 29, no. 4, pp. 17–37.

Yahagi, Toshiyuki (1993c) 'Konbiniensu sutoa no senryaku hikaku' [Comparison of strategies of convenience stores) *Keiei shirin*, vol. 30, no. 2, pp. 53–68.

Yahagi, Toshiyuki (1993d) 'Kyôdôteki maachandaijingu to torihiki kôzô' [Collaborative merchandising and trade structure], *Keiei shirin*, vol. 30, no. 3, pp. 59–72.

Yahagi, Toshiyuki (1993e) 'Soshiki kourigyô no hatten' [Development of organized retailing], in Nikkei Ryûtsû Shinbun (ed.), *Ryûtsû gendaishi* [Modern history of distribution], Tokyo: Nihon Keizai Shinbunsha, pp. 56–87.

Yahagi, Toshiyuki (1994) *Konbiniensu sutoa shisutemu no kakushinsei* [Revolutionary features of the convenience store system], Tokyo: Nihon Keizai Shinbunsha.

Yahagi, Toshiyuki (1997) *Kouri inobeeshon no gensen – keiei kôryû to ryûtsû gendaika* [The sources of innovation in retailing – exchange between management and modernization of distribution], Tokyo: Nihon Keizai Shinbunsha.

Yamada Denki Co. Ltd (2001) *Yuho Report Fiscal Year Ended March 31, 2001*, retrieved from http://www.tecc.co.jp/.

Yamamoto, Hiroshi (1971) 'Chotto matta! Seisen shokuhin no puripakkeeji to serufuka' [Wait a little longer! Pre-packaging of fresh food and development of self-service], *Hanbai kakushin*, October, pp. 121–124.

Yasuda, Yoshiaki (1993) *Kokusai jidai no ryûtsû seisaku* [Distribution policy in the international era], Tokyo: Mineruba Shobô.

Yoshida, Hideo (1982) *Suupaa no genten* [Origin of the the supermarket], Tokyo: Yûshindô.

Yoshino, M. Y. (1971) *The Japanese Marketing System*, Cambridge, Mass.: MIT Press.

Yui, Tsunehiko (ed.) (1991a) *Sezon no rekishi, jôkan* [The history of Saison, first volume], Tokyo: Libro Port.

Yui, Tsunehiko (ed.) (1991b) *Sezon no rekishi, gekan* [The history of Saison, second volume], Tokyo: Libro Port.

Yûseishô (Ministry of Post and Telecommunications) (2000) *Tsûshin Hakusho* [White paper on telecommunications], Tokyo: ôkurashô Insatsukyoku (retrieved from http://www.yusei.go.jp/policyreports/japanese/papers/h12/index.htm).

Index